The Bolshevik Poster

Stephen White

1988
Yale University Press
New Haven and London

103216

Designed by Mary Carruthers
Set in Linotron Bembo by Best-set Typesetter Ltd., and
printed and bound in Yugoslavia by Papirografika, Ljubljana.

Library of Congress Cataloging-in-Publication Data

White, Stephen, 1945–
  The Bolshevik poster.

  Bibliography: p.
  Includes index.
  1. Posters, Russian.   2. Posters – 20th century –
Soviet Union.   I. Title.
NC1807.S65W48   1988   741.67′4′0947   88-14275
ISBN 0-300-04339-2

Previous page illustrations are details
from Plates 5.10 and 4.21.

Contents

Preface   vi

Chapter 1   Origins   1

Chapter 2   Apsit and the Early Soviet Poster   18

Chapter 3   Moor, Deni and the Military-Political
            Poster   39

Chapter 4   Mayakovsky, Cheremnykh and
            the Rosta Windows   65

Chapter 5   Themes and Impact   91

Chapter 6   The Bolshevik Poster and After   119

Notes   131

Note on Sources   143

Bibliography   144

Illustration Credits   149

Index   150

Preface

The early Soviet period was a time of extraordinary ferment in the arts – in literature and theatre, in the cinema, in dance and music, in porcelain and dress design. It was also a time of experiment and achievement in the graphic arts, particularly in a form of graphic art of great importance for the new regime, the political poster. Although there had been some developments in this area in the late Tsarist period and, like elsewhere, during the war, there had been little to suggest the emergence in the years just after the revolution of a series of bold images which have become and enduring part of the iconography of the civil war, and a creative achievement from which poster artists of other times and countries have never ceased to learn. Some of these images – Dmitri Moor's *Have you Volunteered?*, his famine poster *Help* or El Lissitsky's *Red Wedge* – have been widely reproduced and imitated and are well-established classics of their kind. Others, however (and nearly 4,000 posters were produced between 1918 and 1921), have been less widely noted but are no less worthy of attention; and the whole complex of questions associated with the production and distribution of the civil war poster has scarcely begun to be investigated, in the USSR or in the West. This book is an attempt to do so.

Many of the posters reproduced in this volume, admittedly, will not be entirely unfamiliar to Western readers, particularly those who have consulted the collections of reproductions issued by Soviet publishing houses over the past decade or so. Collections of this kind, however, suffer from several serious shortcomings. In the first place, they are anything but comprehensive: even the largest include no more than two dozen or so posters of the civil war years, as compared with the total of well over 100 that are reproduced in this volume. In the second place, the illustrations are very variable in quality, particularly where colour plates are concerned. Thirdly, and perhaps most important, collections of this kind are highly selective, in that several categories of poster are wholly or almost entirely excluded. This applies most obviously to posters depicting Trotsky or other oppositionists, or including quotations from such authors in their texts; but it also applies to posters of a militantly revolutionary character (such as those that called for a Soviet Poland in 1920), posters of an overtly allegorical or symbolic character, and posters that draw attention to the 'dark sides' of Soviet life, such as the deserter problem during the civil war. My aim in this volume has been, first of all, to redress these shortcomings and provide a generous, properly reproduced and historically representative selection of the posters that appeared during the civil war years, a selection drawn almost exclusively from non-Soviet sources; and then secondly, in the text itself, to outline and explain the emergence, flowering and subsequent decline of the Soviet civil war poster, examining the changing subject matter of the posters, the people who prepared and distributed them, their impact upon contemporaries, and their subsequent evolution into the Soviet poster of more recent years.

In preparing this study I have drawn upon a wide variety of sources, both in the USSR and outside it (full details of all of these sources are given in the bibliography at the end of this study). My first group of sources has been the posters themselves, both those that are held in Soviet libraries and archives and those that are held in several substantial and important Western collections, particularly those in Uppsala and Paris. Secondly, I have had access to a considerable number of Soviet archival sources, both of individuals (particularly the poster artists themselves) and of societies and institutions such as the School of Painting, Sculpture and Architecture in Moscow, the State Publishing House (Gosizdat) and the State Academy of Art Studies. I was also given access, for I believe the first time so far as a Western scholar is concerned, to the Central State Archive of the State Army, although this yielded only a single and, as it turned out, unimportant file. Finally, I have drawn extensively upon the printed sources that are available for a study of this kind, including a great deal of contemporary journal, memoir and other literature as well as the scholarly studies that have been produced in more recent years. Discussions with a small number of contemporaries were also helpful, particularly in adding the kinds of personal information and impression that published sources (certainly Soviet ones) tend very often to leave out.

This study has taken the best part of a decade to complete and in the course of my work I have accumulated obligations to a large number of individuals and institutions. I must first of all thank the British Council, which made possible three extended research visits to the USSR under the terms of the Anglo-Soviet cultural exchange agreement, and whose support remains indispensable to the serious study of Soviet affairs by British-based scholars. Within the USSR itself I am indebted to the staff of the Department of the History of Russian and Soviet Art, headed by Professor D. V. Sarabyanov, for their willingness to receive me and to facilitate my studies; in this connection I am above all indebted to Rafuil S. Kaufman for his practical assistance and for his recollections of the poster artists of the civil war period, with most of whom he was personally acquainted. I am also grateful to the University of Glasgow and to the Economic and Social Research Council (through its exchange scheme with the HSFR) for making possible a short and then a more extended visit to consult the very important collection of posters and other material at Uppsala and elsewhere in Sweden. I am glad to be able to record my thanks to Margareta Lindgren, Åsa Hennigsen and the staff of the Maps and Prints Department of Uppsala University Library for their hospitality as well as practical assistance. The Economic and Social Research Council helped to make possible a visit to Paris, where Mme Cécile Coutin of the Musée d'histoire contemporaine at the Invalides was particularly helpful. My visit to North America was supported by the Carnegie Trust for the Universities of Scotland; I would like to thank the staff in the New York Public Library Slavonic Division (particularly Edward Kasinec) and in the Maps and Prints Department of the Library of Congress for their assistance.

My debts to other individuals and scholars are no less considerable. At Glasgow, those who know him will not be surprised to learn that René Beermann was a constant source of advice and enthusiastic encouragement. Other colleagues at Glasgow have helped in various ways, including Martin Dewhirst, Evan Mawdsley and Tony Pearson. I owe a particular debt of thanks to James D. White for his assistance with the translation of material from Latvian, and to Yekaterina Young for the translation of material from Ukrainian and Hungarian. I am also grateful to the University's Photographic Unit for their skill and patience in dealing with a large number of sometimes complicated requests. Elsewhere I am grateful to the following for their advice or assistance on particular points: David Wedgwood Benn; Julie Curtis; Bridget Fowler; Peter Frank; Patricia Grimsted; Neil Harding; Larissa Haskell; Ann Helgeson; Malcolm V. Jones; Frank Kämpfer; David King; Martin McCauley; Rosemary Miles of the Victoria and Albert Museum, London; Daniel N. Nelson; Maurice Rickards; Marilyn Rueschmeyer; Peter Rutland; W. F. Ryan of the Warburg Institute, London; Paul Smith of the Open University Library; Richard Taylor; and John Willett. Myra Stewart and Ishbel White advised on the selection of illustrations and other matters; John Nicoll of Yale University Press gave me the benefit of his experience on the presentation of a volume of this kind for the press, and encouraged the project from the outset.

Finally, some technical points: I have followed the system of transliteration by the journal *Soviet Studies*, except that I have omitted diacritics in the text itself and have also followed more familiar forms where these have become established usage. The notes, which sometimes incorporate additional information, include full details of each item on its first citation in each chapter, and thereafter use a short title form. Soviet archives are cited by archive or *fond* number, inventory (*opis*) and storage unit (*edinitsa khraneniya*). Full details of the principal items cited, other than periodical articles, are also given in the Bibliography.

ПОЖАЛУИ СТА ѠДАИ МНЕ КАКЪ НЕСТЫ НО ТЕБЕ ·
ТЕБЕ ВТО ПОТЕХИ · АМНЕ ХОДЫА СМЕХИ ·:· ✵
И ВОЛИШЪ ЗАМНО БРЕТИ · ДА ГОТОВО ДУНЕС
ТИ ТОЛКО СТАНОВИ · КУВШИ ВПЕЧЬ ДА ГОТО ГДЕ ·
НАМЪ ЛЕЧЬ · НЕ ДАРОМЪ ТЫ УМЕНА ПОД ПИВА
ЛА · НЕ БОЕ З ТЕПЕРЬ САМА ВРУКИ ТЫ ПОПАЛА ✵

1.1 Anon, *Pozhaluista otdai mne . . .* (Give Me the Bucket), coloured woodcut, second quarter of the eighteenth century, 37 × 28.5 cm.

CHAPTER ONE
Origins

The Soviet political poster is conventionally described in Soviet publications as an 'offspring of the socialist revolution ... indebted for its birth to the Great October revolution, a grandiose, historically unprecedented turning-point which radically changed the fate of the peoples of our country'.[1] More discriminating Soviet as well as Western scholarship is generally inclined to the view that the political poster of the early Soviet period had, in fact, at least four pre-revolutionary sources. Two of these, the *lubok* (or illustrated broadside) and the icon, connect the Soviet political poster with some of the oldest traditions of Russian graphic art; the other two, the satirical journals and the pre-revolutionary advertising poster, similarly connect the Soviet political poster with the efflorescence in the graphic arts which occurred, in Russia as in many other European countries, in the late nineteenth and early twentieth centuries. The political poster of the early post-revolutionary years, with which this book is concerned, was much more than simply the product of these earlier forms of communication; but equally, it drew many of its themes, its composition, its use of colour and even (in some cases) its subject matter from these various antecedents. Indeed, given that the task of the political poster was above all to communicate, it could scarcely avoid resorting to a visual language which was familiar both to those who prepared the posters and to those who were supposed to be influenced by them.

For some early Soviet scholars the Soviet political poster was, in fact, simply a continuation of the *lubok*, the peasant illustrated woodcut or broadside which developed in Russia from the early seventeenth century onwards.[2] The word *lubok* is of uncertain origin: according to some scholars it derived from the limewood block (*lub* or *lipovaya kora*) from which it was printed,[3] although it appears more probable that the word derives from the bast baskets (*lubochnye koroby*) from which the pictures were offered for sale.[4] It has also been suggested that the word may derive from the Lubyanskaya Square in Moscow where many of the pictures were produced and sold;[5] or conversely, that the square itself may have taken its name from the manufacture and sale of *lubki*.[6] There is more general agreement that the first *lubki* were produced in Kiev, and that they were influenced by West European engravings, which were by then being imported in significant numbers, as well as by the native traditions of icon painting and the decorative arts as a whole.[7] The *lubok* typically combined illustrations with text, and its subject matter included religion and folklore as well as political developments and social issues of the day. For its readers, as a contemporary Soviet scholar has remarked,

1.2 Anon, *Myshi kota pogrebayut* (The Mice Bury the Cat), coloured woodcut, first half of the eighteenth century, 32.8 × 57.3 cm.

the *lubok* served as a '*sui generis* encyclopedia, newspaper, satire sheet, book and entertainment';[8] it could also serve as a song-book, a guide to polite manners and a repository of literature, poetry, folk-tales and fables.[9]

The earliest *lubki* consisted of paper copies reproduced from a carved wooden block. They became so popular that in the second half of the eighteenth century a transition was gradually effected to copper engravings, which allowed much larger numbers of copies to be reproduced with little loss of quality. Still later, in the nineteenth century, *lubki* began to be reproduced by lithographic means and in still larger quantities (the printing house of I. D. Sytin in Moscow alone produced over 50 million *lubok* pictures annually at this time).[10]

Early *lubki* were predominantly allegorical or fantastic, and often drew heavily upon established figures of Russian folklore such as the witch lady Baba-Yaga, or the knightly hero Ilya Muromets. Heroic and religious themes were also depicted. From the eighteenth century onwards, however, *lubki* began to represent realistic figures from the social world of the time, such as members of the officer class or the court, as well as hunting, pastoral, amorous or other scenes.[11] The first pornographic *lubki* made their appearance at this time,

inspired, Soviet sources agree, by foreign and particularly French models.[12] In the nineteenth century the *lubok* began to pay more attention to social problems and issues, such as drunkenness, the law courts, poverty, the position of women and the social life of the merchant class.[13] By the late nineteenth century they had begun to be produced in very large numbers but their aesthetic quality deteriorated sharply, and by the early twentieth century, when they began to be reproduced by chromolithography for a mass market, they had almost entirely lost their earlier distinctiveness as a popular graphic art form.[14]

From an early stage the *lubok* served as a means of commenting upon political as well as other developments, although generally in an indirect and allegorical manner. The *lubok The Mice Bury the Cat* (Plate 1.2), of which several different versions exist, was thought at first to have been a satirical commentary on the funeral of Pope Pius V or Gregory XIII, or even Ivan the Terrible. In the late nineteenth century, however, the eminent lawyer and ethnographer D. A. Rovinsky was able to establish that the satire was in fact directed against Peter the Great. Peter had also been buried in a sledge drawn by eight horses, and an orchestra had played at his funeral (this meant that the picture must have been produced after 1698, when this practice had been permitted for the first time). The mice accompanying the picture were identified as coming from territories that Peter had conquered in his wars against Sweden; and one of the mice was smoking a pipe, the general sale of tobacco for which had first been permitted during Peter's reign. These and many other clues appeared to leave little doubt that this was a satire directed against Peter the Great and his reforms, probably by Old Believers who were opposed to Peter's reform of the Orthodox Church.[15] Later lubki dealt in a more direct manner with political subjects, such as the victory over Napoleon in 1812, the progress of the Crimean War, the opening of the Moscow-St Petersburg railway and conscription into the armed forces.[16] The government, for its part, took an increasingly close interest in lubki and imposed progressively more detailed forms of censorship upon them from the 1820s onwards.[17]

The lubok and popular arts generally had a profound influence upon many of the professional artists of later times such as the book illustrator and member of the 'World of Art' group Ivan Bilibin (1876–1942) and early Soviet painters such as Boris Kustodiev (1876–1927) and Viktor Vasnetsov (1848–1926), as well as more obviously upon 'neoprimitivist' artists such as Mikhail Larionov (1881–1964) and Natalya Goncharova (1881–1962).[18] The artist Vassily Kandinsky (1866–1944), in a recently published letter, described the lubok as a 'marvel' and wrote that his dream was to have a 'print to the Last Judgement, as old as possible, primitive (with serpent, devils, high priests, etc.)'.[19] The celebrated nineteenth-century master Ilya Repin is reported to have told his pupils that those who wished to create a major popular work should seek their inspiration in 'lubok creations, and of the most primitive character'.[20]

The influence of the lubok was also felt in the staging of operas, for instance those by Rimsky-Korsakov, and in theatrical design.[21] In literature, the simple rhyming verse which often accompanied lubki is held to have influenced Demyan Bedny, Sergei Esenin and other poets of the early Soviet period.[22] Close links have been established between some of the poetry of Vladimir Mayakovsky and the art of the lubok; certainly, it is known from the testimony of the poet's sister Lyudmilla that among his favourite occupations in his early years was the perusal of Rovinsky's vast and still unsurpassed collection of lubok pictures.[23] The influence of the lubok was also apparent upon popular and applied arts such as embroidery, table cloths and gingerbread moulds.[24]

The influence of the lubok upon the political poster was still more direct. Although lubki in their traditional form had largely ceased to exist, at the beginning of the First World War the Russian government established a publishing house, 'The Contemporary Lubok', which in turn commissioned and produced a series of lubki of a broadly patriotic character. Several of those who later became prominent in the production of political posters, such as Mayakovsky and Dmitri Moor, became involved in this work, a fact to which modern Soviet sources do not generally draw attention.[25] Established painters such as Kasimir Malevich (Plate 1.3) were also engaged. The lubok had perhaps its greatest impact upon the 'Rosta Windows', produced between 1919 and 1922, with which Mayakovsky was directly involved and which consisted, like many lubki, of a sequence of frames telling a story accompanied by simple rhyming verse. Other Soviet poster artists such as Aleksei Radakov (see for instance Plates 5.40 and 5.51) similarly made use of the simple narrative style of the lubok to convey their message, particularly in posters that were intended for the countryside. There was also some continuity in terms of subject and composition between the wartime lubki and later Soviet posters: for instance, the depiction of one's own side as a mounted warrior impaling tiny opponents on his lance, or the representation of the enemy as a mythological monster surrounded by skulls.[26] Attempts to revive a distinctively Soviet lubok in later years were not successful: social conditions in town and countryside had changed too much, particularly with the elimination of illiteracy and improved communications. The boldness, energy, humour and popular appeal of the lubok have nonetheless remained among the most important elements of the Russian graphic art tradition, and it was among the most important of the sources from which the political poster of the early post-revolutionary years took its origin.

A further and still older influence upon the Soviet political poster was the ancient Russian tradition of icon painting. Icons (from the Greek eikon, 'image' or 'likeness') are the distinctive art form of the Orthodox Church; they serve not only as aids to worship but also as pictorial commentaries upon theological doctrines. Icons grew out of the mosaic and fresco traditions of early Byzantine art; they were used to decorate the wall and floor surfaces of churches, baptisteries and sepulchres, and were later carried on standards in times of war and in religious processions (many were held to have miracle-working properties). From the time of the conversion of Kievan Russia to Christianity in 988 up to the reforms of Peter the Great pictorial art in Russia was devoted almost entirely to the interests of the Christian religion and the Orthodox Church, and it was based in turn upon the iconic tradition that came from Constantinople and Eastern Christianity. Painters and craftsmen came to Kiev from Byzantium together with

Greek priests and monks; they brought with them their alphabet (the Russian Cyrillic script originated from the ninth-century Greek missionaries Saints Cyril and Methodius), their philosophy and also their pictorial traditions. Greek icons themselves were imported; one of the earliest of such importations, the late eleventh-century *Virgin of Vladimir*, now in the Tretyakov Gallery, was traditionally believed to have been painted by St Luke and to have saved Moscow from the armies of Tamurlane. No icon enjoyed greater renown or was more widely copied.[27]

At first the painters brought from Constantinople were in charge of the major workshops, with Russian artists as their assistants and pupils, but local artists soon assimilated the Byzantine tradition and over the course of several centuries developed a rich and powerful indigenous art form. The earliest surviving Russian icons are those from Novgorod, where a distinctive icon-painting school appeared in the twelfth century. Other important icon-painting schools developed in the twelfth and thirteenth centuries at Pskov, Vladimir, Yaroslavl and Suzdal as well as Novgorod and Kiev. Despite local variations, a common Russian style of

icon-painting developed whose characteristic features included two- rather than three-dimensional treatment of their subjects, rich ornamentation and expressive use of colour. New saints were introduced into the Byzantine hierarchy, among them Vladimir, Boris and Gleb, and particular emphasis was laid upon the Byzantine *umilenie* or 'tenderness' tradition in which the Mother and Child were the central focus of the composition.

Some of the greatest of the early icon painters were foreigners who came to work in Russia at this time. Among them was Theophanes the Greek (Feofan Grek), active in the late fourteenth century, who worked first in Novgorod and then in Moscow, where the finest examples of his work are preserved in the iconostatis of the Cathedral of the Assumption in the Kremlin. Icon painting, however, reached the highest point of its development in the early fifteenth century, above all in the work of Andrei Rublev (*c.* 1360–1430), a Russian monk who worked at the Trinity monastery of St Sergius at Zagorsk and later in Moscow and Vladimir. Adopting the techniques imported by Theophanes the Greek, with whom he may have collaborated in his youth, Rublev went on to achieve an extraordinary

1.3 Kasimir Malevich, *Nu i tresk-zhe, nu i grom-zhe, byl ot nemtsev podle Lomzhi* (What a crash and what a thunder the Germans are making near Lomzhi), coloured lithograph, 1914/15, 38 × 56 cm.

Ну и трескъ-же, ну и громъ-же
Былъ отъ нѣмцевъ подлѣ Ломжи!

1.4 Andrei Rublev, *Troitse* (Trinity), tempera on panel, *c*, 1411, 142 × 114 cm.

logically remote and, for obvious reasons, discounted by most orthodox Soviet scholars,[29] the connection is in fact a close and important one. In part this was a matter of colour – red, in particular, was a colour greatly favoured by Russian icon painters as well as (for political and other purposes) by poster artists in the Soviet period. Red represented the blood of martyrs and the fire of faith; the Russian word for 'red' (*krasnyi*) itself incorporates a characteristic duality, meaning both 'red' and 'beautiful'. Icon painters, like later poster artists, also 'coded' their compositions through their use of colour: the Virgin, for instance, was typically represented with a dark cherry-red cloak, the Apostle Paul with an ochre cloak, and so forth.[30] Poster artists, rather later, employed similar colour conventions to mark out the proletarian (red), the bourgeois (black), the Pole (green or yellow) and other figures in their work.[31]

The connection between the icon-painting tradition and the political posters of the Soviet period was also apparent in the adaptation of theological subjects to secular and propagandistic purposes. St George, for instance, was one of the most venerated saints of the Byzantine Church, and the theme of his victory over the dragon – an allegory for the victory of the Christian faith over paganism – was one of those most favoured by Russian icon painters. After the revolution it came

1.5 Viktor Deni, *Selyanskaya bogoroditsa* (Village 'Virgin'), two coloured lithograph, 1919, 46 × 33 cm., BS 589.

synthesis of luminosity and colour with great intensity of religious feeling. His Old Testament *Trinity* (*c*. 1411) (Plate 1.4), now in the Tretyakov Gallery, represents his art at the very peak of its achievement. Although its theological interpretation is still disputed, the *Trinity* is widely agreed to represent Christ (the central figure) indicating his willingness to offer his own life as a supreme sacrifice in the presence of God the Father (on the left, his face expressing extreme grief) and the Holy Ghost (on the right, acting as a comforter). The composition as a whole is in the form of a circle, representing harmony and peace.[28] The heritage of Theophanes the Greek and Andrei Rublev in turn served as points of departure for the more personal and mystical art of the Moscow master Dionysius, a layman active in the late fifteenth century, who was much admired for his elegant figures, delicate colour and attention to detail. Later, in the sixteenth century, religious painting lost much of its original inspiration; icon painters began to range more widely in their choice of subject, and purely decorative and portrait work become more common. After the reforms of Peter the Great secular rather than religious themes became predominant and the tradition became almost entirely debased.

Although the links between political posters of the post-revolutionary period and icon painting are chrono-

to be used, with suitable adaptations, to symbolise the proletariat's victory over the bourgeoisie. There was also some direct borrowing of religious motifs as, for instance, in Viktor Deni's *Village 'Virgin'* (Plate 1.5), a loose adaptation of the Mother and Child theme strongly reminiscent of the fifteenth-century *Virgin Hodigitria* now in the Tretyakov Gallery in Moscow. The poster substituted the Socialist Revolutionary Viktor Chernov for the Mother and the White Admiral Kolchak for the Child; above, left and right respectively, were two 'saints', the White leaders Yudenich and Denikin. Kolchak holds a placard in his hands demanding 'Shoot every tenth worker and peasant', and the work is signed 'Icon-painter Deni'. According to the testimony of the poet Demyan Bedny, the poster was widely reproduced by local artists in Siberia during the early post-revolutionary period; they made a version as big as a door and carried it about in a parody of a religious procession.[32]

Another adaptation of the Mother and Child theme caused a sensation in the village in which the emigre writer Lev Kopelev was living in the early 1920s, west of Vinnitsa in the Ukraine. He recalled that one morning three girls rushed into his courtyard, appalled and out of breath, to report that a 'terrible picture' of the Mother of God had been put up outside the local shop. Kopelev ran out of the yard and crossed the street. On the door of the shop was a yellowish-brown poster of Lord Curzon, the British Foreign Secretary, cast in the form of a Virgin, holding a bearded Chernov in his lap. 'Holy Virgin, what's going to happen! What a sin!', the girls cried out in horror.[33] A more imaginative adaptation, this time of Rublev's *Trinity*, was produced by the Petrograd 'Rosta Window' artist V. I. Kozlinsky: he substituted the Polish leader Pilsudsky, Lloyd George and the French Premier Millerand for the Father, Son and Holy Ghost in Rublev's original.[34] Other 'icons' of Emile Vandervelde, the Belgian Socialist, and of Viktor Chernov were paraded in Moscow during the trial of the Socialist Revolutionaries in 1922.[35]

Adaptations of this kind were not confined to icons and poster art. The marches and demonstrations of the Soviet period, for instance, drew much of their inspiration from the ecclesiastical processions of the pre-revolutionary period, as well as from secular manifestations such as the celebration of the third centenary of the Romanov dynasty in 1913.[36] Parallels have also been drawn between the public displays of the Soviet leadership on major national occasions and the 'intercessory row' or *deesis* of the Russian iconostasis, which shows Mary and John the Baptist, assisted by apostles and saints, interceding with Christ on mankind's behalf. In both the touched-up photographs of the leadership and

in the *deesis* the facial images are idealised rather than actual, and in both cases the order of precedence is from the centre outwards rather than from side to side.[37] Similar continuities have been suggested between the use of the image of Lenin after his death and the display and veneration of icons in the pre-revolutionary period, and between the display of icons in the corners of pre-revolutionary houses and the 'red corners' of contemporary Soviet buildings in which official messages are displayed for public attention.[38] The first Soviet Constitution of 1918 directly incorporated the words of St Paul's Second Epistle to the Thessalonians, 'He who does not work, neither shall he eat'; Anatoly Lunacharsky, the first People's Commissar for Enlightenment, could write as late as 1921 of the Communist Party leading the working class 'through the desert to the Promised Land'.[39]

Not all adaptations of this kind, admittedly, were entirely successful. Andrei Platonov, for instance, in his short story *The Secret Person* written in the late 1920s, recalled that all kinds of posters had been displayed in the early post-revolutionary years. One poster, in particular, was a repainted version of a large icon on which St George had been contending with a dragon in the depths of Hell. In the repainted version St George had been given the head of Trotsky, and the dragon had been given the head of a bourgeois. The crosses on St George's vestment had similarly been replaced by stars, the Red Army's new symbol, in line with the revolutionary idiom in which the painting had been recreated. The paint, however, had been of poor quality, and with the passage of time the crosses were re-emerging from under the stars that had been superimposed upon them.[40] This may have been related to another and rather more effective version of St George, used in a *Soviet Calender* of 1920, in which Trotsky, mounted on a white horse, is seen meting out death to a bowler-hatted serpent labelled 'counter-revolution' (Plate 1.6). The artist, as in the *Mother and Child* adaptation, was Viktor Deni.

Apart from thematic continuities of this kind, the influence of icons upon the early Soviet poster has been attested to by some of the poster artists themselves. Perhaps the most prominent of all of them, Dmitri Moor, argued in an unpublished lecture that posters had acquired their modern form in Paris in the work of Jules Chéret (1836–1932). The poster form, however, had appeared much earlier than this in peasant woodcuts and 'especially in the religious paintings of the vestibules of churches [and] in a certain number of icons, particularly of the fifteenth century'. Moor found the use of colour in icons particularly remarkable, together with their ability to make the broadest possible popular appeal.[41]

1.6 Viktor Deni, *Georgii pobedonosets (L. Trotsky)* (St George (L. Trotsky)), from *Sovetskii kalendar* [Moscow: Giz, 1920], courtesy of David King.

In his unpublished autobiography Moor remarked upon the impression that the study of icons had made upon his own artistic development. Although a convinced atheist from the age of fifteen, he had made a close study of icons as the most purposive and effective form of popular art that was then available. Moor concentrated particularly upon the composition of icons, their use of colour, their narrative and illustrative techniques, and their form, which was very simple and yet extraordinarily effective. 'All this', Moor later recalled, 'lay at the foundations of my own work'.[42] During the 1920s he had become actively involved in anti-religious journals such as *Bezbozhnik* (The Godless), in which his own work, it was sometimes suggested, depicted his heavenly opponents in an unduly kindly manner. Moor himself insisted that he had simply decided that 'you have to study your enemy'.[43] Soviet poster art, as Moor's experience suggested, owed much to the iconographic tradition, perhaps most of all to its use of colour, its simple but unified composition, and its direct appeal to the viewer.

Still a further influence, and the most important for some Soviet scholars,[44] was the Russian tradition of newspaper and journal graphics, particularly the satirical cartoons that such publications increasingly contained

from the later nineteenth century onwards. Although satirical writings such as those of M. E. Saltykov-Shchedrin (1826–89) were a well-established part of Russian literature, satirical graphics as such were a relatively late development. The first Russian satirical journal of any significance was probably *Iskra* (The Spark), which appeared in St Petersburg from 1859 onwards and became one of the most popular satirical publications of the 1860s. Increasingly radical, it was forced to appear without illustrations from 1870 onwards and three years later had to close down altogether. One of *Iskra*'s editors, the cartoonist N. A. Stepanov, left the journal in 1865 and launched an illustrated satirical journal called *Budilnik* (Alarm Clock), which was published first in St Petersburg and then from 1873 in Moscow, where it appeared on a weekly basis. *Budilnik* published writing as well as cartoons, and in the 1880s Chekhov was among those who appeared on its pages. Perhaps the most celebrated and successful of the illustrated satirical journals was *Satirikon*, which appeared as late as 1908 in St Petersburg, based upon a humorous weekly journal called *Strekoza* (Dragon Fly) which had appeared since 1875.[45] In all, about eighty-nine satirical journals, not all of them illustrated, made their appearance in Russia during the nineteenth century, far fewer than in the first decade of the century that followed.[46]

Early Russian satirical magazines were often highly derivative of the best West European journals of the same period. The French cartoonist Caran d'Ache (1858–1909), who was in fact a Russian by nationality (his name was a version of the Russian word for 'pencil'), was among those most widely imitated by the cartoonists of *Satirikon*. Moor, later the pre-eminent Soviet poster artist, was strongly influenced by the work of Olaf Gulbransson (1873–1958), a Norwegian whose work appeared in the German journal *Simplicissimus*, a very influential, democratically-inclined publication which appeared in Munich (later Stuttgart) from 1896 onwards.[47] The late nineteenth century was, of course, a time when in most Western countries the illustrated satirical journal was developing rapidly, in part as a result of advances in printing technology. The British *Punch* had appeared since 1841 and the German *Fliegende Blätter* since 1844; now they were joined by new journals such as *Le Rire* and *L'Assiette au beurre* (published in Paris from 1894 and 1901 respectively), *The Yellow Book* (published in London from 1894 onwards) and *Judge* and *Life* (which appeared in New York from 1881 and 1883 respectively). The art of the poster itself began to receive serious attention at about the same time in publications such as *The Poster* (1898–1900), *Les Maîtres d'affiche* (1895–1910) and *Das Plakat* (1910–19).

Russian satirical journals developed greatly both in number and in editorial boldness during the early years of the twentieth century. The period of the first Russian revolution, which followed the Tsar's October Manifesto of 1905 and the inauguration of a limited freedom of the press, was especially remarkable. According to the most recent calculations, no fewer than 249 satirical journals made their appearance during the short period 1905–7, excluding journals of a general political and literary character and those which had begun to appear before 1905 or continued to be published after 1907.[48] Earlier computations, less severe in their exclusions, variously recorded 380 or even 429 satirical journals which were published at some time during the same period.[49] The number of satirical cartoons published in journals of this kind during 1905–7 is estimated to have exceeded 3,000;[50] their total print run is estimated to have approached 40 million copies.[51] Many leading artists were involved in the work of the new satirical journals, including Valentin Serov (1865–1911), the 'World of Art' painter Ye. Ye. Lansere (1875–1946), Ilya Repin, Boris Kustodiev and Ivan Bilibin, as well as many of the future poster artists including Moor, Radakov and others. Prominent writers were also

1.8 B.M. Kustodiev, *Moskva I. Vstuplenie* (Invasion), *Zhupel*, 1905, no. 2.

involved including Maxim Gorky, Ivan Bunin and Kornei Chukovsky.[52]

The satirical journals of 1905–7 were remarkable not simply for their number and the aesthetic quality of those whose work appeared in them. More important, at least in terms of their subsequent contribution to the development of the political poster, was the fact that the satirical journals of this period became increasingly open and direct in their criticisms of government and established institutions (many of them, for this reason, appeared only once or twice before being closed). *Pulemet* (Machine-Gun) was seized the moment it appeared in St Petersburg, in November 1905; its back cover featured the Tsar's 'Most High Manifesto' with the bloody hand of D. F. Trepov, the repressive governor-general of St Petersburg, superimposed upon it. All the issues of the journal were confiscated, and the editor was placed in jail; the modified Manifesto was, however, reissued in large numbers in postcard format, in effect a 'pocket poster'.[53] In an equally audacious move a publicity poster issued on behalf of the Singer company, illustrating their premises on Nevsky Prospekt (now the city's largest bookshop), was modified by the printers: the figure of Konstantin Pobedonostsev, the Tsar's Procurator of the Holy Synod, was placed among the strolling crowds, and the shop windows were altered to display slogans such as 'Collectivism', 'Labour and capital' and 'Marx and Engels'. Once again all available issues were swiftly confiscated.[54] Mstislav Dobuzhinsky's *October Idyll* (Plate 1.7) appeared in the

1.7 M. V. Dobuzhinsky, *Oktyabr'skaya idilliya* (October Idyll), *Zhupel*, 1905, no. 1.

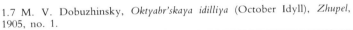

first issue of *Zhupel* (The Bugbear) in November 1905; it drew attention to the gap between liberal proclamations and the reality of bloody repression. Boris Kustodiev's *Invasion* (Plate 1.8) appeared in the second issue of *Zhupel* at the end of the year; it testified to the brutal suppression of the Moscow workers' rising in December 1905.[55]

As the case of the modified Manifesto has already suggested, cartoons and political graphics generally circulated widely during these years as postcards and in other forms as well as in satirical journals. The eminent Soviet historian N. M. Druzhinin (1886–1986), for instance, recalled selling postcard versions of some of M. M. Chemodanov's poorly drawn but effective political cartoons as a student in 1905 in order to raise funds for political exiles and other purposes. Many of the card sellers were arrested or attacked, and Chemodanov himself was imprisoned, apparently because of a caricature of Nicholas II. He died shortly after his release.[56] Another postcard which circulated widely at this time was the celebrated *Social Pyramid* (Plate 1.9), published by the Bolshevik publishing house Forward. This was based upon a drawing by N. N. Lokhov first published in 1901 in Geneva by the Union of Russian Social Democrats.[57] Its tiers read successively: 'We drink for you' (a bar-room scene); 'We shoot you' (soldiers); 'We deceive you' (priests); 'We govern you'

1.10 Nikolai Kochergin, *Kapital i Ko.* (Capital and Co.), coloured lithograph, 1920, 45 × 25 cm., BS 242.

1.9 Anon, *Sotsial'naya piramida* (Social Pyramid), drawing, origin unknown based upon postcard of 1905–6.

(ministers); and finally 'We rule you' (the Tsar and Tsarina). The bottom level, consisting of workers and peasants with Bolshevik banners, was labelled 'We work for you' and 'We feed you'. Hierarchical schemes of this kind were adapted for a number of Soviet political posters, among them Nikolai Kochergin's *Capital and Co.* (Plate 1.10), which showed a vast, ermine-clad Capital reposing upon the Western allies and their money-bags, defeated counter-revolutionaries and (in the bottom row) priests, speculators, kulaks, landlords, underground anarchists and others.[58]

The artistic world more generally was strongly influenced by the political sentiments of the period. This was particularly the case in Moscow, where the influence of the socially conscious group of artists known as the 'Wanderers' was greatest and where there was less emphasis upon the formal skills and classical, often foreign, subject matter that were favoured by the Academy in St Petersburg. At the Moscow School of Painting, Sculpture and Architecture, for instance, which was socially less exclusive than the St Petersburg Academy, classes were cancelled in February 1905 shortly after 'Bloody Sunday', when the police had fired on a peaceful demonstration in the capital and hundreds had lost their lives or been injured. During the general strike which took place in October 1905 teaching staff at the school, with the support of the local Socialists, organised a catering service and an infirmary for those who had been wounded. The School was finally closed the following month, but meetings involving staff and students continued on other premises.[59] At the Stroganov Art School in Moscow, where the student body was still more socially representative, meetings and concerts were organised in support of the strikers and a strike committee was established. There were many arrests in the School after the December uprising had been crushed.[60]

In St Petersburg too the student body was particularly affected by 'Bloody Sunday': classes were interrupted in all higher educational institutions, including the Academy, and meetings and demonstrations were held on Academy premises with substantial public participation. After a meeting in October 1905 at which more than 3,000 were in attendance the Academy itself was closed.[61] The artist Valentin Serov (1865–1911), who personally witnessed 'Bloody Sunday' from his rooms in the Academy, later resigned his membership and depicted the terrible scene in a painting reproduced in the first number of *Zhupel*. Repin, Tadeusz Makovsky and other artists responded in similar if less demonstrative terms.[62] Bilibin, at this time a radical, was briefly arrested for his sketches in *Zhupel* including *Donkey 1/20 Size* (Plate 1.11), which was seen as an indirect attack upon the autocracy.[63] Journals of this kind circulated in large numbers (up to tens of thousands) and appear to have had a considerable public impact; they were certainly in demand and for confiscated numbers particularly large sums were paid.[64]

In political and perhaps also in aesthetic terms this was the high point of pre-revolutionary Russian satirical graphics. By 1907 most of the satirical journals had either been suppressed altogether or had been subjected to more effective government control. Journals like *Satirikon*, which began to appear in 1908 on a weekly basis, were less controversial in their activities, although they continued to attract artists of high repute such as Alexander Benois (1870–1960), Lansere, Lev Bakst (1868–1924) and others. *Budilnik*, which continued to appear in Moscow, was on the whole more sharply

1.11 I. Ya. Bilibin, *Osel v 1/20 natural'noi velichiny* (Donkey 1/20 size), *Zhupel*, 1906, no. 3.

critical in its political stance than *Satirikon*, to some extent reflecting the different political and social milieux of the cities in which the two journals were published. From 1913 up to 1918, however, some of the staff of *Satirikon* published *Novyi Satirikon* (New Satirikon), which was politically more radical than its parent journal and which published the work of, for instance, the young Mayakovsky as well as more established writers and artists. Vladimir Lebedev, Nikolai Radlov and Vladimir Kozlinsky were among the artists who worked in *Novyi Satirikon* and then went on to play a prominent role in Soviet poster art after the revolution. The journal broadly supported the February revolution but opposed the Bolshevik seizure of power in October 1917, and its editor, Nikolai Remizov, was compelled to emigrate soon afterwards when the journal itself was closed down.[65]

Thus, continuities between the Soviet political poster and pre-revolutionary graphic art were of several kinds. In the first place, as has already been noted, many of the poster artists of the Soviet period had come to prominence and developed their art in the pre-revolutionary satirical journals. Among them were, for instance, Moor, who contributed his first sketches to the satirical journals *Kimval* (Cymbal) and *Utro vechera mudrenee* (Morning is Wiser than Evening) in 1907 and then from 1908 up to 1917 was an active participant in *Budilnik*.[66] Other prominent poster artists who made their debut on the pages of pre-revolutionary satirical journals included Viktor Deni (a frequent contributor to *Bich* (Whip), *Budilnik* and others), Aleksei Radakov (a member of the editorial boards of *Novyi Satirikon* and *Galchonok*), Ivan Malyutin (who worked for *Budilnik* and other journals), and Sergei Chekhonin, an active illustrator in satirical magazines during 1905–7 who was later known particularly for his revolutionary porcelain designs.[67] Although the satirical journals, especially those of 1905–7, were generally liberal in their editorial inclinations, it did not necessarily follow that the artists who appeared in their pages supported the Bolshevik and revolutionary cause; in fact some of them, notably Bilibin and Lansere, later lent their services to the White armies. Those who remained in the country, however, whatever their politics, had little choice but to seek an alternative outlet for their talents after the revolution, as the satirical journals had either collapsed or been suppressed (a Bolshevik satirical journal, *Solovei* (Nightingale) was established in December 1917 but brought out only two issues).[68] For many graphic artists who remained on Soviet territory, poster work was the only form of employment that was realistically available.

As well as continuities of personnel there were continuities of theme and subject. The 'Before and After' type of poster, for instance, which was employed after the revolution to contrast the Soviet with the Tsarist period (see for instance Plate 1.13), had its origin in the political postcards that were issued during the 1905–7 period.[69] Viktor Deni's *The Spider and the Flies* (Plate 1.14), produced as an anti-religious poster in October 1919, had appeared in substantially the same form as a cartoon in the journal *Bich* in 1917.[70] A more remarkable example of continuities of this kind was a picture by a young artist, I. I. Mushketov, which was exhibited at the Academy of Arts in St Petersburg in 1906. Entitled *Clock*, it depicted the head of a worker at the top of clock face towards which the hour hand, in the form of a sharp sword, was steadily advancing. The picture appeared in the St Petersburg journal *Niva* the following year, where it came to the attention of the artistic community.[71] Rather later, in 1919, the idea of a clock face with its advancing hand was adapted by M. M. Cheremnykh for an illustration on the front page of the newspaper *Bednota* (The Poor) on 1 January, where it was entitled *Happy New Year, Bourgeois! It is Five Minutes to Midnight*. The head of a capitalist had been substituted for the figure 12, the hour hand was pointing towards it and the minute hand, in the form of

1.12 Viktor Deni, *Poslednii chas!* (The Last Hour!), coloured lithograph, 1920, 62 × 49 cm., BS 470.

a sword labelled 'communism', was advancing rapidly in the same direction.[72] In another version, entitled *Five Minutes to October*, the capitalists of Britain, America and France were shown trying to hold back the progress of the clock hands towards midnight; in a further version, issued in the summer of 1920, the clock face included the heads of Nicholas II and a series of counter-revolutionary leaders including Baron Wrangel, who was advancing upon Soviet-held territory from the south at this time and who was added to the clock face while the poster was still in production.[73] Deni's poster for the Red Army in Kazan in 1920 (Plate 1.12) drew most of its inspiration from Cheremnykh's original.

Finally, and most obviously, the political poster of the Soviet period drew upon the traditions established by the commercial, publicity and other posters that had been produced in Russia, as in most of the other European countries, during the later nineteenth century (the author of the most substantial and near-contemporary study of the civil war poster, Vyacheslav Polonsky, in fact regarded the earliest Soviet posters as simply a continuation of the commercial posters of the pre-

1.13 D. S. Moor, *Prezhde: Odin s soshkoi, semero s lozhkoi; Teper': kto ne rabotaet, tot ne est* (Before: One with the Plough, Seven with a Spoon; Now: He who does not Work shall not Eat), coloured lithograph, 1920, 46 × 33 cm., BS 483.

ПАУК И МУХИ.

Дили - бом !.. Дили - бом !..
Стоит церковь -божий дом,
А в том доме - паучек,
Паучек - крестовичек,
Паучек семи пудов,-
„Все от праведных трудов":
Нахлобучивши клобук,
Ухмыляется паук
И трезвонит целый день:
Делень - день !.. Делень - день !..

Паук весело живет,
Паутиночку плетет,
В паутину ловит мух:
Молодаек и старух,
Молодцов и стариков-
Богомольных мужиков.
Мухи жалобно жужжат,
Пауку несут деньжат,
Все, что нажили горбом.
Дили - бом !.. Дили - бом !..

Ой вы, братцы - мужики,
Горемыки - бедняки,
А давно уж паука
Взять пора вам за бока:
Ваши души он „спасал"-
Вашу кровушку сосал
Да кормил жену и чад-
Паучиху, паучат,
И пыхтел, осклабив рот:
- Ай дурак - же наш народ!

Демьян Бедный·

№ 45

1.14 Viktor Deni, *Pauk i mukhi* (The Spider and the Flies), coloured lithograph, 1919, 54 × 35 cm., BS 3352.

revolutionary period).[74] In Russia, as elsewhere, poster advertising was essentially a development of the late nineteenth and early twentieth centuries, and, as in other countries, some of the most prominent artists of the time became involved in it. Among the Russian artists who contributed most notably to the pre-revolutionary poster were Mikhail Vrubel (1856–1910), Lansere, Bakst, and the brothers Viktor (1848–1926) and Apollinary Vasnetsov (1856–1933). Among the most notable examples of their work were, for instance, Bilibin's posters advertising *New Bavaria* beer (1903) and the *Caucasus and Mercury* shipping company (1911) and a series of posters produced by Valentin Serov for the visit of the Russian ballet to Paris in 1909 including Anna Pavlova in *Les Sylphides*.[75] Posters were also produced to advertise books and journals, exhibitions, and cinema and theatrical performances.[76]

Russian poster art, despite these developments, was nonetheless less well advanced than in many other European countries at this time; when the first international exhibition of the artistic poster was organised in Paris in 1897, for instance, only 28 of the 727 items on display came from Russia.[77] This in turn reflected the country's low level of urbanisation and the very limited development of an indigenous commercial capitalism. Socio-political posters in particular were in an 'embry-

1.15 Anon, *Voennyi 5½% zaem. Posil'noe uchastie v zaime – patrioticheskii dolg kazhdogo* (War 5½% Loan), coloured lithograph, 1916, 61 × 50 cm.

onic state' before the First World War.[78] During the war, however, as in most other belligerent nations, posters played a prominent part in appealing for recruits and for additional funds for war purposes.[79] The earliest wartime posters in Russia, which appear to have enjoyed little success, were essentially proclamations making much use of imperial symbols such as the double-headed eagle in conjunction with a lengthy text. Within a year or two, however, they had been superseded by posters appealing in more graphic terms for subscriptions to a 5½ per cent war loan, for which a competition was organised in 1916.[80] One of these posters addressed itself rather tactlessly to the propertied classes: 'Do not forget those behind whose backs you are drinking coffee', it urged. Others made heavy use of the theme of St George and the dragon, a subject favoured by the artists of other belligerent nations.[81] There were, however, more effective and imaginative posters, some of them by members of the Academy of Arts or of the 'Wanderers' group such as A. F. Maksimov, I. A. Vladimirov and V. V. Belyaev.[82] In posters of this kind, which became increasingly common as the war dragged on, ordinary Russian soldiers came to occupy a more prominent place than before and to be depicted, without false heroism or pretence, as straightforward working people who were carrying out a dangerous and thankless task.

These features were particularly apparent in the posters that were issued to appeal for funds for war victims, orphans and refugees. Several of these, by masters such as the Vasnetsov brothers and Isaac Brodsky, were later adapted by Bolshevik poster artists appealing for support for victims of the civil war.[83] One of the most remarkable was by Leonid Pasternak, a member of the St Petersburg Academy of Arts and father of the poet. Pasternak's poster, issued soon after the war had started, was entitled *Help for War Victims* (the drawing of a wounded soldier which served as the basis of the poster is reproduced in Plate 1.16). The poster was prepared at the request of the Moscow municipality, who sent a deputation to Pasternak to ask him to prepare an illustration that could be used in conjunction with an appeal for donations for the benefit of war victims. Pasternak, who was spending the summer in the countryside, asked for a fully armed soldier to be sent to him as a model. As the artist later recalled, the poster enjoyed an enormous and unexpected success. It was put up all over Moscow on the day of the collection; crowds gathered before it, and women burst into tears. A postcard version was prepared which sold in hundreds of thousands of copies; and versions appeared on the wrapping papers of sweets, on labels and on stickers. Rodzianko, chairman of the quasi-parliament of the period, the State

1.16 L.B. Pasternak, Sketch for *Na pomoshch' zhertvam voiny* (Sketch for 'Help to War Victims'), *The Studio*, vol. 64, February 1915.

under a jury headed by Maxim Gorky, for the best posters to advertise a 'Freedom Loan' (as support for the war effort was now presented). Two posters were approved in Petrograd (as the former imperial capital was now known), Boris Kustodiev's *Freedom Loan* (Plate 1.18), which won first prize, and P. Buchkin's *Freedom Loan*: *War until Victory* (Plate 1.17), which came second. Other posters were approved in similar contests in Moscow and elsewhere.[85] Some of the posters that were produced during 1917 boldly accused the Bolsheviks of being in German pay, such as Bilibin's *How the Germans bought up the Bolsheviks*.[86] Posters were also produced for the elections to the Constituent Assembly in November 1917. It is generally agreed that those produced by the peasant-based Socialist Revolutionary Party were the most effective in terms of numbers, size and richness of colour; some of them, in the view of Polonsky, were among the best of all the posters that were produced during the revolutionary period.[87] Other posters of note were produced by the liberal Cadet Party, by industrial and trade groupings, and by the Social Democrats. The Bolsheviks them-

1.17 P. Butchkin, *Zaem svobody*. *Voina do pobedy* (Freedom Loan. War until Victory), coloured lithograph, 1917, 101 × 68 cm.; courtesy of the Imperial War Museum, London.

Duma, personally appealed to Pasternak to supply him with several tens of thousands of copies. The Tsar himself was less satisfied, reportedly remarking in disgust that '*his* soldiers conducted themselves bravely, and not like this!' Four years later, in August 1918, Pasternak, returning from the countryside to Moscow, found that his poster had been adapted yet again, this time as a Soviet anti-war poster (in fact the very first issued under the auspices of the new regime). The only change was that the title had been altered from *Help for War Victims* to *The Price of Blood*. The head of the publishing house explained to Pasternak that all the work he had previously produced was now state property and could be reproduced without his permission and indeed without payment. Unabashed, he invited Pasterak to undertake further work in the same style; Pasternak, however, produced no more posters (although he did make some sketches of Lenin) and in 1921 emigrated to Germany.[84]

Further developments occurred after the February revolution and the establishment of a Provisional Government, which was still committed to the war effort. Soon afterwards a competition was organised,

1.18 B. M. Kustodiev, *Zaem svobody* (Freedon Loan) coloured lithograph, 1917, 101 × 67 cm.

1.19 Viktor Deni, *Antanta pod maskoi mira* (The Entente under the Mask of Peace), coloured lithograph, 1920, 49 × 34 cm., BS 842.

demurely feminine mask from his beast-like and aggressive features.

In general, as Polonsky has justly remarked, 'the Russian poster in a qualitative sense moved far forward' in the months from February to October 1917,[90] and the contribution of the graphic art of this period and of the wartime years to the Bolshevik political poster was a direct and important one.

selves produced a single poorly-printed sheet in two colours, headed simply 'Vote for List No. 4'. Depicting a soldier and a worker hoisting a red banner, it served as the basis for many Soviet posters in the post-revolutionary period but at the time attracted little public attention.[88]

Another direct link between the pre- and post-revolutionary periods was a poster prepared by A. Zelinsky for elections to the Constituent Assembly on behalf of the Cadet Party. Entitled *Remember to Vote only for [List] No. 2*, it showed a large mask, from behind which the ugly features of a policeman were peering out with a lazy grin. So little did the appearance of the poster accord with the manner in which the Cadets would have wished to present themselves that it has been argued that it may have been modified by Bolshevik printing workers or even produced by the Bolsheviks themselves.[89] At all events, the motif of a mask being removed to reveal the real nature of one's political opponents was repeatedly employed by Soviet poster artists in the post-revolutionary period, for instance in Deni's *The Entente under the Mask of Peace* (Plate 1.19), which depicted a bowler-hatted bourgeois removing a

CHAPTER TWO
Apsit and the Early Soviet Poster

It was not until August 1918, nine months after the new regime had been established, that the first distinctively Soviet political posters appeared on the streets of Petrograd. There were nonetheless several circumstances which suggested that the Bolsheviks were likely to devote considerably more attention to the political poster and other forms of mass persuasion than preceding administrations had done. The first stemmed from the fact that the new Soviet regime was intended to represent a qualitative change from all previous forms of state power in that it was to be constituted through the informed participation of all citizens, particularly ordinary workers and peasants. The Constitution of the Russian Socialist Federal Soviet Republic (RSFSR), adopted in July 1918, declared its fundamental aim to be the

> abolition of all exploitation of man by man, the complete elimination of the division of society into classes, the ruthless suppression of the exploiters, the establishment of a socialist organisation of society and the victory of socialism in all countries.

In line with these objectives political power was reserved 'wholly and exclusively' for working people and their elected representatives.[1] The new Programme adopted by the ruling Communist Party in March 1919 similarly committed the new regime to the Soviet form of government by which the vast majority of the population, workers and poor or semi-proletarian peasants, were to become the 'permanent and exclusive basis of the whole state apparatus, local and central'.[2] In order to realise the full potential of this new form of rule and (not least) to build up their own support, the Bolsheviks had for their part to commit themselves to what the Party Programme described as a 'continually rising standard of culture, organisation and self-activity on the part of the masses',[3] transforming levels of political knowledge and activity to those required and presupposed by the new forms of state and party organisation.

If the new regime did wish to carry out a 'cultural revolution', as Lenin evidently intended, it followed that non-printed forms of political communication would receive particular attention. One of the most important reasons for this was the low level of literacy of the Soviet population at this time, particularly outside the major towns and European areas. The first census of the Russian Empire, carried out in 1897, found that only 28.4 per cent of the total population aged between nine and forty-nine was literate; the proportions varied enormously from an almost wholly literate Estonia (96.2 per cent) to an almost wholly illiterate Central Asia (Uzbekistan, for instance, was no more

2.1 V. I. Lenin, photographed by Pavel Zhukov, 1920.

common with other sectors, had been seriously affected by the disruption of revolution and civil war. Stocks of paper were at a low level, in part because of the loss of the Baltic provinces which had previously supplied about half of total requirements.[5] The printing works themselves were often out of action, partly because of the loss of qualified staff, partly because of a lack of spare parts, equipment and fuel, and partly also because of the hostile attitude of the pro-Menshevik printers' union. By 1921, it was calculated, only about half the printing presses that had been in operation before the war were still working.[6] The position was still worse outside Moscow and Petrograd.[7] The public transport system, which was responsible for the distribution of books and newspapers outside the major urban areas, was in a state of chaos as a result of military action and a lack of fuel and equipment. The circulation of newspapers in the early post-revolutionary years, for reasons such as these, was relatively low by comparison with both earlier and later years. The daily print of *Pravda* during the civil war, for instance, was about 138,000 copies per issue, and the total daily print of Red Army newspapers, of which there were about 25, was rather less than 250,000.[8] Book production was also at a low ebb: the number of titles produced between 1918 and 1920, for instance, was only a sixth of the pre-war average, and the number of copies produced was down by more than half.[9] Clearly, even allowing for multiple readership, reading aloud and other such devices, the printing press was not likely to provide an effective means of communication with even the literate minority in a total population which in the early 1920s was already approaching 150 million.[10]

In an attempt to respond to these circumstances a wide variety of forms of mass communication was employed in the early years of Soviet rule, particularly during the civil war (roughly 1918 to 1920). Among the first was a plan to replace memorials to the Tsar and members of their court with memorials to socialists and revolutionaries. This, Lenin's plan of 'monumental propaganda', was first adumbrated in a discussion with Anatoly Lunacharsky, the People's Commissar for Enlightenment, in April 1918.[11] Lenin explained to Trotsky that he was

> anxious to have as many revolutionary monuments erected as possible , even if they were of the simplest sort, like busts or memorial tablets, to be placed in all the towns, and, if it could be managed, in the villages as well, so that what had happened might be fired into the people's imagination, and leave the deepest possible furrow in the popular memory.[12]

A decree of April 1918 provided for the removal of

than 3.6 per cent literate). The RSFSR itself was close to the national average with 29.6 per cent literacy. By the time the next census was carried out, in 1920, the overall level of literacy within the territory under Soviet rule had increased to 44.1 per cent, but there were still marked variations between the areas inhabited by different nationalities, between men and women, and between urban and rural areas (73.5 per cent of whose who lived in urban areas were literate, but only 37.8 per cent of those who lived in the countryside). In rural areas, in which the overwhelming majority of the Soviet population lived and in which the tasks of political mobilisation were most urgent, the new regime had to operate, at least until the late 1920s, in circumstances of majority illiteracy which meant that particular emphasis had to be placed upon visual rather than printed or textual forms of communication and persuasion.[4]

In the immediate post-revolutionary years there were, in any case, major obstacles to the widespread circulation of printed propaganda materials, particularly of books and newspapers. The printing industry, in

2.2 Monument to Alexander III brought down, Moscow, 1918 (courtesy of David King).

statues of members of the Tsarist court (see Plate 2.2); a further decree of July 1918 set out a list of those who were to be honoured in their place in Moscow and other cities.[13] Lenin personally unveiled the monument to Karl Marx and Friedrich Engels in Moscow on 7 November 1918, the first anniversary of the revolution (Plate 2.3), and he also unveiled a bas relief *To the Fallen in the Struggle for Peace and Friendship of the Peoples* on the Senate Tower of the Kremlin.[14] The first of the memorials to be unveiled was a bust of Alexander Radishchev, the eighteenth-century radical; other monuments were dedicated to the Ukrainian poet Taras Shevchenko, the nineteenth-century radical writers Alexander Herzen and Nikolai Ogarev, and figures of artistic and cultural distinction such as Fedor Dostoevsky, Andrei Rublev and the composer Skryabin. Foreigners were also honoured, among them Spartacus, Danton and Robespierre, Garibaldi, Robert Owen and Florence Nightingale. In Moscow alone at least thirteen monuments had been erected by the end of 1918 and twenty-five by the end of 1921; by the same date more than fifteen had been erected in Petrograd.[15]

A particularly wide range of activities was undertaken on anniversaries or other notable occasions, when Moscow, Petograd and other towns and cities were decorated with large-scale banners and other forms of display. The first festive decorations of this kind took place on 1 May 1918; they were repeated on 7 November 1918 and on other revolutionary and public anniversaries and holidays. Special arrangements were made for these occasions by local party committees; in Moscow, for instance, these covered the route the demonstration should take, the forms of public decoration, the content of speeches and even the possibility of hostile inter-

20

2.3 Lenin speaking at the unveiling of a memorial of Karl Marx and Friedrich Engels in Moscow, November 1918.

Saints Cyril and Methodius, and others depicted popular but non-socialist figures such as the peasant leader Stenka Razin.[17] The work was varied in style and execution, and some of it was almost exaggeratedly avant garde: the lawns, flower-beds and trees in front of the Bolshoi Theatre, for instance, were coloured purple and red,[18] and the shops along Okhotnyi Ryad (now Marx Avenue) in the centre of Moscow were painted in brilliant carnival colours.[19] Similar displays were mounted in other Soviet cities by local artists, both on orthodox lines and particularly in Vitebsk and its environs, where Chagall, Malevich, El Lissitsky and others were involved) on more experimental lines as well.[20]

Considerable attention was devoted to the organisation of public demonstrations of all kinds, and to the floats that were displayed on such occasions. In some cases groups of workers paraded behind large representations of the goods they produced: a file factory, for instance, brought a huge diagram representing its production achievements for the previous few months, and brewery workers paraded behind a car on whose roof were barrels of various sizes showing the nature of their output. Other displays were more directly political: workers in a fur factory, for instance, displayed dolls representing Lloyd George, Mussolini and other Western leaders in a large cage, and the Association of Chemists carried a huge tablet with a doctor's prescription upon it, which read: 'For the sick proletariat of Western Europe: one part general strike, one part united front, and one part soviet republic. Ordered by Doctor Vladimir Ilich Lenin. Dose: as much as is required.' Another device was to stage open-air 'trials' of political opponents, or re-enactments of revolutionary events (the most celebrated of these was a re-run of the storming of the Winter Palace in 1920 involving real troops and many of the original participants). There were street theatre performances, and concerts in

2.4 Decoration of the Town Duma building (now the Central Lenin Museum), Moscow, 1918.

ventions during the proceedings.[16] Special committees were set up to undertake detailed arrangements which worked in close cooperation with the Fine Arts section of the Moscow Soviet and with Proletkult, an organisation of originally non-Bolshevik character whose purpose was to help to develop proletarian culture as one of the means by which the socialist revolution was to be attained. In these early years civic decorations took a variety of forms and were not wholly Bolshevik in inspiration: one of the decorative panels erected in Moscow in November 1918, for instance, honoured

2.5 Figures of Lloyd George, Millerand, Kerensky and Milyukov in front of the Kremlin, Moscow, 1921 (courtesy of the Radio Times Hulton Picture Library).

which, in line with the spirit of the times, industrial as well as ordinary musical instruments were used. These 'factory whistle symphonies' were held in major towns from 1918 onwards; the first on a large scale took place in Baku in 1922 and involved the whole of the Caspian fleet as well as two batteries of artillery, machine guns and masses choirs. This 'concert', not surprisingly, could be heard 'far from the walls of the town of Baku'.[21]

Festive decorations and processions were largely confined, for practical reasons, to the larger towns and cities. Visual propaganda was extended to the countryside by a variety of other means, among them the agitational trains and other forms of transport which made their first appearance in 1918. The idea of 'agittrains', according to contemporary sources, originated in the Military Department of the publishing house attached to VTSIK (the All-Russian Central Executive Committee), the body which served as the Soviet legislature at this time. The Department regularly despatched compartments full of political literature to various parts of the country on ordinary passenger trains, accompanied by couriers. It soon occurred to those responsible that a carriage or even a whole train could be filled with literature of this kind, and that the sides of the carriages could be decorated with agitational pictures and slogans (ordinary posters were torn off by the wind or washed away by rain).[22] The first 'agit-train' of this kind, the 'Mobile Military Front-line Literary Train Named after V. I. Lenin', left Moscow for Kazan in August 1918 for a two-week visit to a part of the country then held by the Czech Legion. The experiment was judged a success, and arrangements for further trains of this kind were entrusted to a commission headed by Vyacheslav Karpinsky (1880–1965), a Bolshevik journalist who was a member of VTSIK, and Konstantin

2.6 The Girl Corps, Soviet Red Cross, marching in Red Square, Moscow, 1921 (courtesy of the Radio Times Hulton Picture Library).

Eremeev (1874–1931), another Bolshevik journalist who had personally taken part in the storming of the Winter Palace. Agit-trains distributed literature at points along their route, and produced their own newspapers in up to 15,000 copies. All had bookshops and other services, and some had travelling cinemas with seats for up to 150 people. Their sides were highly decorated by poster artists in a style suitable to the territory through which they were to travel.[23] VTsIK was also responsible for the *Red Star* agitational ship (Plate 2.7), which toured the Volga and Kama rivers after the defeat of Kolchak in the summers of 1919 and 1920; and there is also mention of an 'agit-barge'.[24]

Agitational trains, in practice, were subject to very little control on the part of the party and state bodies to which they were nominally accountable. Some government administrators, it appears, were actually hostile to the idea of measures of this kind, seeing them as little better than 'sanatoria' for sick and overworked officials where they could rest and recuperate, and some poor choices were made in the selection of political workers to accompany them. There were also delays in equipping the agit-trains; the fifth and last was ready for service some two years after it had been commissioned.[25] Altogether five agitational trains were in service between the summer of 1918 and the end of 1920, each of them making up to twelve separate journeys.[26] On one of them the Soviet President, Mikhail Kalinin, was present in person (this train was known as 'VTsIK on wheels'). His train, the *October Revolution*, left Moscow in April 1919 to visit areas near the Kolchak front; it consisted of twelve carriages, including a printing works which produced a train newspaper, a restaurant,

a radio station, and presents for ill and wounded soldiers, as well as living and sleeping quarters for its staff. A further carriage contained a garage with a car which allowed Kalinin to visit areas up to fifty miles on either side of the railway line.[27] On another occasion, in the summer of 1919, Lenin's wife, Nadezhda Krupskaya, together with Vyacheslav Molotov, travelled on the 'Red Star' agitational ship.[28] Altogether, it has been calculated, agitational trains and ships visited almost all regions of Soviet Russia during the civil war years, spending 659 days in the field and receiving 2.8 million members of the public at 775 different locations.[29]

Polonsky called the agitational train a 'mobile poster' or 'poster-train'.[30] Posters of a more orthodox kind took some time to make their appearance, but in August 1918, as the civil war was just beginning, the first two posters of the Soviet period were published by VTsIK. The first, already mentioned, was a version of Leonid Pasternak's *Help for War Victims* with the title changed to *The Price of Blood* and some verse added to commemorate the fourth anniversary of the outbreak of the First World War. Two versions were printed, one in Moscow under the auspices of VTsIK, the other in Petrograd under the auspices of the city Soviet.[31] At about the same time a second poster, *Tsar, Priest and Kulak*, was issued by VTsIK (Plate 2.8), the work of an artist called Pet.[32] Also somewhat static and decorative in nature, the poster was issued not only in Russian but also in Ukrainian, Belorussian, Polish, Tatar, Hebrew, Chuvash, Latvian, Lithuanian, Estonian, Mordovian and Mari, with appropriate changes in the figures depicted (the version in Estonian, for instance, substituted a Lutheran pastor for the Orthodox priest and merchant for the kulak; the version in Tatar introduced

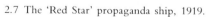

2.7 The 'Red Star' propaganda ship, 1919.

23

2.8 Pet, *Tsar, pip ta kulak (glitai)* (The Tsar, the Priest and the Kulak), two coloured lithograph, 1918, 70 × 61 cm., BS 708, text in Ukrainian.

4). The posters he produced for VTSIK consisted of a sequence of frames, normally in black and white, conveying a political message but in a humorous and imaginative manner. Cheremnykh himself drew the posters and supplied the accompanying text. His *Concerning the Toiler, the Priest and the Parasite*, for instance (Plate 2.9), produced in late 1918, told the story of a hard-working peasant who had been robbed of all his possessions by a priest and a parasite, who had persuaded him that (in line with Christian doctrine) he should give his shirt to his neighbour, shelter the destitute and feed the hungry. The priest and parasite turned up themselves and ate and drank their fill, finally chasing the poor peasant out of his own home. Prayers, candles and contributions to the church brought no end to his suffering. Finally, despairing, he climbed into the sky, found there was no god and realised he had been fooled. Returning home, he threw out the parasite, reclaimed his house and property, and began to bring his land back into cultivation. The parasite returned

2.9 M. M. Cheremnykh, *Pro trudyashchegosya, popa i tuneyadtsa* (Concerning the Toiler, the Priest and the Parasite), black and white lithograph, 1918, 71 × 53 cm., BS 494.

the figures of a mullah and a bey.[33]) The text of the Russian-language original began by noting that priests and kulaks were lamenting the end of Tsardom because it had allowed them to prosper at the people's expense. Soviet power had deprived them of their privileges, and they were now uniting to overthrow it. Those who wanted the return of landlords and the Tsar should support them; those who wanted to retain their land and liberty should resist them, ideally through committees of poor peasants (most later posters were less wordy).[34]

The triptych of Tsar, priest and kulak, though simply executed, was reproduced on a smaller scale in many other posters of the civil war period and has been described as a kind of 'symbol of the epoch'.[35] Also influential, although still very simply produced, was a series of posters produced by the Siberian artist Mikhail Cheremnykh for VTSIK during the latter part of 1918 and the early months of 1919. Cheremnykh was in his late twenties at this time, and had just graduated from the Moscow School of Painting, Sculpture and Architecture (his life and work are considered more fully in Chapter

24

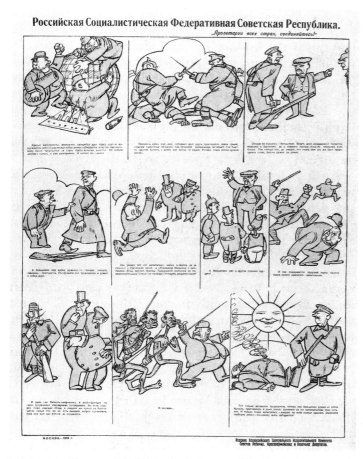

2.10 M. M. Cheremnykh, *Krichat kapitalisty* . . . (The Capitalists cry out), two coloured lithograph, 1919, 78 × 54 cm., BS 285.

with arms to take his revenge; in the final frame the peasant, despite the priest's best efforts, enlists in the Red Army in order to defend his possessions more securely.[36]

In another poster produced in the early months of 1919, Cheremnykh turned to the theme of the civil war. The poster is remarkable among other things for its inclusion of one of the very first recognisable depictions of Lenin. Again in the form of a series of frames with a brief linking commentary, the poster's main theme was that the revolution could ultimately be defended only by force of arms (Plate 2.10). Capitalists, the poster began by suggesting, had fought with each other to divide up the world in their own interests. Having failed to reach agreement they had started a war in which ordinary working people had shot and gassed each other and millions had lost their lives. At this point 'a Bolshevik' (clearly Lenin) had intervened, pointing out that the workers were in fact killing their own class brothers. The workers had then returned home with their weapons in their hands. Russian capitalists, in a panic, appealed to their allies, 'the American Wilson and

Co.', to save them. Bolshevism (once again inspired by Lenin) had meanwhile made its appearance in other countries and workers had risen up against their own capitalist class. Doubting the loyalty of their own soldiers in such circumstances, Wilson and the Allies had despatched semi-naked African troops to achieve their purposes. Russian workers, now understanding why the Bolsheviks had been reluctant to allow them to disarm, defeated this new offensive and disposed of those who had led it.[37] Other posters produced by Cheremnykh during the same period included *How the Deserter helped the Capitalist, The Worker turned out the Capitalist* with another depiction of Lenin (Plate 4.5), and *The Bourgeoisie lived well* (Plate 4.4), in which Lenin again puts in an appearance.[38]

Undoubtedly the master of the early Soviet political poster, however, was Alexander Apsit (Aleksandrs Apsitis), a Latvian who had previously worked mainly in the field of book and journal illustration. Apsit was born in Riga on 25 March 1880, the son of a blacksmith

2.11 Aleksandrs Apsit (reproduced from *Latviešu tēlotāja māksla 1957* [Riga: Latgosizdat, 1958])

and a spinning-mill worker.[39] He spent his early childhood in Pardaugava, one of the city's working-class districts. When Apsit was just five years old his father died and the family's material circumstances worsened considerably. His mother, who was Estonian, moved with her son to Tartu and eked out the family's existence by taking in laundry. The family still remained in some financial difficulty. Apsit, according to his own account, began to make a contribution to the family budget while still at school by decorating the book-covers of his more prosperous colleagues for two or three kopeks a time, or (as he was good at drawing) by making sketches or carrying out exercises in calligraphy. During his free time, whenever the travelling circus was in town, the young Apsit earned extra money by carrying out all sorts of tasks for them, acting as a barker or playing walk-on parts in pantomimes. When Apsit was fourteen his mother moved again, this time to St Petersburg, where he took on other casual jobs but gave as much time as he could to his favourite occupation, which was art. He began to copy paintings by the landscape artist, Ivan Shishkin, and others, and did so with such a degree of proficiency that dealers began to sell them as originals. While working in this way Apsit came into contact with the then celebrated St Petersburg artist Lev Dmitriev-Kavkazskii, who became interested in the young Latvian's ability and invited him to come to work in his studio.

The Dmitriev-Kavkazskii studio had been established in St Petersburg in 1895 with the aim of preparing its pupils for higher schools of art and academies. Profiting from the instruction with which he was provided without charge, Apsit's talents developed rapidly and within a year he had become a professional artist, painting the portraits of various influential figures in St Petersburg. These casual commissions, however, yielded too little money to provide a decent living. Fed up with his constant poverty, Apsit allowed himself to be influenced by one of his friends, Olshansky, who had also been a student in Dmitriev-Kavkazakii's studio, and was persuaded to go with him to Mount Athos in Greece to make sketches and earn some money. The journey was not a success: the two friends fell out, Olshansky returned home, and Apsit was left in a strange country with no means of support. He was compelled to become a novice in Mount Athos monastery, with which the Russian Orthodox Church had traditionally close relations, and came under strong pressure to remain permanently as a monk-illustrator. In the end the Russian consul had to intervene before Apsit was allowed to return home; his mother, who had had no word from him for nine months, had already given him up for dead. Dmitriev-Kavkazskii later bought the

sketches Apsit had made at Mount Athos and exhibited them with great success. Apsit now came to the attention of the leading journals and began to work for *Rodina, Niva* and other publications, becoming one of the most popular and best-paid illustrators in the city. He moved to Moscow at the turn of the century and was equally successful, supplying, as the engraver Ivan Pavlov recalled, 'almost all pre-revolutionary Moscow with posters, illustrations and drawings'. Like others, he turned to 'patriotic' poster work during the war.[40]

Apsit welcomed the October revolution, although he was making a luxurious living under the old regime and the depth of his political commitment should not be exaggerated. He did, however, become involved at an early stage in poster and propaganda work for the new regime, which itself lost no time in availing of his considerable talents. Konstantin Eremeev, through his contacts with VTSIK, invited Apsit to come and work under its auspices, and during 1918 and 1919 Apsit worked almost exclusively on political posters, for the most part for VTSIK. Apsit's first Soviet poster *A Year of the Proletarian Dictatorship* (Plate 2.12), a coloured lithograph celebrating the first anniversary of the revolution, made its appearance in the autumn of 1918. It showed a worker and a peasant, arms in hand, standing on the broken chains and other symbols of the imperial past and guarding the gate to a scene of industrial and agricultural prosperity, with a child in the foreground to represent the new life. Apsit used a variety of pseudonyms throughout his career, perhaps to disguise his extraordinarily prolific output: they included 'Skif', 'Chustka', 'A. Petrov', 'N. Osinin', 'A-t', and the zigzag device which appears in the corner of Plate 2.12. His illustrations were often accompanied by the verses of a revolutionary poet, most often Demyan Bedny, who had a considerable popular following at the time as the self-consciously proletarian bard of the new regime. Apsit, however, spent less than two years engaged in work of this kind; in late 1919, hearing that Denikin's army was approaching Moscow, he began to fear that (as he put it) he might be 'hung by the Whites for his posters' and left with his family for Ekaterinoslav (now Dnepropetrovsk) in southern Russia.[41] Apsit eventually found his way back to his native Latvia where he lived from 1921 onwards, working again as an illustrator for the major Riga journals and book publishers. He died in Germany in 1944 in obscure circumstances.[42]

While he was living in St Petersburg in the late 1890s Apsit made the acquaintance of the engraver Ivan Pavlov, who has left us an entertaining memoir of this period. They met, Pavlov recalled, around the billiard table in the 'Golden Anchor' bar. Apsit, although thoroughly irresponsible, attracted Pavlov by the

2.12 A. Apsit, *God proletarskoi diktatury* (Year of the Proletarian Dictatorship), coloured lithograph, 1918, 105 × 71 cm., BS 89.

warmth of his sociability and his undoubted talent. In fact he found it difficult to live without company, and spent much of his time in drinking sessions. He was an 'extremely original and eccentric person, especially when he found himself under the influence of Bacchus' Pavlov recalled. Once, while walking drunkenly around St Petersburg and bumping into pedestrians, an elderly man remarked to him that he was a fool 'and a long-haired one at that'. Apsit went immediately to the hairdresser's and had all his hair cut off. His mother failed at first to recognise him and asked what he had done; Apsit reassured her, saying 'It's all right, mama, now I'm brainy'.[43] On another occasion, Apsit was awaiting the arrival of a train in a station buffet with a group of companions. The conversation turned to legendary drinking bouts, one of the group remarking that he had heard of people who drank their glass and then ate it. Apsit immediately proposed that everyone drink an glassful and then announced: 'And now, friends, I will drink three glasses in a row and have the fourth as *hors d'oeuvres.*' He threw down the glasses one by one and then put the fourth into his mouth and crunched it into little pieces. Several of his more highly-strung companions found this too much to bear and fled; Apsit himself calmly took the pieces out of his mouth and offered them around to those who remained. He had lost all his teeth from repeated 'experiments' of this kind.[44]

Until quite recently Apsit's poster art was treated severely by Soviet commentators. Early Soviet posters of this kind, wrote Polonsky in 1925, were distinguished neither by their vividness of colour nor by their originality of composition or revolutionary inspiration; from the technical point of view they were simply 'banal popular pictures' of a kind that had been mass produced before the revolution. He described Apsit, who had been almost the only supplier of these lithographs in the early post-revolutionary years, as a 'mediocre draftsman' who had all the faults of the artists who had filled the illustrated boulevard journals with this kind of material in earlier years. Apsit, he went on, had been given his themes and had followed his instructions closely, so that his posters were in effect collective rather than individual creations; indeed they should not properly be called posters at all. Despite their 'noisy success', the only merit of posters of this kind was that they were among the first attempts to make use of lithography for the purposes of agitation and propaganda.[45] Dmitri Moor wrote some years later that Apsit's posters were a 'conglomerate of cinema poster pseudodramatics, cheap vulgar symbolism and the external elements of old-fashioned romanticism', reflecting a 'purely philistine, petty-bourgeois understanding of the revolution which was reactionary in its passivity'. Instead of appealing for action and showing the real friends and enemies of the revolution, Apsit's abstract

2.13 A. Apsit, *Narodnoe dvizhenie v smutnoe vremya* (The Popular Movement in the Time of Troubles), coloured lithograph, 1918, 36 × 52 cm., BS 359.

compositions simply disorientated the working class and its allies. The struggle against 'Apsitism', Moor declared, was in effect a struggle for the 'politicised, concrete, proletarian poster'.[46] Even after the Second World War Apsit was accused of tendencies towards bourgeois commercialism and of being excessively abstract and decorative.[47] More recent scholarship has however taken the view that, while much of his early work was unduly abstract and for this reason not always successful in agitational terms, Apsit was the first real master of the Soviet political poster and a figure of genuine distinction in the development of Soviet graphic art.[48]

Apsit's poster work in fact included much that was entirely straightforward in character. His *Popular Movement in the Time of Troubles* (Plate 2.13), for instance, was an uncomplicated depiction of the popular uprising of the early seventeenth century led by Ivan Bolotnikov,

2.15 A. Apsit, *Grud'yu na zashchitu Petrograda!* (Stand up for the Defence of Petrograd), black and white lithograph, 1919, 70 × 104 cm., BS 1022.

2.14 A. Apsit, *Vpered, na zashchitu Urala!* (Forward, to the Defence of the Urals!), black and white lithograph, 1919, 106 × 73 cm., BS 946.

a slave whose support came mainly from the poor and oppressed. This was one of a series of posters on historical themes which have been held to establish Apsit as one of the founders of the Soviet revolutionary-historical poster.[49] His *Forward, to the Defence of the Urals* (Plate 2.14), brought out in 50,000 copies by the main military publishing house in the early summer of 1919, was widely reproduced at the time and was again entirely realistic. Apsit's *Stand up for the Defence of Petrograd* (Plate 2.15), which appeared under the same auspices in the late spring of 1919, was conceived, carried out and printed in the course of a single day as the White leader Yudenich was approaching the former capital. Much later it served as the model for Vladimir Serov's *We will Defend the City of Leningrad*, produced in 1941 as German armies began their siege.[50] Apsit's *Day of the Wounded Red Army man* (Plate 2.16) was again entirely representational in character. His *Retreating before the Red Army*, produced in the autumn of 1919 (Plate 2.17), presented what was at least intended to be a realistic picture of the fate of the countryside as the White armies retreated. Apsit's splendid *To Horse, Proletarian!* (Plate 2.18), issued early in 1919 with a supporting text by Trotsky, is among the finest examples of heroic-revolutionary poster work of the whole civil war period. Even Apsit's *First of May* (Plate 2.19), issued in early 1919 on the thirtieth anniversary of the workers' festival, showed an entirely realistic worker planting a red flag on the surface of the globe; it was used as the cover illustration for at least one contemporary edition of the Party Programme.[51]

Apsit's more allegorical work evokes rather less approval even among sympathetically-inclined Soviet

2.16 A. Apsit, *Den' ranenogo krasnoarmeitsa* (Day of the Wounded Red Army Man), three coloured lithograph, 1919, 80 × 109 cm., BS 1022.

2.17 I. Osinin [A. Apsit], *Otstupaya pered Krasnoi Armiei, belogvardeitsy zhgut khleb* (Retreating before the Red Army), coloured lithograph, 1919, 65 × 100 cm., BS 1510.

НА КОНЯ, ПРОЛЕТАРИЙ!

№ 52

Рабочая революция должна создать могущественную красную конницу. Коммунист должен стать кавалеристом.

Л. Троцкий.

2.18 A. Apsit, Na Kanya, Proletarii (To Horse, proletarian!), two coloured lithograph, 1919, 104 × 71 cm text by Trotsky.

2.19 A. Apsit, *I Maya* (Ist May), three coloured lithograph, 1919, 95 × 71 cm., BS 434.

commentators and is generally held to reflect the pernicious influence of the newspaper drawings and popular prints in which he had engaged before the revolution.[52] A more considered judgement must surely place them among the most notable achievements of poster art of any period. Apsit's allegorical posters were generally large in format, bold in their use of colour and striking in their use of symbolism and allegory. *The Tsar, the Priest and the Rich Man on the shoulders of the Labouring People* (Plate 2.20), for instance, produced at the end of 1918, posited the same association between the autocracy, the church and the capitalist class that had been suggested in the very first but much less impressive Soviet poster, *The Tsar, the Priest and the Kulak* (see above, Plate 2.8). The same poster was produced with a different title, *Vengeance on the Tsars*, also under the auspices of vtsik; this time the text consisted of the 'Varshavyanka', a Polish working-class song which had been translated into Russian by G. M. Krzhizhanovsky in 1897 and had become popular in the socialist movement.[53] Another allegorical poster, *The Interna-*

tional (Plate 2.21), produced in late 1918 or early 1919, depicted workers pulling down a monstrous beast resting on a golden pedestal labelled 'Capital'; the text consisted of three of the verses of the 'Internationale', which had been translated into Russian in 1902 and adopted by the Russian Social Democrats in 1906 and then by the Soviet state in 1918 as their official anthems.[54] Another poster of late 1918, *To the Deceived Brothers* (Plate 2.22), depicted a peasant hero despatching the hydra-headed monster of Tsardom. Altogether, including both his realistic and his allegorical work, Apsit produced about forty political posters during the first year of so of civil war, from the autumn of 1918 up to the latter part of 1919;[55] it is thus not unreasonable to consider him the founder of the Soviet political poster.

Apsit was by no means the only Soviet poster artist who drew heavily upon allegory and myth at this time. Boris Zvorykin, for instance, a Moscow artist born in

2.20 A. Apsit, *Tsar', pop i bogach na plechakh trudovogo naroda* (The Tsar, the Priest and the Rich Man on the Shoulders of the Labouring People), coloured lithograph, 1918, 105 × 70 cm., BS 709.

„Пролетарии всѣхъ странъ соединяйтесь!"

ИНТЕРНАЦИОНАЛ.

ВТОРАЯ ГОСУДАРСТВЕННАЯ ТИПОГРАФІЯ.
Москва, Триумфальный пер., 8.

Издательство Всероссійскаго Центральнаго Исполнит. Комитета Совѣтовъ Рабочихъ, Крестьянск., Красноарм. и Казачьихъ Депутатовъ.

2.21 A. Apsit, *Internatsional* (The International), coloured lithograph, 1918/19, 107 × 72 cm., BS 221.

2.22 A. Apsit, *Obmanutym brat'yam (v belogvardeiskie okopy)* (To the Deceived Brothers), coloured lithograph, 1918, 105 × 70 cm., BS 1481.

1872, produced his *Struggle of the Red Knight with the Dark Force* (Plate 2.24) for the state publishing house in late 1919 in connection with the second anniversary of the revolution. Zvorykin's worker-hero was not entirely traditional in style: he fought with a hammer rather than a sword, and his shield was decorated with the hammer and sickle. This was nonetheless a heavily allegorical resolution of the struggle between capital and labour. Another artist who worked in this way, also of the older generation, was Vassily Spassky, a Moscow artist who was born in 1873 and died in 1924. His *Towards the Lighthouse of the Communist International*, for instance, was issued in the spring of 1919 to mark the International's first congress. It depicted a shipwrecked mariner, adrift on a stormy sea, steering towards a distant lighthouse on an open book with the words, 'Workers of all Countries, Unite!', spread across its pages. In the background a ship, its Tsarist flag still in

place, was slipping below the surface. 'Simple logic', it has been noted, 'suggests the unavoidable conclusion that if the ship has already sunk, an exhausted worker, barely able to steer his craft, will hardly make it on the pages of a book'.[73] Spassky, however, was also capable of more straightforward work, for instance *A Great Battle is Coming* (Plate 2.23), with its depiction of a dying Red Army man writing 'For socialism . . .' on the wall with his own blood. During the following year or so Spassky produced over thirty other posters, mostly representational in character, dealing with educational, public health and related themes.[74]

The early Soviet years were in fact very rich in their invention or popularisation of symbols and imagery which have had a significant influence upon the graphic art of other countries as well as upon Soviet political art up to the present day. The device of a worker breaking free from the chains that constrain him, for instance, had appeared in the publications of

2.23 V. Spassky, *Gryadet velikaya bitva* (A Great Battle is Coming), coloured lithograph, 1919, 71 × 54 cm., BS 95.

БОРЬБА КРАСНОГО РЫЦАРЯ С ТЕМНОЙ СИЛОЮ.

ГОСУДАРСТВЕННОЕ ИЗДАТЕЛЬСТВО.

ВТОРАЯ ГОСУДАРСТВЕННАЯ ТИПОГРАФИЯ.
Москва, Триумфальный пер., 9.

2.24 B. Zvorykin, *Bor'ba krasnogo rytsarya s temnoi siloyu* (The Struggle of the Red Knight with the Dark Force), coloured lithograph, 1919, 107 × 70 cm., BS 15.

2.25 B.M. Kustodiev, Cover of *Kommunisticheskii internatsional* (Communist International), no. 1, 1 May 1919.

2.26 Anon, *Rabochii! Tol'ko razbiv tsepi t'my, pridesh' k sotsializmu* (Worker! Only having Broken the Chains of Ignorance will you reach Socialism), three coloured lithograph, 1919, 73 × 106 cm., BS 3367.

the socialist movement before the war, but it received new and powerful expression in Boris Kustodiev's cover for the journal *Communist International* (Plate 2.25), the first issue of which appeared in the spring of 1919. Kustodiev prepared two other versions of the cover, both of which lacked the dynamic central element of the worker with his hammer and neither of which was for this reason quite so effective.[56] The emancipation of man from his chains of servitude contained echoes of the Greek myth of Prometheus, on which radical writers such as Shelley had also drawn; more obviously, perhaps, it drew upon the *Communist Manifesto* with its well-known conclusion that the workers of the world had 'nothing to lose but their chains'.

The hammer and sickle was another potent symbol of Soviet rule which became firmly established in these early years. It seems to have made its first appearance on the emblem of a local authority in Saratov in 1917, and swiftly became popular thereafter.[57] The first Soviet constitution, adopted in July 1918, established it as the new state symbol of the RSFSR ('a golden sickle and hammer, crossed, with handles pointing downward,

against a red background in the rays of the sun'). In 1924, in the first Constitution of the USSR, a five-pointed star was added to the upper part of the state arms.[58] The red star itself had been approved as a symbol for the newly-formed Red Army in April 1918, with a crossed hammer and plough superimposed upon it to represent the social forces form which the Army was supposed to draw its strength. The design, by an unknown artist, may have been inspired by Alexander Bogdanov's utopian novel *Red Star* (1908) which was reissued in large editions immediately after the revolution.[59]

The representation of the new regime in the form of a worker and a peasant also became established during the civil war years. It may have owed something to an influential drawing, *Brothers-in-Arms*, which appeared on the front cover of *Zritel* (Spectator) in 1905, and which depicted a worker, a peasant, a soldier and a sailor in a close and symbolic union.[60] The 'worker-peasant' imagery was repeated in many forms during these early post-revolutionary years: it was, for instance, a 'Worker-Peasant Red Army' and a 'Worker-Peasant Red Fleet' that were established in 1918, and a 'Worker-Peasant Inspectorate' that was established in 1920.

Another important symbol of the new regime was the sun, which had traditionally represented knowledge and new life. The sun was widely used to illuminate distinctively Soviet scenes, such as education and female emancipation, in contrast to the misery and oppression of the old regime (see for instance Plates 2.26 and 27). Individual elements soon became established artistic currency: a strong arm, for instance, to represent the working class, a red bayonet to represent the Red Army, and a fortress to represent the invincible Soviet Republic.[61] The notion of the 'locomotive of history'

2.27 I. Simakov, *Da zdravstvuet solntse! Da skroetsya t'ma*! (Long Live the Sun! May the Darkness be Hidden!), three coloured lithograph, 1921, 49 × 61 cm., BS 3266.

was reflected in further visual imagery: a red locomotive, for instance, was used to represent the Soviet state proceeding forwards, or to point to the motive agencies of social change (as a poster produced by an unknown artist for the railwaymen's union put it, 'Revolutions are the locomotives of history').[62]

Not all the new imagery, admittedly, was appropriate or successful. The Russian traditional, Biblical, classical and French revolutionary canons were raided fairly freely, and all kinds of associations might be suggested. Deliverers, for instance, were frequently depicted on Pegasus-style winged horses (see Plate 5.43). Freedom might be represented as a young maiden in classical dress.[63] Nike, the Greek god of victory, was enlisted to applaud the success of the proletarian cause.[64] The collapse of capitalism was represented as the 'fall of bourgeois Pompei'[65] and even Egyptian pharaohs were pressed into service in the proletarian interest.[66] There were also some 'mistakes' or at least inconsistencies in the new imagery. Moor, for instance, was taken to task

some years later by a group of Moscow art workers for having used colour incorrectly: in one of his posters, they pointed out, he had depicted White generals as well as Red Army bayonets in red.[67] Again, although the eagle was the accepted symbol of Tsardom, one of the proposals for a new state emblem in 1918 was an old eagle, plucked and stripped of its regalia, adorned with red stars and wearing a Red Army cap on its head, holding a stick and a stone in its respective wings.[68] A poster was in fact issued in 1919 entitled *Red Eagles of the World, Unite*!, showing a sinister looking bird, painted red, beside an aeroplane.[69] The cross, clearly a Christian rather than a socialist image, appeared in some early political posters;[70] so too did red angels, bringing peace and happiness to the world.[71] Another early poster of 1918 proclaimed the 'Ten Commandments of the Proletarian' (Plate 2.28); in another curious case Bernini's statue of David ws used as the basis of a poster, with a ship's wheel substituted for the Biblical sling.[72] On the whole, however, these

2.28 Anon, *Desyat' zapovedei proletariya* (The Ten Commandments of the proletarian), two coloured lithograph, 1919, 107 × 71 cm., BS 166.

and at other times. There was still, however, a tendency to purely decorative work with an excess of detail, and allegory and myth were often over-emphasised to the extent that they appear to have hindered understanding. The texts that accompanied the drawings were often lengthy and obscure, and religious, classical and other traditions were drawn upon rather indiscriminately. Above all, perhaps, there was still a tendency towards descriptive representation and passivity compared with the urgency, simplicity and direct appeal to the viewer of the posters of the years that immediately followed. It was during these years, essentially the years of the civil war (1919 and 1920), that the varied elements studied in this chapter were drawn together and fused into the classic Bolshevik poster.

early years were notable for their relatively swift development of a visual language which was effective, appropriate to the needs of the moment, and of lasting significance for Soviet political inconography.

The Soviet political poster in these early, post-revolutionary years had achieved some notable advances. A poster production and distribution system had come into being, dominated by the publishing house attached to VTSIK in Moscow and its local affiliates. A corps of poster artists, most of them already established as illustrators in books, magazines and newspapers, had been recruited and pressed into service. Elements of a new and distinctively Soviet imagery had begun to be developed, based upon symbols such as the hammer and sickle and the figures of worker and peasant (sometimes also Red Armyman) for whom the new regime claimed to stand. A number of posters of distinction and influence had been produced, to judge at least from the extent to which they were reissued of copied in other places

CHAPTER THREE
Moor, Deni and the Military-Political Poster

3..1 Unknown photographer, Leon Trotsky (1879–1940).

If the first two years of Soviet poster production were associated with vtsik, the civil war years were connected above all with Litizdat, the publishing house established in the summer of 1919 under the auspices of the Political Directorate of the Revolutionary Military Council of the RSFSR (*Revvoensovet*). This, the Soviet high command, was presided over by the People's Commissar for Military and Naval Affairs (from 1918 until 1925, Leon Trotsky) and had, during these years, the status of a department of the party's Central Committee apparatus.[1] There had, in fact, already been a considerable amount of military publishing under the auspices of a variety of other bodies. A *Soldiers' Pravda* had been published from April 1917 to March 1918 and it was swiftly followed by other publications intended for a military readership (by the latter part of 1918 at least ninety specifically military newspapers and journals were being published). The first publishing activities within the army itself began on 7 February 1918, just ten days after the Red Army had been formally established, with an emphasis from the outset upon agitational and instructional materials as well as upon official information. The first specialised military publishing house came into being in July 1918 under the auspices of vtsik, publishing a wide range of popular military materials, and the military academies which began to be established from late 1918 onwards issued a series of more specialised literature in smaller quantities.[2] There was still a great shortage of all kinds of publications for military purposes, as well as a lack of coordination among those bodies that were producing material of this kind. To remedy this situation a 'Literary-Publishing Department' (Litizdat) was established in June 1919 under the Political Directorate of Revvoensovet and under the technical supervision of Gosizdat, the state publishing house which had been established earlier the same year.[3]

The official decree of October 1919 confirming Litizdat's existence entrusted it with three tasks. The first of these was the 'preparation and issuing of periodicals, posters, pictures, drawings [and] proclamations of a military-agitational character'. Litizdat was also given responsibility for preparing and issuing books, brochures, posters and other material of a military-technical or military-educational nature, and for the preparation of periodicals, proclamations, posters and other material for distribution among the soldiers of the White armies and those of the Entente. In view of the 'exceptional importance and extraordinary urgency' of its work Litizdat was given 'complete independence' in organising the printing of its publications and every kind of technical assistance was to be made available to it, including the use of printing works and whatever stocks of paper and other material that might be needed. Litizdat was also empowered to absorb the activities and budgets of all other military publishing organisations in order to reduce duplication and to give more effective guidance to all work of this kind.[4]

Within Litizdat three separate sections were formed, political, technical and educational, the first of which assumed responsibility for the production of posters and other agitational materials.[5] A very high proportion of Litizdat's production during 1919 and 1920 was devoted to such purposes: almost 70 per cent of the 29.8 million copies of publications in all categories between June 1919 and January 1921, for instance, were proclamations, appeals, posters or open letters to the troops, and posters and *lubok* pictures alone accounted for some 20 per cent of total production over the same period.[6] Military publishing, sometimes in considerable quantities, was also undertaken under the general auspices of Litizdat by army headquarters at the various fronts. The publishing department attached to the armies on the western front, for example, issued almost 35 million copies of publications in seven different languages during the civil war years; its output included El Lissitsky's famous poster *Beat the Whites with the Red Wedge* (Plate 3.2), of which 2,000 copies were produced in 1920.[7]

Litizdat was headed from the outset by Vyacheslav Polonsky (real name Gusin), who thus became in effect the organiser of the military-political poster of the civil war years. Polonsky, according to his unpublished autobiography, was born in June 1886 to a Jewish watch-maker of modest means who lived near St Petersburg. His formal education came to an end in the second class of his grammar school because his father was unable to keep up his payment of the fees. It was for this reason, Polonsky believed, that he developed a passion for books, as a kind of compensation for the proper education of which he had been deprived. School friends helped him to get hold of what he needed, and he spent the long winter evenings reading. Almost an

3.2 El. Lissitsky, *Klinom krasnym bei belykh* (Beat the Whites with the Red Wedge), two coloured lithograph, 1920, 54 × 72 cm., BS 1215.

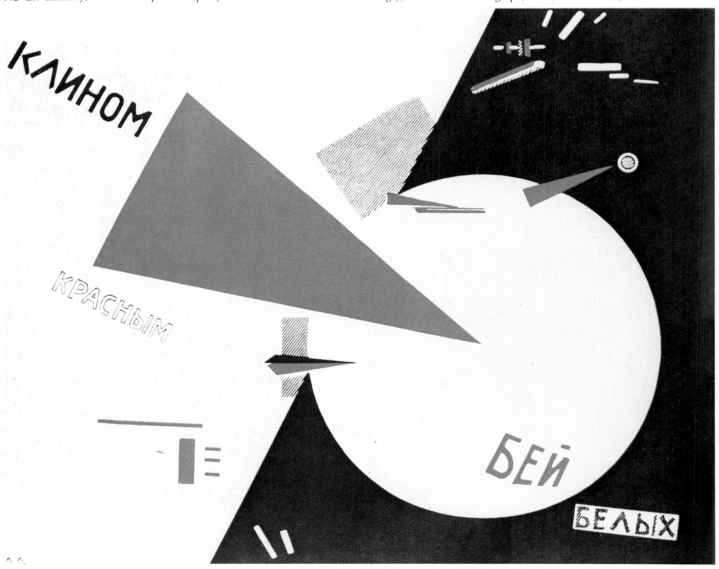

orphan at this time, he recalled, his playmates were poor children whose parents worked in the factories in the locality. Polonsky began to earn his living at the age of fourteen, first by transcribing letters and other documents, and latterly by working for the Chinese Eastern Railways. At the same time he attended classes at a commercial college as an extramural student. Here, Polonsky later recalled, he first heard of Marx and began to study political economy and socialist writings. In 1905, at the age of nineteen, he became involved in political activities, first of all as a Menshevik (he met and collaborated with V. A. Antonov-Ovseenko who was then also a Menshevik and later one of the leaders of the assault on the Winter Palace). Sacked from his job at the railway company in December 1905, Polonsky continued his studies, took his examinations successfully and became a teacher of history and Russian at a trade school. He had also begun to publish articles on literary themes from about 1908.

Polonsky worked for four years at the trade school, meanwhile extending his studies into medicine, until in the spring of 1911 he was arrested with other student radicals and sent into exile in the northerly Olonets region. He returned to St Petersburg in 1913 after an amnesty, was arrested again but soon released. He had meanwhile married and established a family, and found it necessary to do whatever he could to supplement his meagre earnings (his wife, in addition, had become seriously ill).

When war broke out in 1914 Polonsky was in the Caucasus, lecturing. He returned to St Petersburg (now Petrograd) and began to associate with the literary circles around Maxim Gorky, who had adopted a moderately 'patriotic' attitude towards the war effort (at first, Polonsky later admitted, he had not correctly understood the war's essentially imperialist nature). Polonsky continued to undertake literary work during these years, for Gorky's paper *Novaya zhizn* (New Life) among others, and also worked as a statistician for the Ministry of Land. He took an active part in the February revolution from the outset, touring the Romanian front on behalf of the Petrograd Soviet (he had meanwhile become a Menshevik-Internationalist and was temporarily a member of Trotsky's Interdistrict group). Polonsky initially opposed the Bolshevik seizure of power, believing it to be premature, but in 1918 he announced his resignation from the Mensheviks and became associated with the Internationalist section of the Russian Communist Party and later with the Bolshevik party proper. Between 1918 and the spring of 1919 Polonsky worked in VSNKh (the Supreme Council of the National Economy); he served briefly in the army, and was then given responsibility for the organisation of Litizdat from its foundation. He directed Litizdat

throughout the civil war years, later turning to other forms of literary work including the editorship of *Novyi mir*.[8]

Writing in *Izvestiya* on Polonsky's death in 1932, Moor and Deni, on behalf of the artists who had worked with him during the civil war, recalled Polonsky as a 'great figure, impetuous and emotional, [who] understood the mechanics of the artist's creative processes'; his 'enthusiasm, sincerity [and] fervour' compelled the artist to do his 'very utmost to respond to the appeal for creativity'.[9] The writer Lev Nikulin (1891–1967) remembered Polonsky as a 'man of 1919', as the editor of the Red Army paper *Krasnoarmeets*, and as the instigator of 'thousands of posters and *lubki*, with which the nearby front and rear had been saturated' during the civil war years. At that time, he recalled, the formerly magnificent flat in the huge house by the Sretensky gates in Moscow was a place where the editors of Red Army newspapers, artists and political workers would meet; around Polonsky himself there was a constant atmosphere of 'poetry, and the smell of paint and printer's ink, and . . . gunpowder'.[10]

The association between Polonsky and Moor, Deni and other artists was absolutely central to the creation and development of the Soviet political poster during these civil war years, in which it reached the height of its development. Polonsky, a figure whose own background was in the creative arts, was able to maintain a good working relationship with the often temperamental artists with whom he had to deal, and as head of Litizdat was able to ensure that their work was produced and distributed with a minimum of delay. Polonsky himself has left the fullest early accounts of the development of poster work during these years, first in an article in 1922 and then in a copiously illustrated volume published in 1925.[11]

Soviet poster art developed in two main directions during the civil war years: the heroic and the satirical. These were in turn associated with the two leading practitioners of the early Soviet poster, Dmitri Moor and Viktor Deni, respectively. Of the two it was perhaps Moor who was more distinctively a poster artist, Deni's work being closer in style to newspaper cartoons and caricature (it generally lost little by being reproduced in much smaller format, for instance in newspapers or on postcards). Dmitri Stakhievich Moor (real name Orlov) was born in October 1883 in Novocherkassk, the town in southern Russia which served as the capital and cultural centre of the Don Cossacks. His father, a mining engineer, was himself a Cossack, and in later life Moor often wore the distinctive clothing and headgear of his place of birth.[12] Moor's schooldays were spent in Kiev, Kharkov and finally in Moscow, where his family moved towards the end of the century. Already by this time Moor had shown a proclivity for art, producing an illustrated 'journal' for his younger sister, brother and school friends.[13] Moor went on from school to Moscow University, spending two years in the physics and mathematics faculty and then changing to the law faculty. He did not, it appears, have any ambition to practise as a lawyer at this time, or indeed any other definite career ambitions, and spent a lot of time furthering his own education, reading Marxist literature among other things (in school, according to his own perhaps romanticised recollection, he had been actively involved in radical student politics).

In 1905–6, at this time a university student, Moor took part in the revolutionary movement which was sweeping the country, and during the December 1905 uprising in Moscow he was entrusted with the safe keeping of the arms of the group of insurgents to which he belonged. He also took part in meetings and demonstrations and helped to put up barricades, and in 1906 he helped to set up an underground printshop with equipment smuggled out of the printing works in which he was then employed. His experience at this time, he later recalled, 'could not but leave a deep impression on my biography'; or as he put it in another memoir, 1905 had 'decided [his] fate': all his life he retained the 'youthful dreams' of that year.[14]

Moor had married by this time (his wife, Evgeniya Dneprova, was the daughter of one of the editors of the important paper *Russkie vedomosti*[15]) and had taken up employment in Mamontov's printing works to supplement his modest income. He was often required to work late at night. One evening, trying to keep awake, Moor began to make some sketches of Tsarist ministers. The editor of one of the evening papers produced at the works passed by, saw the sketches and invited Moor to contribute something to his paper. Moor carried out the editor's instructions and received his first royalty, the then considerable sum of 3 rubles. He had never previously thought of becoming an artist and had wished if anything to become an opera singer. Now, however, he hurled himself into his new career, spending not just his leisure time but whole nights sketching. In the end Moor never took his degree, nor did he receive any formal instruction in art apart from a few months spent in the studio of P. I. Kelin, an artist of some distinction at the time whom Moor referred to as the 'poor man's Serov'.[16]

Moor's first cartoons appeared in *Kimval* and *Utro vechera mudrenee* in 1907, and were mildly rather than sharply satirical in flavour.[17] In 1908 the much more important journal *Budilnik* accepted his first contribution, a cartoon of the former Prime Minister Witte for which he received the princely sum of 10 rubles (this

3.3 D. S. Moor, Self-portrait (1934).

was about a quarter of his monthly salary at the printing works). From this time onwards his cartoons and sketches, signed 'Dor', began to appear more and more frequently in the leading Moscow newspapers and journals. The pseudonym 'Dor' was derived from the first letter of his Christian name and the first two letters of his surname. A contemporary journalist by the name of O. L. d'Or, however, objected, and Moor began to sign his work 'Mor'. Rather later, influenced by a character in Schiller's play *The Robbers*, he changed his signature to Moor. During the First World War the editors of *Budilnik* had to reassure their readers that the rather foreign-sounding artist Moor was not in fact a German but a Russian whose real name was Orlov.[18]

Moor continued to work as a political cartoonist up to the end to the Tsarist period. Some of his work maintained a sharp satirical edge, for instance a cartoon produced on the occasion of the elections to the Third Duma in 1912 in which a row of candidates, every fifth one a priest, was depicted standing beside a stern-looking policeman, 'Vote for every fifth candidate', he commanded.[19] With some other young artists and writers, among them Demyan Bedny and Ivan Malyutin, Moor began to produce a satirical review called *Volynka* (Bagpipe), although none of its four issues got past the censor. Some of Moor's caricatures of members of the Tsarist government, dressed up in fezes and labelled 'Turkish ministers', were however, allowed into print.[20] Moor's work became increasingly popular:

he was invited to contribute to *Satirikon* and appeared in the leading journals of the time such as the liberal dailies *Russkoe slovo* (Russian Word) and *Utro Rossii* (Morning of Russia).[21] When the war began in 1914 Moor became involved in the production of patriotic *lubki*, producing a whole series of sketches on the 'heroic deeds of Kozma Kryuchkov', a fictionalised ordinary soldier on the lines of the British Tommy Atkins.[22] In 1916 he became one of the editors of *Budilnik*, evidence in itself of the prominent position he had now acquired. In 1917, after the February revolution, he produced the first caricature of Nicholas II; it appeared in *Utro Rossii* just five days after the Tsar's abdication and elicited a flood of letters, many of them scandalised by the disrespectful manner in which the former autocrat had been depicted.[23] *Budilnik*, which had reflected the generally patriotic spirit of the times at the outbreak of the war, now renamed itself *Free Budilnik* and began to assume a more radical posture. It was hardly, however, 'close to Bolshevik positions', as Moor was later to claim, and in fact it shifted its position several times in the course of the year, as did Moor himself.[24]

After the October revolution Moor continued to work in the field of newspaper graphics, but he began at the same time to seek an artistic form which (as he later put in) could 'resound on an equal basis with the speech of a political orator'. This form he found in the political poster.[25] Altogether, over the civil war years, Moor produced just over fifty political posters, the great majority of which (thirty-three, produced in 1.3 million copies) were for Litizdat.[26] Moor usually produced about two or three posters a month at this time, but his output varied from one to five, depending upon the circumstances. He worked ahead whenever he could, preparing a May Day poster, for instance, the previous March, but this degree of deliberation was rarely possible. More often Polonsky would come to him and say 'All Europe is looking at us. This poster must be done within the hour'.[27]

Moor was one of the very few Soviet poster artists who were willing to sign their work at his time; many other members of the cultural intelligentsia, fearing that the new regime would not survive, were reluctant to identify themselves publicly with it in this way. As Polonsky later recalled, the numbers of artists who were willing to work for him on political posters, never very large, declined significantly when Denikin advanced on Tula in the summer of 1919 with every prospect of advancing further. Only Moor, exhausted, cold and hungry, had continued to put out poster after poster with his own name on them, although it was clear that if Denikin took Moscow he would not 'sit' in prison but would be guaranteed a 'hanging' position.[28]

In the later civil war period Moor resumed his work in newspapers and journals; from 1919 his cartoons began to appear in *Izvestiya* and *Krasnoarmeets*, and from 1920 they began to appear in *Pravda*. He was involved in the decoration of Moscow for festive occasions; for the first May Day celebrations in 1918, for instance, he prepared the decoration of the Historical Museum near Red Square. He was also involved in the decoration of the first agitational trains, and took a minor part in the 'Rosta Windows' which appeared between 1919 and 1922 (Moor seems personally to have been responsible for no more than about five or six of these productions, so far as can be established[29]). After this time he became more closely involved in satirical magazines such as *Krokodil* (from 1922) and in the illustration of anti-religious books and journals such as *Bezbozhnik* (from 1923 onwards).[30] So skilful were Moor's sketches of the saints, the engraver Ivan Pavlov recalled in his memoirs, that peasants used to put them up in their hall corners and pray to them, not noticing their satirical intentions.[31] Moor continued to produce political posters, although less frequently, and became involved in theatrical design and book illustration. During the Second World War he returned more actively to work in the field of political posters, both in Moscow and in Samarkand, to where he had been evacuated. Together with his artistic work, Moor became a leading figure in the world of Soviet art education (the Kukryniksy and Alexander Deineka, for instance, were among his pupils[32]). He was awarded the title of 'Honoured Art Worker', was elected to the presidium of the Union of Revolutionary Poster Workers in 1931, and in 1935 he was even elected to the Moscow City Soviet. Moor called himself 'a Bolshevik, although an illiterate one' and did not join the Communist Party until the end of the 1930s; in the view of one of his fellow artists, Deineka, he was nonetheless the 'commissar of propagandistic revolutionary art'.[33]

Moor, according to his own account, was strongly influenced by French painting and by German graphic art, and perhaps most of all by *Simplicissimus* and its leading cartoonist Olaf Gulbransson (he was even known for some time as the 'Russian Gulbransson'[34]). From an early age, as we have noted, he devoted himself to the study of icon painting, admiring its use of colour, form and composition even though he no longer shared its religious assumptions.[35] Mikhail Cheremnykh, who held Moor in the highest regard, believed that Moor had also been influenced by the Russian graphic artist Mechislav Dobrokovsky (1895–1937).[36] His poster style in fact took some time to develop, but as it did so these earlier influences gradually lost their direct purchase upon his work. Moor's first post-revolutionary poster, for instance, was issued by vTsIK in 1918; entitled *Before and After*, it contrasted the well-dressed rich

ЦАРСКИЕ ПОЛКИ И КРАСНАЯ АРМИЯ

ЗА ЧТО СРАЖАЛИСЬ
ПРЕЖДЕ

ЗА ЧТО СРАЖАЮТСЯ
ТЕПЕРЬ

3.4 D. S. Moor, *Tsarskie polki i Krasnaya Armiya*, (The Tsarist Regiments and the Red Army), coloured lithograph, 1919, 49 × 75 cm., BS 1853.

Regiments and the Red Army (Plate 3.4) also made use of the 'before and after' motif and was more of a *lubok* than a proper poster. One Soviet commentator has suggested that the figures of the worker, peasant and Red Army man in the right-hand frame reflected the influence of the icon-painting tradition; another more contemporary critic suggested that it showed the influence of the *style russe*.[38] His *Death to World Imperialism* (Plate 3.6), produced in the summer of 1919, was clearly allegorical in form; so also was his *The Enemy is at the Gates* (Plate 3.5), with its figure of a skeleton-like Death with the Tsar on its arm approaching the fortress of the RSFSR.

This was Moor's last strongly symbolic poster; his *We will not Surrender Petrograd* (Plate 3.7), produced in the spring of 1919, already showed an evolution towards a more directly representational style (perhaps not coincidentally, it was the first poster commissioned from Moor by Litizdat). His *Soviet Turnip* (Plate 3.8) adopted a somewhat different approach, tending toward the *lubok* although with a very different motif. It showed 'Monsieur Capital', assisted by a counter-revolutionary grandmother, her reformist grandson and a dog, discovering that the turnip he had hoped to steal while.

and badly-dressed poor before the revolution with the more equitable arrangements that had been introduced by the Bolsheviks, in which rewards were directly proportional to the work that people did.[37] Moor's *Tsarist*

3.5 D. S. Moor, *Vrag u vorot! On neset rabstvo, golod i smert!* (The Enemy is at the Gates!), two coloured lithograph, 1919, 71 × 102 cm., BS 950; courtesy of the Musée d'histoire contemporaine, Paris.

СМЕРТЬ МИРОВОМУ ИМПЕРИАЛИЗМУ

3.6 D. S. Moor, *Smert' mirovomu imperializmu* (Death to World Imperialism), coloured lithograph, 1919, 106 × 70 cm., BS 602.

3.7 D. S. Moor, *Petrograd ne otdadim* (We will not surrender Petrograd), coloured lithograph, 1919, 104 × 70 cm., BS 1528.

Army. Simple, bold and dynamic, it represents Moor's poster art at the height of its achievement. The poster was produced in a single night in June 1920, and in June, it has been pointed out, 'the nights are short'.[40] It was originally entitled *Will You Volunteer?*, but Moor discarded this wording in favour of the bolder, more direct appeal of the version he finally adopted. Some 47,455 copies of the poster were produced by Litizdat and distributed nationally.[41] The writer Valentin Kataev came across the poster in Odessa. Many posters of the time, he wrote shortly afterwards, called for the swift organisation of a Red Army. 'The most widely distributed was a poster depicting a Red Armyman, pointing at the viewer with a large and insistent index finger. He asked "Have you enrolled yet in the Red Army?" Everyone joined up'.[42] Moor himself recollected that the poster had provoked a lot of discussion; some had told him that it made them 'ashamed not to volunteer'.[43]

The recruiting officer with his pointing finger was not, admittedly, an entirely novel theme in the poster

3.8 D. S. Moor, *Sovetskaya repka* (Soviet Turnip), three coloured lithograph, 1920, 71 × 45 cm. BS 605.

no-one was looking was in fact a Red Armyman.[39] Moor's *Labour* (Plate 3.9) similarly depicted, in successive rows, agricultural workers tending to the needs of the landlord and industrial workers toiling for a bowler-hatted capitalist, assisted by a priest, until in the final row the working people resolved to end this 'slave labour' and work for themselves rather than their oppressors. *Christmas* (Plate 3.10), published towards the end of 1921, contrasted the pilgrimage of the privileged towards the East with the movement of workers, peasants and Red Armymen towards the red star of the revolutionary cause. Its style, again, owed something to the *lubok*.

Perhaps Moor's most celebrated poster and one which has become enduringly associated with the iconography of the revolutionary period is his *Have You Enrolled as a Volunteer* (Plate 3.12), which was inspired by the need to accelerate recruitment into the Red

46

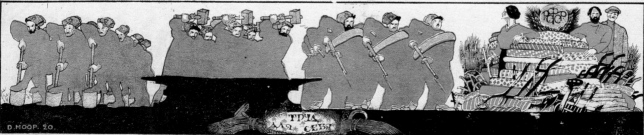

3.9 D. S. Moor, *Trud* (Labour), three coloured lithograph, 1920, 70 × 53 cm., BS 2434.

3.10 D. S. Moor, *Rozhdestvo* (Christmas), coloured lithograph, 1921, 71 × 107 cm., BS 3371.

art of the period. Perhaps the most celebrated war poster of this kind was Alfred Leete's Lord Kitchener with his ringing declaration, 'Your country needs YOU', which was first published in September 1914. Leete's poster in turn served as the model for James Montgomery Flagg's recruiting Uncle Sam and for others of a similar kind.[44] A Hungarian poster produced in that country during the short-lived Soviet republic of 1919 showed a soldier pointing at the viewer and demanding 'You! Counter-revolutionary in the dark, Tremble!'.[45] Moor may have been influenced by a British poster, similar in style to Leete's Kitchener, which showed John Bull in front of an empty space in a row of troops asking 'Who is absent? Is it YOU?'.[46] Moor, it appears, did not himself see this poster, but it was included in a display of British wartime art in Moscow in 1916 of which he was informed by Polonsky.[47] Moor's version was at all events a creative achievement in its own right, and one that has enjoyed enormous influence in the USSR and abroad ever since. Other posters produced in the following months, for instance,

asked 'What have you done for the front?' (Plate 3.11), or whether the viewer had joined the Society of Friends of the Air Force and Fleet.[48] The same device was employed by Moor himself during the Second World War (see Plate 6.5); later still, in the 1980s, it was used to ask what those who saw it had done to assist Gorbachev's campaign of acceleration and *perestroika*.[49]

3.11 Anon, *Chto ty sdelal dlya fronta?* ('What have You done for the Front?'), two coloured lithograph, 1920, 44 × 71 cm., BS 1890.

3.12 D. S. Moor, *Ty zapisalsya dobrovol'tsem?* (Have You Enrolled as a Volunteer?), two coloured lithograph, 1920, 106 × 71 cm., BS 1798.

3.13 D. S. Moor, *Pomogi* (Help), black and white lithograph, 1920, 106 × 71 cm., BS 2762.

he had thought all the testimony he could collect about the famine was of such significance that it must be used, and conceived of a poster based upon a starving peasant surrounded by evidence of all the horrors by which the famine had been accompanied. In the end he decided to focus upon a single detail: a bare, dried-out and broken ear of corn, transfixing the body of a starving peasant. In this single ear of corn, he recalled, he had tried to represent the 'scorched and barren steppe lands, and the animals swollen with hunger, and the tears of the mothers, and the frightened eyes of the children'. His purpose would not have been achieved, however, if he had not at the same time indicated some means by which those who saw the poster and were affected by it could contribute towards a solution. This was achieved by the simple slogan 'Help'; the word, in Russian, is in the second person singular, deliberately chosen so as to appeal to everyone who saw it in a personal and individual way.[51]

Moor's other posters of the civil war years covered a wide range of topics. Some of the more attractive but less well-known ones appealed 'To the people of the Caucasus' (Plate 3.15) and to 'Comrade Muslims' (Plate 3.17) in connection with the southern campaigns of the Red Army in 1919 and 1920 respectively. His *The Red*

3.14 D. S. Moor, *Krasnyi soldat na fronte ne obut, ne odet* (The Red Soldier at the Front is without Footwear and Clothing), black and white lithograph, 1920, 71 × 51, BS 1296.

Moor enjoyed a comparable degree of success with his poster *Help* (Plate 3.13), which was produced in 1921 in connection with the famine which had overwhelmed the lower Volga basin. Nearly 20 million people lived in the area concerned and an enormous relief effort was organised, on an international scale as well as within the USSR itself. Moor's resolution of the theme was again a simple but extraordinarily effective one: an elderly and emaciated peasant, simply dressed and without shoes, making an anguished appeal for assistance. It was in Moor's own view the most successful of all his posters, and the only one he was willing to compare with the work of Mayakovsky.[50] He had begun to work on the poster following his participation in an exhibition in Moscow devoted to the famine. The exhibition made an enormous impression upon him, and he resolved to do what he could to mobilise assistance. To begin with

3.15 D. S. Moor, *Narodam Kavkaza* (To the Peoples of the Caucasus), coloured lithograph, 1920, 71 × 106, BS 358.

Soldier at the Front is without Footwear and Clothing (Plate 3.14), issued in October 1920, urged mothers and housewives to open their trunks and give all they could to those who were defending them. Various other features of the home front were treated in, for instance, *Priests help Capital and Hinder the Worker* (Plate 3.16), which foreshadowed Moor's later anti-religious work, and the posters that were devoted to deserters and saboteurs (see for instance Plate 5.17). *Soviet Russia is an Armed Camp* (Plate 3.18), based on a version of the Red Army emblem, showed how every section of the population – youth and women as well as workers, peasants and party members – could contribute to the war effort. Several of Moor's civil war posters were devoted to particular occasions, such as the third anniversary of Soviet rule (Plate 3.19) or the First of May (Plate 3.20). Most of his posters, however, reflected the progress of the civil war itself, both the struggle against Denikin and other domestic opponents (see for instance Plates 5.23 and 24) and the Russo-Polish hostilities of 1920 (see Plates 5.1, 15 and 18).

Perhaps surprisingly, in view of the uncompromising and sometimes ferocious nature of his work, Moor was personally a mild, sociable and good-humoured

3.16 D. S. Moor, *Popy pomogayut kapitalu i meshayut rabochemu. Proch' s dorogi!* (The Priests help Capital and Hinder the Workers), three coloured lithograph, 1920, 74 × 108 cm., BS 3359.

Товарищи Мусульмане! Под зеленым знаменем Пророка шли вы завоевывать ваши степи, ваши аулы. Враги народа отняли у вас

родные поля. Ныне под красным знаменем Рабоче-Крестьянской революции под звездой армии всех угнетенных и трудящихся собирайтесь с востока и запада, с севера и юга. В седла товарищи! Все в полки Всевобуч!

ОБРАЩАЙТЕСЬ ЗА СПРАВКАМИ ИНСПЕКЦИЯ
Кавалерийских Формирований Центр. Упр Всевобуч.
Всеросс. Главн. Штаба.
Москва. Малый Ржевский, 3.

D.MOOP.

Издание Центр. Управл. Всевобуч.

مسلمانلار ایبڭ شلر !
عسكرلك که اویده تو اداره سی توزو کدن آتلی مسلمان عسكر
لری پولقینه یازلڭز !
او ز کزنڭ اویوکزنی ، یبرلرکزنی هم ایدرکزنی او زکزکند صاقلی آلورسیز !

3.17 D. S. Moor, *Tovarishchi Musulman'e!* (Comrade Muslims), coloured lithograph, 1919, 95 × 70, BS 1766.

man who latterly suffered from poor health. The cartoonist Boris Efimov, meeting Moor for the first time in 1922 in the offices of the newly-established magazine *Krokodil* (Crocodile), had expected someone 'severe and haughty, with a frown on his brow'. Moor, on the contrary, turned out to be 'remarkably simple, sociable and merry'. Moor, Efimov recalled, took a supremely indifferent attitude to all worldly matters and creature comforts. In summer he wore a simple half-buttoned belted blouse, and in winter a service jacket under a peasant coat, open at the front, with a high-pointed Cossack hat upon his head. An enormous home-made cigarette was usually clamped between his teeth.[52] The engraver Ivan Pavlov, who first met Moor as a young man at a literary evening, remembered him as a 'very interesting, lively and chatty' person, with a sharp sense of humour. His sketches of actors from the Arts and Maly theatres, including Stanislavsky and others,

3.18 (*left*) D.S. Moor, *Sovetskaya Rossiya – osazhdennyi lager. Vse na oboronu!* (Soviet Russia is an Armed Camp), coloured lithograph, 1919, 97 × 73 cm., BS 1714.

3.19 (*below*) D. S. Moor, *Oktyabr' 1917 – oktyabr' 1920. Da zdravstvuet vsemirnyi Krasnyi Oktyabr!* (October 1917 – October 1920. Long Live the Worldwide Red October!), two coloured lithograph, 1920, 69 × 107 cm., BS 394.

3.20 D. S. Moor, *1-e Maya – prazdnik truda* (1st of May – a Festival of Labour), two coloured lithograph, 1920, 107 × 71 cm., BS 448/9.

were then in vogue. Moor later developed into an artist and caricaturist, so effective, Pavlov recalled, that questions were asked about his work in foreign parliaments and the Pope even excommunicated him. (Pavlov's remarks appear in fact to refer to a cartoon by Boris Efimov, published in *Izvestiya* in December 1926, in which the British Foreign Secretary and the Polish Prime Minister were shown applauding an announcement that four Lithuanian Communists had been executed; this did indeed lead to an official diplomatic protest.)[53]

Moor was a great lover of animals, especially birds. As Pavlov recalled, he had converted one of the rooms of his flat into an aviary, where he kept as many as 200 pigeons of various kinds. Moor gave his birds humorous name: one of them was called 'Wilhelm II'.[54] It was far from easy to feed so many birds in Moscow in the early post-revolutionary years, but Moor somehow managed to cope, keeping a box of corn in his hall for this purpose. The house manager, dissatisfied with these arrangements, took Moor to court on a charge of 'using living quarters for pigeons'. The court, however, found in Moor's favour.[55] According to some popular verse which appeared in *Krokodil*, Moor used to talk to his pigeons for hours on end. He also had a raven called Vanka who, in answer to the question 'Who is strongest of all in the world?', would reply 'RKKA' (the Worker-Peasant Red Army).[56] Apart from his birds, Moor had a mongrel dog called Fifka, and (as a Cossack) considered himself an excellent judge of horses and often attended races.[57] He lavished no such attention upon his own surroundings: he had a small flat on the fifth floor of an elderly apartment building which he made no attempt to decorate, and had given away the car with which he had been provided by Sergo Ordzhonikidze. Moor and his wife entertained regularly, and the three small rooms of their flat on Serebryanicheskii Lane was usually full of young artists, actors and musicians. Their only son unfortunately died at an early age, a loss Moor found very hard to bear.[58]

Moor was a great favourite with younger artists, who found him an attractive, kindly figure in whom they could confide.[59] Nikolai Dolgorukov, who was one of his pupils at the Higher Artistic-Technical Institute (VKHUTEIN) and later a distinguished poster artist in his own right, came into contact with Moor in the early 1920s. Like Efimov he had expected him to be austere and forbidding, but found him instead a large, heavy, noisy man, with light blue and very direct eyes his most notable feature.[60] By this time Moor was already suffering badly from asthma, and going up the stairs he would stop several times to regain breath. In particularly bad weather he would not leave home as he found too much difficulty in breathing.[61] Giving a lecture, he

3.21 Unknown photographer, Viktor Deni (from *My, nashi druz'ya i nashi vragi v risunkakh Deni* [Moscow-Leningrad: Gosudarstvennoe izdatel'stvo, 1930]).

would simply sit down somewhere on the edge of the table and begin to talk. 'Charming, lively, with a sharp sense of humour, Moor immediately fascinated people and charmed them', Dolgorukov recalled.[62]

Dologorukov was one of those who visited Moor at home and experienced his spartan and unusual life style at first hand. Fifka attacked him at the door, and from inside a crow could be heard. Although it was the early afternoon Moor was still breakfasting, as he slept poorly and usually worked into the night. He offered Dolgorukov a glass of Riesling. When Moor was younger he had sung well, Dolgorukov recalled; he had an excellent musical memory, and could sing more than one opera from beginning to end. He loved to listen to musical broadcasts at night on his radio, especially La Scala of Milan.[63] Although easy-going at a personal level, Moor was nonetheless a stern critic of any kind of sloppiness or routine in the field of art.[64]

Moor was slightly older than Viktor Deni, the other leading figure in Soviet poster art during the civil war period. Moor nonetheless characterised him, in an article written in the late 1930s, as an 'oldster', one of those whose artistic formation had predated the October revolution.[65] Viktor Nikolaevich Deni (real name Denisov) had been born in February 1893 in Moscow; his father was an impoverished member of the gentry who had died three years after Deni was born.[66] Deni was sent to a school for orphaned members of the gentry, where he first displayed his excellent visual and musical memory. He was not, apparently, a particularly diligent pupil, preferring to spend his time drawing and studying art, in which he was much influenced by a number of distinguished visiting teachers. Deni's particular heroes at this time, and indeed in later life, were Ilya Repin and Valentin Serov. He began to publish his sketches in *Budilnik* at the end of 1910, acting on the advice of an older brother who worked as a satirical poet for the journal. Soon his work began to appear not only in *Budilnik* but also in the newspaper *Golos Moskvy* (Voice of Moscow), the theatrical journal *Rampa i zhizn* (Footlights and Life) and elsewhere. By this time he had begun to employ the pseudonym 'Deni', or less frequently 'Visov'. Deni, a contraction of his own name, may also have been suggested by the name of the leading *Satirikon* cartoonist Re-mi (Nikolai Remizov).[67] Deni published frequently in *Budilnik* between 1910 and 1912, as well as contributing sketches of well-known writers and cartoons on international themes to *Golos Moskvy* and other journals.[68]

A year before the First World War broke out Deni moved to St Petersburg, where he was an immediate success. He was taken up by N. G. Shebuev, artistic director of the journal *Solntse Rossii* (Sun of Russia), and began to publish regularly both here and in *Vesna* (Spring), *Satirikon* and other satirical journals. He himself became the artistic director of the satirical-humorous weekly journal *Bich*, while continuing to place his work in *Budilnik* and elsewhere. His work began to be collected, and he was invited to undertake theatrical designs. Deni appears to have been particularly popular with the opera singer Fedor Shalyapin, who amassed a considerable collection of his work.[69] During the wartime years there were fewer outlets for Deni's satirical talents, because of censorship as well as the jingoistic atmosphere of the time, but in February 1917 conditions became easier and satirical journals re-emerged in sharper and more combative form. Deni worked mainly for *Bich* at this time, which itself came under the control of a new and outspokenly anti-Bolshevik editor, A. Amfiteatrov. *Bich* had welcomed the overthrow of the autocracy but had already opposed the revolutionary movement; under Amfiteatrov's editorship it moved still further to the right and began to take part in anti-Bolshevik press campaigns. Lack of a clear understanding of what was happening in the

3.22 V. N. Deni, *Tov. Lenin ochishchaet zemlyu ot nechisti* (Comrade Lenin Cleans the World of Filth), coloured lithograph, 1920, 68 × 44 cm., BS 634.

country led Deni, in the words of his Soviet biographer, to an 'incorrect assessment' of the activities of the Bolsheviks and to an 'inaccurate representation' of the role of the working class.[70] Soon after the October revolution *Bich* was closed down, its editor emigrated and Deni had to look elsewhere for employment.

Deni wrote at this point to Anatoly Lunacharsky, People's Commissar for Enlightenment, to offer his services as an artist to the new regime. Lunacharsky well remembered the occasion on which Deni had come to see him, as he later wrote in a preface to a collection of Deni's sketches. He seemed very young but also very ill, and had told him 'not without melancholy' that he welcomed the revolution and wished henceforth to devote its talents to its service. This he had done.[71] Deni was given work under the auspices of Litizdat and was attached initially to the artistic section of the Volga military district, where he became involved in poster work and also in newspaper caricature and lectures on fine art to soldiers and the local population. Several of Deni's first Soviet posters appeared in Kazan, where he was stationed, for instance the poster *The Last Hour* (see Plate 1.12), and his poster *In the Waves of Revolution*, which showed 'Wilson, Clemenceau, Lloyd George and Co.' drowning in the sea while bubbles labelled 'Plan of Struggle with Communism' burst above their heads.[72] Deni's poster *Comrade Lenin Cleans the World of Filth* (Plate 3.22), based upon a cartoon by Cheremnykh which had appeared in *Bednota* in October 1918, also appeared in Kazan.[73]

Some years later, piqued by the republication of some of his old *Bich* cartoons in the satirical magazine *Krasnyi perets* (Red Pepper), Deni wrote a letter to *Pravda* in which he tried to place a better complexion upon his early attachment to the revolutionary cause. His service to the new regime had begun, he wrote, 'not in the distant rear and not in the sixth year of existence of Soviet power' but in Kazan, which had at that time been in the forefront of the struggle against Kolchak. 'Here', he went on, 'observing the heroic struggle of Soviet power and becoming aware of the real nature of the revolution', he had resolved to dedicate himself to the Bolshevik cause. In Kazan his works, reproduced in great quantities, had made a considerable popular impression. Trotsky, while stopping over in the town, had been shown his work and had made the artist's personal acquaintance in his own train; he hoped Trotsky would remember the occasion. His services had also been required by Lunacharsky. Since that time, he wrote, he had faithfully supported the new regime and given all his energies to the establishment of the new life.[74] *Pravda* itself supported Deni against *Krasnyi perets*'s real or implied attack.[75] The poet Demyan Bedny also made Deni's acquaintance in Kazan at this time. 'How it came about', he recalled a few years later, 'that the puny, ailing, hothouse blond, as we knew Deni, turned into a staunch, brave, even cheeky agitator – that amazed everyone'.[76]

Deni was most active in the production of political posters during 1919 and 1920, when the best-known of his sharply satirical poster work appeared. His *Denikin's Band* (Plate 3.23), for instance, appeared under the auspices of Litizdat in the autumn of 1919, with accompanying verses by Demyan Bedny. It depicted Denikin, in the centre of the front row, together with a priest, a kulak, a right-wing politician with a picture of the Tsar, a policeman and two casks of spirits, under a banner reading *Beat the Workers and the Peasants*. Deni's *"Liberators"* (Plate 3.24) was also directed against Denikin; at 113,500 copies, it was the most widely reproduced of all civil war posters. Deni's *At the Grave of the Counter-*

Revolution (Plate 3.25), produced for Litizdat in the autumn of 1920, depicted a weeping priest and capitalist at the grave of Kolchak, Denikin and other anti-Bolshevik leaders, while behind them the apparation of a dead Tsarist soldier floated in the sky. Deni's *Manifesto* (Plate 3.26), also produced in late 1920, showed a priest, a bourgeois and Baron Wrangel grouped together under imperial regalia behind a placard reading 'All power to the landlords and capitalists! Whip the workers and peasants!'.

Deni devoted a comparable degree of attention to the Russo-Polish war of 1920. His *Entente under the Mask of Peace* (Plate 1.19), for instance, produced in the summer of 1920, was intended to show the real aims of the Western powers at this time despite their peaceful overtures; it showed Deni's sometimes exaggerated tendency to bestialise his opponents, giving them porcine faces, fang-like teeth, slavering jaws and pointed ears. His *Sow prepared in Paris* (Plate 3.27) was similarly intended to suggest that the Poles, supported by the French, would be content with nothing less than the restoration of the 'frontiers of 1772'. Deni's *Peasant* (Plate 3.28), produced during the Polish advance into Soviet Russia in the early summer of 1920, suggested that the Polish landlords would go so far as to reintroduce slavery in the lands they conquered; his *Hangmen torture the Ukraine*, showing a distinctly Christ-like figure being nailed to a cross by a Polish officer assisted by the counter-revolutionary leader Petlyura, suggested that for some there might be a fate that was still worse.[77]

Deni extended his satirical talents to a variety of other subjects including the League of Nations (Plate 3.29), which he represented as a grouping of major Western powers under the heading 'Capitalists of the world, unite!'. The League, which formally came into existence in January 1920, was widely seen as a capitalist conspiracy in Soviet Russia at this time, although the USSR did eventually become a member in the 1930s; the USA, depicted at the centre of the new organisation, was not in fact a member of the League at this or any subsequent time. Deni's *Capital* (Plate 3.30), produced in a massive 100,000 copies in late 1919, involved him in collaboration with Demyan Bedny, who provided the verse for many of Deni's civil war posters. Simple but expressive, it has been described as 'one of the most outstanding satirical sheets of the whole civil war period'.[78] The spider and web motif, already apparent in *Capital*, was addressed more directly in Deni's *The Spider and the Flies* (Plate 1.13), produced at about the same time, again with verses by Demyan Bedny. It was one of Deni's posters attacking organised religion; his *All Men are Brothers – and I like to Take from Them* was in a similar vein.[79] His *Third International* (Plate 3.31) appeared

3.23 (*left*) V. N. Deni, *Denikinskaya banda* (Denikin's Band), coloured lithograph, 1919, 100 × 68 cm., BS 1081.

3.24 (*right*) V. N. Deni, "*Osvoboditeli*", ("Liberators"), coloured lithograph, 1919, 65 × 95 cm., BS 1498.

3.25 (*below left*) V. N. Deni, *Na mogile kontrrevolyutsii* (At the Grave of the Counter-Revolution), 1920, 93 × 70 cm., BS 1412.

3.26 (*below right*) V. N. Deni, *Manifest. Vsya vlast' pomeshchikam i kapitalistam! Rabochim i krest'yanam plet'* (Manifesto), coloured lithograph, 1920, 68 × 52 cm., BS 1357.

3.27 V. N. Deni, *Svin'ya, dressirovannaya v Parizhe* (A Sow prepared in Paris), three coloured lithograph, 1920, 48 × 33 cm., BS 579.

3.28 V. N. Deni, *Krest'yanin! Pol'skii pomeshchik khochet sdelat' tebya rabom. Ne byvat' etomu!* (Peasant!), two coloured lithograph, 1920, 53 × 36 cm., BS 1214.

3.29 V. N. Deni, *Liga natsii* (The League of Nations), coloured lithograph, 1919, 98 × 75 cm., BS 303.

3.30 V. N. Deni, *Kapital* (Capital), three coloured lithograph, 1919, 54 × 35 cm., BS 237.

rather later, in early 1921, and in only 5,000 copies; it was one of the last posters that Deni produced at this time. Altogether Deni composed nearly fifty posters, most of them for Litizdat, between 1918 and 1921.[81] Like Moor and other poster artists he subsequently became more and more involved in newspaper cartoon work and from 1921 was a regular contributor to *Pravda, Izvestiya, Krasnaya Niva* (Red Cornfield) and other publications, specialising in foreign policy themes. Deni returned to poster work during the Second World War, re-using some of his old compositions; he died very shortly afterwards, in 1946.[81]

Deni's poster art has been subject to a variety of interpretations, both at the time and subsequently. Polonsky, for instance, who directed Deni's work for Litizdat, described him as a 'brilliant caricaturist' to whom the spirit of the poster proper was 'alien'. He had prepared a series of sketches for Litizdat, 'very interesting and sharp', but they were on the whole not posters in the accepted sense of the word but 'large satirical painted drawings'. All of Deni's posters, for this reason, could be reproduced without loss or even to their advantage on the pages of an illustrated journal or newspaper, or they could be framed like a picture.[82] Moor, in Polonsky's view a more 'posterly' artist, himself described Deni as a 'genuine newspaperist' whose satirical skill enabled him to see the ugly realities behind what were often pleasant-seeming exteriors. A background or interior were often lacking, allowing Deni to concentrate all his attention upon the psychological features of the face or of the body. In Moor's view, Deni's work had two main faults: he had some difficulty in coping with themes that fell outside his usual repertoire, and he also suffered from a certain stylistic inertia – his work of the early 1920s and the late 1930s, for instance, was almost identical in formal terms.[83]

A much more kindly view was taken by Lunacharsky, who appears in effect to have acted as Deni's patron at this time. 'In Deni', he wrote, 'we have a combination of a sharp political mind, faultlessly understanding situations and the relations between us, our friends and our enemies, and a formidable artistic gift.' Deni, he went on, was 'not only a draftsman' but a 'poet, a *littérateur* of the pencil'. His characteristics included an 'unusually gentle humour, which he plays in a friendly way upon the shoulders of one or other of us or of our friends', but he was also capable of the 'highest degree of anger and scorn' where the imperialist bourgeoisie was concerned.[84] Lunacharsky wrote personally to Lenin on Deni's behalf in March 1920 to try to secure him better living conditions. Deni, he explained, was 'one of the most sincere and talented of our friends', who had created the 'best posters that we have'. His work had been used for

agitational purposes and was very well known; some of it had even been reprinted in foreign journals. He was very keen to continue this work, but he was a sick man. In view of this he must be given more reasonable living conditions, for which he would certainly reward them with marvellous, sharp and well-aimed posters. Lunacharsky asked Lenin personally to arrange for Deni to receive some comfortable and well-heated accommodation in Soviet government premises, if possible in the Kremlin itself, together with the right to eat in the government canteen or at least to receive an adequate supply of foodstuffs at his own address.[85] Deni also approached Lenin directly and sent him a folder of drawings, which the Soviet leader apparently examined with great approval; both Lev Sosnovsky, editor of the peasant paper *Bednota*, and Lenin's wife Krupskaya confirmed that he looked through albums of Deni's work with some amusement while recuperating at Gorky in 1923.[86]

Boris Efimov is one of those who have left us their recollections of Deni during these early post-revolutionary years. Meeting Deni in the offices of *Pravda* in 1922, Efimov was struck, as he had been with Moor, by the discrepancy between art and artist. Deni's poster work was striking, full-blooded, and full of optimistic humour; Deni himself, however, was misanthropic, ailing, and overly concerned about his state of health. Deni disliked open windows, lifts or other populated places, fearing infection, and whatever the weather he wrapped up in a warm scarf. Although Deni was a smoker he took the most elaborate precautions: first of all he cleaned the cigarette paper with a wad of cotton that he kept in a special box, then he disinfected the mouthpiece with a burnt match, and finally he smoked it out of the side of his mouth so that the smoke went to the side. In later life these hypochondriac tendencies gained ground, and he was rarely seen at all in public although he continued to work actively.[87] Nikolai Dolgorukov similarly recalled Deni as an isolated figure, thin, mournful and unsociable, who seemed a most unlikely author of his witty, warmhearted cartoons and posters. Dolgorukov made Deni's acquaintance for the first time in the winter of 1930. Deni, wrapped up in a warm black coat with a fur collar, was looking disapprovingly at the small panel in the window which had been opened for ventilation. Dolgorukov once travelled home with Deni and offered him some grapes from a bag he had bought along the way. Deni was appalled: the grapes were unwashed – had Dolgorukov gone mad, or did he want to become ill? Dolgorukov visited Deni's flat at Durasovsky Lane and found it larger and more comfortable than Moor's, but the main dining and working room was rather dark, with just a single window for illumination, and there were cats everywhere – on the floor, on the divan, on the chairs and even on the dining table. Despite his characteristic reserve, Deni suggested that he should collaborate with the younger artist and a series of posters on the first Five Year Plan appeared under their joint signatures.[88]

Perhaps only one other artist deserves attention in the same context as Moor and Deni: Nikolai Kochergin, a rather younger artist whose work must nonetheless be ranked among the most effective and influential as well as aesthetically satisfying of the entire civil war period.[89] Kochergin was born in May 1897 in the village of Vsesvyatsky on the outskirts of Moscow. After education at a village school and in Moscow, where he spent most of his time running and visiting art galleries, Kochergin entered the Stroganov Art School in 1908. As well as his formal studies, he was able to indulge an interest in Greek mythology and met Maxim Gorky. In 1917 a soviet was established at the Stroganov School, and meetings and discussions took place on the working class and its relationship to art. Kochergin was involved in these and had already begun to take an active part in the new artistic world that was developing, contributing to the festive decoration of Petrograd for May Day in 1918 even before he had graduated from the Stroganov School. This he did with a diploma in sculpture in the summer of the same year (Kochergin was in fact one of the few prominent poster artists to have received a formal art training). In the summer of 1918 he joined the Red Army as a volunteer together with ten fellow students, and was sent to the Higher School of Military Camouflage. He took part in the decoration of Theatre Square in Moscow for the anniverary of the revolution, and also prepared agitational handouts which came to the attention of Nikolai Podvoisky, the former chairman of the Petrograd Military-Revolutionary Committee and one of the leaders of the Red Army. Kochergin was invited to join Podvoisky's staff as a military artist.

In the spring of 1919 Kochergin was sent with an agitational team to Kharkov, which had just been taken by the Red Army. He prepared two posters in the train which were published in Kharkov on his arrival, and also took part in street decoration. Later he worked with three other artists in a carriage which was attached to Podvoisky's train, travelling from front to front and producing posters within an hour or two of the events to which they were intended to refer. None of these posters, produced by colour wash on a paper or plywood base, is now extant. In the summer of 1919 Kochergin returned to Moscow; he continued his poster work for Vsevobuch (the military literacy campaign, now headed by Podvoisky) and Litizdat, collaborating with Demyan Bedny and others in this connection. A

poster he produced at this time, *Ukrainian Torments*, produced in 30,000 copies in 1919, was so successful that it was republished twice the following year in comparable quantities. Another poster, *To the Ukrainian Comrades*, appeared in early 1920.[90] His most successful early poster, however, was his *The Enemy is at the Gates! All to the Defence of Petrograd* (Plate 3.34), which was produced and put up in a single day when Denikin was approaching Moscow and Petrograd was in comparable danger. Its influence was felt immediately upon other posters such as Moor's *The Enemy is at the Gates* and Apsit's *The Enemy wants to Capture Tula*, both of which appeared a few days later.[91]

During 1920 Kochergin produced several posters devoted to the subject of economic reconstruction, among them *Dislocation and the Army of Labour* (Plate 3.32), with a text by Demyan Bedny. Kochergin was fully occupied at this time during the day and he had to carry out his poster work during the evenings or at night. He was given a special warrant allowing him to use an 100 watt bulb for this purpose. His other work included part of the decoration of the agitational train 'V. I. Lenin' and a poster for the First of May (Plate 3.33), which was one of the first to reflect a joyful and festive rather than severely military approach to such occasions. Kochergin continued to work on military posters, producing *It's Wrangel's Turn* and particularly *Wrangel is Coming* (Plate 3.37), which was issued in 75,000 copies in the late summer of 1920. Towards the end of 1920 Kochergin was sent to work at the newly-established Soviet mission in Persia, but he contracted typhus on the way and remained in Baku. In February 1921 he helped establish Soviet control in Georgia, and some of his most inventive and decorative work was produced here under the auspices of Rosta (see next chapter). His *First of May* (Plate 3.35), for instance, appeared on 1 May 1921 with its text in Georgian; his *Long Live the Friendship of all the Peoples of the Caucasus* (Plate 3.36) appeared at about the same time and showed some stylistic similarities, particularly the imaginative use of colour which was characteristic of all Kochergin's work and which made him one of the most popular of all the poster artists.[92] From about the end of 1921 Kochergin, like other poster artists, became involved in newspaper cartoon work and also in book illustration and theatrical design, first of all in the south of Russia and later in Petrograd. He died in 1974.[93]

The civil war years – roughly from the summer of 1918, when the first interventionist forces arrived in Russia, up to the autumn of 1920, when the last serious domestic opposition had been defeated – were the years in which the Soviet political poster attained the peak of its achievement. The work of this period was often sim-

3.31 (*left*) V. N. Deni, *III-i Internatsional* (The Third International), three coloured lithograph, 1921, 44 × 36 cm., BS 658.

3.32 (above) N. M. Kochergin, *Razrukha i armiya truda* (Dislocation and the Army of Labour), coloured lithograph, 1920, 53 × 71, BS 2353.

3.33 (*below left*) N. M. Kochergin, *I-e Maya 1920 goda. Cherez oblomki kapitalizma k vsemirnomu bratstvu trudyashchikhsya!* (The First of May), 1920, 70 × 53 cm., BS 451.

3.34 (*below right*) N. M. Kochergin, *Vrag u vorot! Vse na zashchitu Petrograda* (The Enemy is at the Gates! All to the Defence of Petrograd), three coloured lithograph, 1919, 104 × 70 cm., BS 949.

3.35 N. M. Kochergin, *I Maya* (Ist of May), coloured lithograph, no date [1921], 83 × 64 cm., BS 423; text in Georgian.

3.36 N. M. Kochergin, *Da zdravstvuet bratstvo vsekh narodov Kavkaza!* (Long Live the Brotherhood of all the Peoples of the Caucasus), three coloured lithograph, 1921, 88 × 66 cm., BS 99.

3.37 N. M. Kochergin, *Vrangel' idet! K oruzhiyu, proletarii!* (Wrangel is Coming! To Arms, Proletarians), coloured lithograph, 1920, 53 × 71 cm., BS 961.

ple, even crude, by comparison with the elaborately produced posters that had appeared in the first months following the revolution, still more so the work that was to appear in later years. The paper was often very poor in quality, and only a limited range of colours was available or could in practice be employed. As Polonsky pointed out, posters were needed urgently, and might be current for only a few days. Every extra colour that was used meant a longer printing process and a greater delay in publication. As a result, only one or two colours were used in most cases; only in exceptional circumstances, when a week or two was in hand, could three or four colours be employed. Posters produced in this more leisurely manner tended to be on fairly general themes, such as Moor's *Death to World Imperialism* (Plate 3.6) or Deni's *League of Nations* (Plate 3.29).[94]

At the same time the urgency and need to appeal to the widest possible audience compelled poster artists to aim for the maximum of simplicity and directness in their compositions. Distinctively posterly features came to the fore: compositions became stronger and simpler, often based upon a single active figure in the foreground; texts became shorter; a direct appeal was made to the viewer, emphasising action of some kind rather than passive contemplation; and a boldly symbolic use was made of colour, marking out the positive and negative features in every composition in a manner that bound the text and design into a powerful and effective unity. The critic and historian A. A. Sidorov, who lived through these events, has reasonably argued that a poster such as Moor's *Help* is 'a genuinely great work', fully on a par with poems such as Blok's *The Twelve*, and certainly superior to anything that was achieved in the other graphic arts during the same period.[95] In terms of the development of the poster itself the work of Soviet artists in these civil war years represented a level of achievement which has scarcely been improved upon in any other country or at any other time.

CHAPTER FOUR
Mayakovsky, Cheremnykh and the Rosta Windows

The civil war years saw the emergence of a further distinctive form of poster art: the 'Rosta Windows' (*Okna ROSTA*), which took their name from the Russian Telegraph Agency (Rosta) responsible for their publication. Rosta was established by a VTSIK decree of 7 September 1918 on the basis of the old Petrograd telegraph agency and a newly-formed press bureau attached to the Council of People's Commissars.[1] The new Agency was purged of hostile or unsuitable staff members, and then staffed with party journalists and members of the literary intelligentsia who were thought to be friendly to its objectives. In March 1918 it moved from Petrograd to Moscow, which had become the Soviet capital the previous month. From the spring of 1919 until the end of 1920 Rosta was headed by Platon Kerzhentsev (1881–1940), a Bolshevik since 1904 who had lived abroad before the revolution and who took a direct interest in street theatre and the performing arts as well as in journalism and (later) diplomacy.[2] To begin with Rosta was concentrated in Moscow and Petrograd, with only three or four regional branches. In the spring of 1919, however, it was decided to establish Rosta sections in all the regional centres, and this was achieved about a year later. The Council of People's Commissars press bureau had been responsible mainly for informing the press and other bodies of the decrees and decisions of the Soviet government; the Petrograd telegraph agency had had the task of collecting and disseminating domestic and foreign news through the telegraph system. Rosta was given in addition the task of collecting and distributing any other informational material that the Soviet press might find necessary. With the widening in the scope of its work, an increase in the number of newspapers that were published and an expansion in the area under Soviet rule Rosta acquired more and more responsibilities, finally becoming, in Kerzhentsev's works, a 'sort of syndicate of the Soviet press'.[3]

Rosta had three main areas of work: information; agitation; and the supervision of the Soviet press generally. It published a daily bulletin, based upon items culled from foreign radio broadcasts as well as from the foreign press, and this was distributed widely to central and local newspapers. Informational material of this kind began to be divided into two forms: a Radio Bulletin, consisting of about 3,000 words of material, and a shorter Poster Bulletin, consisting of just 500–600 words. The former was sent to the larger newspapers, the latter communicated by telegraph or telephone to local areas and to their party and state committees. Where there were no local papers the bulletin was typed up and displayed on boards; major proclamations on matters of the day were made public in the same way.

ОКНО САТИРЫ РОСТА №5.

1) КРАСНОАРМЕЕЦ, ОТНИМЕМ У БУРЖУА ЗИИ ПОСЛЕДНЮЮ СО-ЛОМИНКУ, - И ОНА ПОЙДЕТ НА ДНО !

2) МДА, ПРИДЕТСЯ МИРИТЬСЯ !

3) ЖЕЛЕЗО КУЙ ПОКА ГОРЯЧЕЕ ЖАЛЕТЬ О ПРОШЛОМ - ДЕЛО РАЧЬЕ.

4) ИЗ ГАЗЕТ: ПО СЛУХАМ, АМЕРИКА НЕ ХОЧЕТ ПРИНИМАТЬ УЧАСТИЯ В ОБСУЖДЕНИИ РУССКАГО ВОПРОСА. ЭЙ, ВИЛЬСОН КАШУ ЗАВА-РИЛ, А РАСХЛЕБЫВАТЬ ЕЕ НЕ ЖЕЛАЕШЬ !?

4.1 V. V. Mayakovsky, *Krasnoarmeets: Otnimem u burzhuazii poslednyuyu solomiku . . .* (Red Armyman! Let us Take from the Bourgeoisie its Last Straw), Rosta Window No. 5, 1919, 100 × 100 cm., BS 1841.

From the spring of 1919 a special daily *Agit-Rosta* bulletin was issued, and from about the same time a Rosta wall-newspaper began to appear, first on a weekly basis and then more often, conveying the latest news in telegraphic style and frequently including cartoons or satirical sketches. Special issues were produced for important occasions, such as anniversaries of the revolution or the periodic mobilisations of troops. Rosta also distributed maps, portraits and other kinds of visual material, and attempts were made to develop 'illuminated' newspapers and posters by projecting coloured slides on to the walls of public buildings in suitable locations. The printing industry was in a poor state and reproduction in colour was almost impossible, so Rosta decided to organise special 'windows' in all its sections containing colour drawings on themes of the day.[4] This was the origin of the 'Rosta Windows', which thus 'combined', as a Soviet scholar has put it, 'the functions of poster, newspaper, magazine and information bulletin'.[5]

The publication of Rosta Windows began in the autumn of 1919 and continued until January 1922. For the last part of this period they appeared under the auspices of Glavpolitprosvet (GPP), a committee for political education attached to the People's Commissariat for Enlightenment. The posters were hung up in busy places, not just in shop windows; in fact 'windows' became a progressively less accurate designation. They could not, however, simply be hung out on the street, because of wind, rain and the attentions of anti-Bolshevik members of the public.[6] Rosta Windows appeared in a single copy to begin with, then for a time were copied by hand, and finally from the spring of 1920 they were duplicated by means of cardboard stencils. Up to 300 copies of each Window could be run off in two or three days.[7] With five artists engaged in their production, each of whom could prepare an average of ten Windows a month, the average monthly production of the Moscow Rosta office alone could reach up to 50,000 separate Windows.[8] Most of them were hung up in Moscow itself; others were sent to Rosta offices in the localities for display or possible republication. The first appeared at the beginning of September 1919 beside the Moscow City Soviet in the window of the former sweet ship Abrikosov and Sons (the building is no longer in existence); it dealt with Denikin and the fall of the Hungarian Soviet Republic.[9] It was labelled 'Rosta Satire Window No. 1', and promised that the text and drawings would be changed weekly. Several more Windows were put up in the same month, on the corner of Petrovka and Kuznetsky Bridge and elsewhere in the city centre. By the beginning of 1920 about ten different sequences of Rosta Windows were appearing in various

different locations. This poses some problems for the numbering of the Windows: there were in fact six 'No. 1s', nine 'No. 2s' and altogether about 100 different Windows numbered between 1 and 21.[10]

The idea of creating the Windows belonged to Mikhail Cheremnykh, who from the beginning of 1919 had been working on the printed Rosta wall-newspaper, contributing sketches and cartoons and latterly orangising a separate wall-newspaper called *Krasnyi bich*.[11] In collaboration with the journalist N. K. Ivanov he produced the first Window and then several others, in effect enlarging a page of *Krasnyi bich* to poster proportions.[12]

Mayakovsky, with whom the Windows are now most closely associated, was not involved in their production at this early stage; but about four or five weeks after the first Window had appeared he came to work at Rosta, and his first Window was No. 5, which was issued in early October 1919. Another 'No. 5' (Plate 4.1), also concerned with the struggle against Denikin, appeared in December 1919. It was, it appears, under the influence of Mayakovsky that the character of the Windows began to change: initially, they had treated several themes more or less in the manner of a satirical journal, but by the end of 1919 they had begun to concentrate upon a single theme treated in a consecutive series of frames in the manner of a comic book. Some themes indeed began to run continuously from one Window to the next. The painter Ivan Malyutin also arrived to work at Rosta at about the same time as Mayakovsky, and these three, Cheremnykh, Mayakovsky and Malyutin, formed the core of the Rosta Window staff. Cheremnykh, strictly speaking, was the head of the Art Department at Rosta, but Mayakovsky, who had no formal title of any kind, soon became the acknowledged director of the whole enterprise.[13]

Neither Mayakovsky nor Cheremnykh chose particular themes for the Windows: these tended to be dictated by the texts, which were written by Mayakovsky or by others whose work was then approved by Mayakovsky. Mayakovsky later claimed that, after the first few weeks, 'almost all the themes and texts were mine'.[14] More precise calculations have established that perhaps as many as 90 per cent of the texts of the Rosta Windows did indeed belong to Mayakovsky, a total of more than 600.[15] Other texts were contributed by N. K. Ivanov (in the first two or three months), Rita Rait (about 70 or 80 texts, six of which Mayakovsky inadvertently included in his own collected works), M. D. Volpin, S. M. Tretyakov, T. M. Levit, B. A. Pesis and Osik Brik. After Mayakovsky had approved them, the texts were given to the artists for illustration.

Mayakovsky thus became the effective director of a political and artistic establishment which employed up

4.2 Mayakovsky, Malyutin and Cheremnykh in 1920.

to 100 people at this time, as many as had worked in the pre-revolutionary stock exchange.[16] Mayakovsky himself scanned *Pravda*, *Izvestiya*, the Rosta wall-newspaper and later *Ekonomicheskaya zhizn* and the railway workers' paper *Gudok*, noting themes that would be suitable for Rosta Windows and composing text or verse as required. Lili Brik recalled that in the summer of 1921 on his journeys from Pushkino to Moscow Mayakovsky would write out fifteen to twenty themes of this kind and sometimes came to the office with the verses already prepared.[17] Mayakovsky worked continuously at Rosta from October 1919 up to January 1922, and later recalled this time as among the happiest of his entire life although the living and working conditions had been very arduous.[18]

A definite system of work was established at an early stage. The drawings were made separately, and them glued on to a large sheet of paper (even a newspaper, if nothing better was available). Their size varied from 90 to 220cm in height and from 70 to 220cm in width; the largest, Glavpolitprosvet Window No. 167, was a massive 422cm high and 230cm wide.[19] Photographs were taken of the Windows before they were stencilled, not simply as a record but because mistakes were sometimes introduced at this stage (punctuation marks might be moved, lines transposed, or mistakes made in gram-

mar).[20] Some 944 numbered Rosta Windows were produced and a further 469 Glavpolitprosvet Windows, making a total (including duplicates or unnumbered issues) of about 1,600 Windows over the whole period.[21] Mayakovsky was himself responsible for about 500 of the illustrations, or just under a third of the total; another third was contributed by Cheremnykh, and a wide variety of other artists contributed the remainder including A. M. Nyurenberg, A. S. Levin, V. O. Roskin and V. V. Khvostenko.[22] As its staff increased, the rate of production became greater: in September 1919 between ten and twelve separate Windows were produced, but the rate gradually increased up to twenty-five a month and in one wholly exceptional month, October 1920, no fewer than 200 separate Windows were produced.[23] Each Window was reproduced on average 150 times, making a total of about 240,000 copies of all Moscow Windows put together, or as many as two million individual frames.[24] In the end fewer than one in ten appeared in shop windows; the great majority were displayed in other locations.[25]

Mikhail Cheremnykh, formally the senior partner in the enterprise, was born in Tomsk in October 1890, the twelfth child of a retired colonel who was a member of the gentry class.[26] His father died when Cheremnykh was only 18 months old, and his young widow was left in difficult circumstances. His father had been a rich man, with his own stable of horses and a fine library, volumes from which were until recently still to be found in Tomsk public library. His army pension, however, provided no more than a modest living, and only Mikhail of all the children was given a proper education. The Cheremnykhs, like many others, spent most of the summer in the countryside, and the young artist was able to spend a great deal of time fishing and playing games. He always retained the great love of Siberia with which he grew up, and his pet-name 'Misha', a diminutive of Mikhail, was based upon the popular name for the Siberian bear, big, quiet and kind-hearted, whom he was supposed in these respects to resemble.[27] Cheremnykh began to draw and paint at an early age, encouraged by his elder brother, who copied pictures from journals for him and gave him paints. His grandfather on his mother's side had been an artist, and his self-portrait hung in the family home; Cheremnykh was even supposed to look like him. His first teacher, a political exile, encouraged his talents further. Cheremnykh began to read widely and developed an excellent memory, reciting *Evgeny Onegin* by heart for his elder brother. He also sang well in the choir, which may have helped him to obtain full marks in his school examinations for religious knowledge.[28]

At the wish of his mother Cheremnykh enrolled in

4.3 M. M. Cheremnykh (from O. Savostyuk and B. Uspensky, intr., *Mikhail Mikhailovich Cheremnykh* [Moscow: Sovetskii khudozhnik, 1970])

4.4 M. M. Cheremnykh, *Zhili sebe, pozhivali burzhui . . .* (Once upon a time the Bourgeoisie lived Well), two coloured lithograph, 1919, 71 × 54 cm., BS 202.

old order. In the final frame, with the interventionists defeated, the worker was able to turn to more peaceful pursuits and began to reap the benefits of the new life (a school and a soviet of people's deputies were shown

4.5 M. M. Cheremnykh, *Vygnal trudyashchiisya kapitalista . . .* (The Worker turned out the Capitalist), two coloured lithograph, 1919, 78 × 53 cm., BS 84.

the medical faculty of Tomsk University, but he stayed there only a year and a half.[29] His explanation in later years was that he had no wish to become a doctor and be woken up at nights. He told his lecturers that what he really wanted to do was to become an artist; they persuaded his mother, and in due course he went to Moscow to enrol in the painting section of the School of Painting, Sculpture and Architecture, where he studied under N. A. Kasatkin and K. A. Korovin.[30] Cheremnykh was allowed to postpone his military service in order to complete his education,[31] and graduated shortly before the revolution. He was, according to contemporary testimony, one of the first to offer his services to the VTSIK publishing house headed by Konstantin Eremeev.[32] Some of Cheremykh's work for VTSIK during 1918 has already been considered (see above, Plates 2.9 and 2.10). Another poster of the same period, *Once upon a time the Bourgeoisie lived well* (Plate 4.4), produced in early 1919, showed a blindfolded worker waiting upon a bourgeois and a priest. For this he was promised a heavenly kingdom in the hereafter. Lenin arrived and opened his eyes; the worker, realising he had been fooled, tore off his chains, kicked out his oppressors, and enrolled in the Red Army to defend his gains when foreign troops were called in to restore the

in the background of this picture of domestic contentment).[33] Cheremnykh's other work of the same period – for instance *The Worker Kicked out the Capitalist* (Plate 4.5) – made similar points in the same simple visual language.[34]

Like most other poster artists, Cheremnykh approached the tasks of political poster making on the basis of a considerable experience of newspaper graphics and cartoons. His first drawing had been published as early as 1910 in the journal *Sibirskaya nov* (Siberian Virgin Soil), which was published in Tomsk.[35] While studying in Moscow Cheremnykh supplemented his modest income by working as a caption writer·for the newspaper *Vechernye izvestiya* (Evening News), and his cartoons and sketches began to appear there from November 1912, signed either 'M. Ch.' or 'Nero'. A political cartoon on the subject of the Triple Alliance appeared in one of the Moscow journals in 1914.[36] Cheremnykh began work on his final-year project in 1916 and showed it at a student exhibition the following year. A gloomy painting entitled *The Blind*, it was clearly influenced by the wartime atmosphere and in the end he did not complete it.[37] Curiously, perhaps, for a Soviet poster artist, Cheremnykh's own favourite painters were Raphael and Picasso;[38] one of his favourite pictures was Raphael's *Sistine Madonna*, now in Dresden[39]; and he greatly enjoyed the singing of Orthodox church choirs.[40]

Cheremnykh continued to publish his work in newspapers and journals after the revolution; his sketched appeared in newspapers such as *Bednota*, *Vechernye izvestiya* and *Rannee utro* (Early Morning),[41] and a cartoon, *The Menagerie of the Future* (Plate 4.6), showing a worker and his son looking curiously at a Tsar, a banker and a Whiteguardist in captivity, appeared in the Petrograd journal *Kommunar* (Communard) in 1918.[42] During 1918 and 1919 Cheremnykh also worked on a more elaborate project, two illustrated volumes dealing in a humorous way with themes of Russian history. Although the work was completed the manuscript was unfortunately lost by the publishers and has not subsequently been located.[43] His cartoons *The Last Hour* and *Comrade Lenin at Work*, as already noted, were taken up by Deni and used as the basis of poster designs (see Plates 1.4 and 3.22). Lenin was reportedly amused by Cheremnykh's cartoon but asked him to spare the German revolutionary Klara Zetkin, then working in the headquarters of the Comintern, as she would be much less sympathetic.[44]

Cheremnykh performed at least one other service for the revolutionary cause before he became involved in Rosta. This was in the spring of 1918, when Lenin began to make plans to repair the clock on the Spassky

4.6 M. M. Cheremnykh, *V zverintse budushchego* (The Menagerie of the Future), drawing for *Kommunar*, Petrograd, 1918.

Tower of the Kremlin which had been damaged by artillery fire in October 1917. It was proposed that the clock's chimes, which had previously rung out the old Russian hymn 'Kol slaven' and the march of the Preobrazhensky regiment, should be retuned so as to play the 'Internationale'. Workmen were easily found to repair the clock itself, but the chimes proved more difficult. The architect N. V. Vinogradov, who was Deputy People's Commissar for State Property at this time, proposed to Cheremnykh that he should take this opportunity to display his musical talents. (Indeed Cheremnykh loved music, had taken music lessons and (like Moor) had even thought of becoming an opera singer.) In two weeks of hard work he managed to adjust the bells and they henceforth played the 'Internationale'. The new chimes were used on the first anniversary of the revolution and at funeral marches of deceased revolutionaries.[45] Trotsky, who made regular use of the Spassky Gate to pass into and out of the Kremlin, recalled that although the chimes themselves had been adjusted, a double-headed eagle and even an icon had still been left in place over the gate, despite his request that a hammer and sickle be placed above them.[46] Lenin was reportedly very pleased with the transformation, not least because of the major saving in public spending that had been achieved (the leading private firm of clock makers had quoted a figure of 200,000 rubles; Cheremnykh received the much more reasonable sum of 8,000 rubles).[47] Cheremnykh him-

4.7 M. M. Cheremnykh, *Istoriya pro bubliki i pro babu, ne priznayushchuyu Respubliki* (The Story of the Bread Rings), coloured lithograph, 1920, 148 × 76 cm., BS 1174.

self, however, ruefully told his wife that ever since that time he had started to go bald as a result of the high winds to which he had been exposed.[48]

The testimony of contemporaries leaves little doubt that Cheremnykh, although a fierce critic of opponents of the new regime, was an open, honest, kindly and rather shy man. In the forty years that he had known him, Boris Efimov recalled, he had never known Cheremnykh to be annoyed or irritable, or at odds with anyone; he could remember no occasion on which Cheremnykh had even raised his voice or lost his temper.[49] His work was not angry and denunciatory, like Moor's, nor was it bitterly ironical, like that of Deni; it tended rather to make good-humoured fun of its subject. In this respect Cheremnykh and Mayakovsky complemented each other, as did the more satirically-inclined Deni and Bedny.[50] Cheremnykh, Efimov added, was a Siberian, and 'everything in him, from his characteristic "Siberian" surname to his deliberate and solid footstep, was weighty, firm, if one can put it like that, bear-like (not for nothing was he called Misha)'.[51] Cheremnykh tended to be taciturn, and if asked for his opinions at meetings he would oblige with the minimum of words in a deep bass voice. A non-drinker, he nevertheless loved life in all its forms: and member together with Moor sang in the *Krokodil* 'choir', which performed at all their parties.[52] In later life he became involved, like many other poster artists, in newspaper cartoon work, in book illustration and in theatrical design, and during the Second World War he produced one of the very first 'Tass Windows'. But of all the work he had done in his lifetime, his wife recalled, he was proudest of his Kremlin chimes and his Rosta Windows which, following the art critic Tukhendkhold, he called the 'flowers of the revolution'.[53]

Cheremnykh directed the Artistic Section of Rosta for two and a half years, and was the author of drawings for about 500 Rosta Windows.[54] If Mayakovsky's name had not been attached to other artists' work he would himself, Cheremnykh believed, have been the most productive of all the Rosta poster artists.[55] He worked quickly and easily at this time and collaborated readily with Mayakovsky, although he was apparently too shy to be a regular guest at Mayakovsky's own home (they addressed each other throughout in the second person plural rather than in the more intimate *ty*).[56] Cheremnykh could complete up to fifty posters in a single night; sometimes he would doze off at his work with sheer fatigue, but 'maintained that on waking up he found the work had been completed by inertia'.[57]

One of Cheremnykh's most popular posters at this time was *The Story of the Bread Rings* (Plate 4.7), to which Mayakovsky supplied the text. It featured a woman who went to the market to sell her *bubliki* (bread rings), but refused to give any to the hungry Red Army men on their way to the Polish front. The Poles, pushing aside their undernourished opponents, duly advanced as far as the market where they found the woman trader and ate her up, together with her bread rings. The moral was a clear one: 'Feed the red men then! Bring your bread and don't complain, otherwise you'll lose your bread and your head as well'. Cheremnykh's *In the Luxury Carriage* (Plate 4.9), produced in the early summer of 1921, was devoted to the mission that the Allied powers proposed to send to Soviet Russia to examine the famine situation at first hand; it was to be led by Joseph Noulens, a known opponent of Bolshevism, and was widely regarded as a covert attempt to destabilise the new regime in its hour of adversity.

Mayakovsky modestly declared that Cheremnykh was the 'best draftsman of the Soviet Union' at this time, and Polonsky considered him the most talented of all the Rosta artists. Cheremnykh, however, believed that this honour should more properly go to the youngest member of the Rosta collective, Ivan Malyutin.[58] Malyutin, born in 1891, had studied at the Stroganov Art School but had not completed his studies there, being tempted away by the opportunity to engage in theatrical design.[59] He worked as a cartoonist in *Budilnik* and the theatrical journal *Rampa i zhizn* and then in a private opera house before moving to Rosta, where he became one of the longest-serving participants. Ivan Pavlov remembered him as a 'brilliant and original figure', absolutely free of routine and convention;[60] and he was, apparently, the only Rosta artist who never copied from anyone else. Some Petrograd cartoonists, visiting Moscow, agreed with Cheremnykh that Malyutin was a very gifted artist, but objected that 'he imitates you a lot, Mikhail Mikhailovich'. Cheremnykh had to point out that the opposite was in fact the case.[61] Malyutin was a temperamental but humorous artist, much influenced at this time by Paul Cézanne (he signed some of his work 'Ivan Malyutin à la Cézanne'). 'Whatever he did', Cheremnykh recalled, 'it always turned out remarkably funny'.[62] After working in Rosta, Malyutin also turned to work in journal and theatrical design; he drew the front cover for the first issue of *Krokodil*, working until 5 o'clock in the morning to complete his task.[63] He died at a relatively young age in 1932 after a long and serious attack of pleurisy.[64]

The dominant figure in the Rosta collective, its formally democratic character notwithstanding, was the poet and artist Vladimir Vladimirovich Mayakovsky.[65] Mayakovsky was born in July 1893 in the village of Bagdadi in the Kutaisi region of Georgia; his birthplace, predictably, is now called Mayakovsky. The young

Mayakovsky went to secondary school in Kutaisi and did well, at least initially, but his education, he later recalled, had really been undertaken by his two sisters, particularly his elder sister Lyudmilla, who had been to Moscow to study drawing and, at some risk to herself, had brought back 'long sheets of paper' covered with revolutionary songs and verse. 'This was revolution', Mayakovsky wrote later in his autobiography *I myself*. 'It was in verse. Verses and revolution somehow fused in my head.[66] Georgia was affected by the unrest of the time (this was during the 1905–7 revolution) and the young Mayakovsky was able to attend meetings and demonstrations. Seeking to make sense of he new concepts and unfamiliar words he began to read political literature and came to regard himself as a Social Democrat.[67]

When Mayakovsky's father died in 1906 the family moved to Moscow, where they lived in very modest circumstances. Mayakovsky himself used to decorate Easter eggs to augment the family budget. In 1908, aged only fourteen but looking older, he joined the Bolshevik wing of the Russian Social Democratic Party, became a propagandist, and was elected to the city party committee.[68] In the same year he was arrested for the first time. Altogether Mayakovsky was arrested three times, on the last occasion spending five months in solitary confinement. After his release in 1910 he drifted away from politics and towards serious academic study, also taking up the study of art under S. Yu. Zhukovsky and then under Petr Kelin, who had also briefly taught Dmitri Moor. A year later, in 1911, he was accepted by the Moscow School of Painting, Sculpture and Architecture, the only institution of this kind that he could enter without a certificate of political reliability.[69] Here he met a somewhat older, experimentally-minded artist called David Burlyuk (1882–1967), who influenced him greatly. Mayakovsky later claimed that Russian Futurism had been born out of their meeting. Encouraged by Burlyuk, Mayakovsky began to write seriously and to conduct himself in such an outrageous manner that he was forced to leave the art school. The Futurists, undaunted, toured Russia, giving lectures and mass performances with drew large audiences, although more cautious publishers still refused to print their work.[70]

His youthful radicalism and self-conscious iconoclasm notwithstanding, Mayakovsky, like most other artists and writers, rallied warmly to the national cause on the outbreak of the First World War. He greeted the war with 'excitement', and tried to volunteer but was turned down because of his political record. According to the writer Ivan Bunin, on the day war was declared he climbed the Skobelev monument in Moscow and

4.8 V. V. Mayakovsky, photographed by A. M. Rodchenko (1924).

recited patriotic verse.[71] Mayakovsky was also involved in patriotic poster work for the government-sponsored Contemporary Lubok publishing house. 'In front of Warsaw and Grodno', ran one of his texts, 'the Germans were beaten in every respect; with us even women are ready to shoot Prussians' (a play on words: the Russian term can also mean 'cockroaches').[72] Another (Plate 4.10) warned the Turks, allied at this time to the Germans, not to advance further.[73]

During the wartime period Mayakovsky made the acquaintance of Maxim Gorky, who arranged a job for him in the Petrograd auto school where several other literary figures with modest technical attainments were also being sheltered.[74] He began to publish short satirical poems in *Novyi Satirikon* at this time to help make

73

1) В ШИКАРНОМ ВАГОНЕ
В ВАГОНЕ САЛОНЕ
ТРИ ФРАНЦУЗА ЕДУТ И
ВЕДУТ МЕЖ СОБОЙ БЕСЕДУ

2) ГОВОРИТ НУЛАНС ТРЯСЯСЬ ОТ
СМЕХА-,,ВОТ БУДЕТ ПОТЕХА –

3) КАК ДОЕДЕМ ДО ГОЛОДНЫХ
МЕСТ СРАЗУ ВЫПУСТИМ МАНИФЕСТ.

4) КТО ХОЧЕТ ЕСТЬ ВСЛАСТЬ
СВЕРГАЙ СОВЕТСКУЮ ВЛАСТЬ

5) ВОТ ВАМ ЦАРЬ ВОТ ЦАРИЦА
А ВОТ РОЖЬ И ПШЕНИЦА.

6) ГОВОРИТ ЖИРО
ПОДМИГНУВ ХИТРО

7) ЭТОГО МАЛО —
МЫ ИХ ПОПРИЖМЕМ СНАЧАЛА

8) ПУСТЬ ПОПОТЕЮТ КАК СЛЕДУЕТ
А ПОТОМ ПООБЕДАЮТ

9) ГОВОРИТ ПО ГЕНЕРАЛ БРАВЫЙ
ЗНАЕМ КОРМИШЬ ВСЕЙ ОРАВОЙ

10) МЫ ИХ ЧИСЛОМ ПОУБАВИМ
ТИХИХ ОСТАВИМ

11) А КТО С НОРОВ ВЗДОРНЫМ
– ТОГО ВЗДЕРНЕМ

12) ДРУЗЬЯ РАСХОДИТЕСЬ ОЧЕННО
РОССИЯ-НЕ ВАША ВОТЧИНА

Главполитпросвет N316

4.9 M. M. Cheremnykh, *V shikarnom vagone, v vagone-salone . . .* (In the Luxury Wagon), Glavpolitprosvet Window no. 316, 1921, 220 × 123 cm., BS 2674.

ЛУБОК. 1914.

Эх, султан, сидел бы в Порте!
Дракой рыла не попорти.

4.10 V. V. Mayakovsky, *Ekh sultan, sidel by v Porte, drakoi rylo ne poporti* (Hey Sultan, Sitting in the Porte, don't Spoil your Mug with such a Fight), coloured lithograph, 1914/15, 38 × 56 cm.

ends meet and worked on several longer compositions, 'A Cloud in Pants', 'The Backbone Flute' and 'Man' among others. In 1915 he had met Osip Brik and his wife Lili, for whom he conceived an extravagant – and eventually reciprocated – passion. Mayakovsky initially welcomed the February revolution, a fact that causes his present-day Soviet biographers some embarrassment,[75] but in October 1917, there was no question as to whether he would support the Bolshevik seizure of power: this was 'my revolution'.[76] VTSIK, which had just been elected by the Second Congress of Soviets, invited the leading artists and writers to the Smolny Institute to discuss future policy; only five or six turned up, among them Mayakovsky.[77]

Mayakovsky had already begun to write and perform for a large public audience, and in the early months of the new regime he found every opportunity to develop further the more publicistic, agitational aspects of his art. He declaimed his poetry nightly in the Poets' Cafe in Moscow; he wrote three film scenarios, and acted in

them himself; and he began to produce cinema posters.[78] His *Mystery-Bouffe* was written in 1918 and performed on the first anniversary of the revolution under the direction of Meyerhold and Malevich as a mass spectacle. It later toured the factories where – according at least to Mayakovsky – it met with a most favourable response; still later a special performance was given in German to the delegates attending the third congress of the Communist International in 1921.[79] A single issue of the *Futurists' Newspaper* appeared in March 1918; copies were pasted on to house walls for greater impact.[80] The new paper included Mayakovsky's 'Open Letter to the Workers' in which he proclaimed the Futurists to be the real revolutionaries in the field of art.[81] Mayakovsky's *Heroes and Victims of the Revolution* appeared in 1918; it consisted of a set of sketches of workers, Red Army men, bankers, landlords and others. His *Soviet Alphabet* (Plate 4.11), which appeared in the autumn of 1919, was turned down by established publishers; in the end Mayakovsky produced it himself and handed it out,

75

4.11 From V. V. Mayakovsky, *Sovetskaya azbuka* (Soviet Alphabet), 1919.

still damp, to troops leaving for the front line.[82] Elements from both of these were drawn upon in his later poster work.

Mayakovsky, in short, had already begun to move beyond the limited world of cafe society and to address a wider and more representative public when in the autumn of 1919 he saw his first Rosta Window and decided to throw his enormous energies into the further development of what was then still a very embryonic form of visual and textual communication.

The Rosta Windows, Mayakovsky later wrote,

> that was a fantastic thing. It meant a nation of 150 million being served by hand by a small group of painters. It meant news sent by telegram immediately translated into posters, decrees into couplets . . . It meant Red Army men looking at posters before a battle and going to fight not with a prayer but with a slogan on their lips.

The Windows, he wrote, were huge, stencilled sheets, which were hung up in stations, at points along the front, and in empty shop windows. The public, even crude character of the Windows was not only a consequence of the lack of paper, it but also a result of the 'mad tempo of the revolution, with which no printing technology could keep pace'.[83] 'Days and nights in ROSTA', he wrote later in his autobiography. 'All kinds of Denikins attack. I write and draw. Made about three thousand posters and about six thousand captions.'[84] 'We don't need a dead temple of art where dead works languish, but a living factory of the human spirit', he wrote. Art must be concentrated, 'not in dead museum-temples, but everywhere – on the streets, in trams, in factories, in workshops and in workers' apartments'.[85] The Rosta Windows were certainly a significant step in this direction.

Rosta posters, in principle, were unsigned, but the different styles of the main protagonists nonetheless emerged clearly. Moor later suggested that the Rosta Windows could be divided formally into three main types: the most lapidary belonged to Mayakovsky; the best drawn belonged to Cheremnykh; and the most painterly belonged to Malyutin.[86] A more recent scholarly assessment has suggested that Mayakovsky's work was the most laconic, schematic and brilliant in its use of colour, while Cheremnykh's work was freer and more varied in its depiction of movement although more limited in its use of colour, and Malyutin's was the most decorative.[87] Still another verdict was that Mayakovsky was the most accessible, the sharpest and clearest of the Rosta artists, while both Malyutin and Cheremnykh were more considered, colourful, individual and detailed.[88] An example of Mayakovsky's work is shown in Plate 4.12, which was issued as Rosta Window No. 742 in December 1920. The subject was taken from Lenin's speech on electrification to the 8th Party Congress the previous year. 'We lit this truth above the world', the text begins, 'this truth was carried throughout the world' (the illustration depicts 'all power to the Soviets'). 'Now we need these lights', the text goes on, showing more conventional forms of illumination, 'may this fire light up Russia!' The 8th Party Congress was also the inspiration for Mayakovsky and Cheremnykh's *At the Moment No-one is Poorer than Us* (Plate 4.16), which promised that Russia would be 'richer than all in a few years' if the congress's plan for electrification was put into effect.[89]

Mayakovsky's other Rosta Windows were more directly concerned with the conduct of the civil war. His first, as already mentioned, dealt with the struggle aginst Denikin in the autumn of 1919. His *Help Voluntarily* (Plate 4.14), issued in the autumn of 1920, called for every assistance from industry and agriculture to defeat the revolution's remaining enemies. His *Remember Red Barracks Day* (Plate 4.13) pointed out that it was not enough to defeat the Russian Whiteguardists while the monster of world capitalism was still at large. The Red Army, in consequence, was still needed and must still be supported. *If We don't Finish off Whiteguardism Completely* (Plate 4.15), issued in the summer of 1920, urged the need for continued vigilance in view of the opposition that still remained on the Polish front and from Baron Wrangel to the south: 'until the red banner has been strengthened', it concluded, 'we can't throw our rifle away'. In all of these Rosta Windows Mayakovsky composed the text and was also responsible for the illustrations.

There were essentially three kinds of Rosta Window, Cheremnykh wrote later: a multi-frame poster with a two-line caption; a major poem by Mayakovsky illustrated with a number of drawings by himself or one of the other artists; or a substantial poetic work illustrated by a single large drawing. Most of the Windows were of the first type.[90] There were, however, still other types of Rosta Windows. Among them were the single frame poster, usually reproduced lithographically, which was often taken from a much larger stencilled Window. Mayakovsky's *Ukrainians and Russians have a Single Cry* (Plate 4.17), for instance, produced during the earlier stages of the Russo-Polish war of 1920, was based upon a single frame of Rosta Window No. 63 together with the caption from another of the frames. Another frame from the same Window also became a separate poster, Mayakovsky's *To the Polish front! Armed! In an Instant!*[91] Several other Rosta posters were devoted to the Polish front in response to an appeal by VTSIK and the Council of People's Commissars, issued in April 1920, which urged all workers, peasants and 'honest citizens of Russia' to go to there. Malyutin's *Only He Deserves Freedom who goes to Defend it with a Rifle* (Plate 4.19) was issued in response to this appeal in the late spring of 1920; so also was Malyutin's *To the Polish Front!* (Plate 4.21), which was issued at about the same time. Malyutin's *One Hand Stretches out to Russia with Peace, while the other Gives Rifles to the Poles* (Plate 4.20) was produced later in 1920 when it appeared that Polish peace overtures were not to be taken at face value. These single-frame posters, although produced by the Rosta studios, did not however form part of the numbered sequence of Windows.

The production of Rosta Windows took place in a suite of interconnected rooms on the fourth floor of No. 16, Malaya Lubyanka, a large and formerly elegant stone building.[92] Mayakovsky's own flat on Lubyansky Passage was nearby. The critic Viktor Shklovsky walked one day with Mayakovsky to the Rosta workshop. 'I have to invent four lines before we reach that house', Mayakovsky told him.[93] Inside the workshop a stove provided some background heat, but there was only limited ventilation and smoke collected below the ceiling, settling at about the level of Shklovsky's fur hat. Mayakovsky was a particularly tall man and had no room to stand up straight. Most of the work was done on the floor; Mayakovsky composed the posters, while others prepared cardboard stencils, and still others used the stencils to make copies. Such was the disorder that Shklovsky lost his way and knocked over a pot of paint, but somehow or other the paint that was spilled was incorporated into the design of the poster on which it had been sitting. Mayakovsky himself worked day and night, sleeping with a log under his head instead of a pillow so that he could wake up more easily. From the window of the workshop the Sukharevsky Tower could be seen, as well as the steam of human breath in the freezing cold outside and a large clock urging the work along.[94] So cold was it in the workshop in winter, another participant recalled, that all the staff wore heavy overcoats, hats and boots, and their hands were swollen with the cold.[95] A student from Siberia called Borisov, who has left the only contemporary account of the Rosta workshop, found it to be a vast labyrinth of doors and passages, in which he had spent half an hour trying to find Mayakovsky. In the poster workshop itself five or six people were sitting on the floor, surrounded by paper and paint, while wooden tables along the wall were collapsing under the weight of the posters, books and other aterials that had been placed upon them.[96] The atmosphere was thick not just with smoke but with the smell of glue, tobacco and rotting paper.[97]

Despite the circumstances, Cheremnykh recalled, 'everyone worked with tremendous enthusiasm'; productivity was very high, and the atmosphere was lively and goodhumoured.[98] Work at Rosta was certainly intensive. As Cheremnykh later explained, all posters, in practice, were 'urgent' ones, and there were even 'races' to complete them. At a given signal all the artists would hurl themselves at a sheet of paper, trying to complete a poster. Mayakovsky was most often the victor in these contests.[99] On one celebrated occasion the artist Amshei Nyurenberg, who was one of the leading members of the Rosta collective, became so engrossed in a discussion of developments in Soviet painting that he forgot the urgent work that was awaiting him at home. It was already midnight when he returned to his accommodation, and he had still to do twenty-five drawings making up three complete Windows. He managed to finish the work by morning. Rolling up the still-damp posters, he rushed off to Rosta, arriving at 12 o'clock, a full two hours late. 'I'm a little late ...' he began hesitantly, hoping to propitiate the stern Mayakovsky. 'I'm clearly ill ...' 'Comrade Nyurenberg', replied Mayakovsky, 'you can obviously get sick. You can even die – that is your own affair. But the posters should have been here by 10 o'clock.'[100] On another occasion Mayakovsky telephoned the artist Denisovsky, also a member of the Rosta collective, and told him that twelve posters had to be ready by 9 am. the following morning for the People's Commissariat of Health.[101] Mayakovsky himself recalled that printing technology was simply unable to cope with the urgency of the work that was being carried out by Rosta. Only posters of long-term significance could be printed; more usually a telegram was received at the Rosta offices and a poster was prepared overnight, which was hung up on the streets the following morning before the newspapers

4.12 (*above left*) V. V. Mayakovsky, *My zazhgli nad mirom istinu etu . . .* (We Lit this Truth above the World), Rosta Window no. 742, 1920, 100 × 74 cm., BS 2047.

4.13 (*above right*) V. V. Mayakovsky, *Pomni o Dne krasnoi kazarmy* (Remember Red Army Barracks Day), Rosta Window no. 729, 1921, 100 × 79 cm., BS 1559

1. Сейчас беднее нас нет

2. Будет Россия всех богаче через несколько лет

3. VIII Сезд дал план

4. Нами должен быть плану ход дан

УКРАИНЦЕВ и РУССКИХ КЛИЧ ОДИН -

РОСТА

ДА НЕ БУДЕТ ПАН НАД РАБОЧИМ ГОСПОДИН!

had appeared. News of a victory at the front, received by telegraph, could be on the streets in poster form within forty minutes to an hour in certain circumstances.[102]

All Rosta work, as a matter of principle, was carried out by a collective of writers, painters and stencillers, and a number of conventions applied to all the work they undertook. A form of colour coding was employed throughout: workers were red, capitalists were black, and the Polish nobles were usually green or yellow. Workers were usually young and thin, the enemy old, fat and whiskered.[103] Factories were buildings with tall smoking chimneys, peasant huts were small buildings with thatched roofs, and fields were represented by parallel strips of land, trees and sky.[104] Within these general conventions particular devices were used by individual artists and then borrowed freely by the others. Malyutin, for instance, had drawn a factory which consisted of ten chimneys and a vast number of windows. It transpired that he had first of all covered the wall of the building with window sashes, and had then coloured the stone surrounds. It was quick and effective, and everyone immediately began to use the same method.[105] Cheremykh himself was the first to place a raven on the smokestack of a broken-down train; this was later used more generally as a symbol of economic inactivity and dislocation.[106] Cheremnykh in turn copied from Mayakovsky the representation of smoke in the from of a spiral, as small children would draw it, and Mayakovsky also pioneered the standard figure of a worker in a cap and blouse.[107] Mayakovsky himself worked closely with Lili Brik and others, who would colour or even complete his sketches according to a standard scheme.[108] So practised did this work become that Mayakovsky could latterly draw the complicated figure of a worker with his eyes closed and yet with perfect accuracy.[109]

Rosta provided a living and indeed sometimes rather more than that for those who were employed there. Amshei Nyurenberg recalled that salaries at Rosta were paid out twice a month. The staff came to the counter with bags in their hands, as they could receive a thick and sometimes rather heavy bundle of notes for their labours. Having received their money, they would then proceed to the nearby Sukharevsky market where they could obtain flour and Ukrainian salt pork from soldiers and street traders.[110] The earnings of Rosta staff were based to a large degree upon an assessment of the complexity of the work they had to undertake, and the largest Windows with the greatest number of individual frames were accordingly presented for inspection. So large were the earnings of the Rosta staff that, according to Lili Brik, the finance director used to post a small boy outside his door, who would warn him when the artists were approaching. Whenever the boy saw Mayakovsky and the other artists making their way towards him in a body he would call out 'The artists are coming! The artists are coming!' and the finance director would slip out through a back door.[111] Cheremnykh, according to his wife, worked very hard at this time but also earned a lot of money. He took to dressing as a dandy, with expensive clothes and patent leather boots. Called before a party committee to explain his large earnings, he was asked if the state would still exist under socialism (one of the workers who interviewed him thought perhaps it would), and finally demoted to the more junior status of candidate. Cheremnykh later wrote on official forms that he had been a party member from 1919 until 1922 but had later 'left mechanically' (vybyl mekhanicheski).[112]

The Rosta collective operated with a good deal of informality and a great degree of political and organisational autonomy. The artist N. K. Verzhbitsky, for instance, who came to work at Rosta in 1919, had no close links with the Bolshevik party at the time and indeed continued to 'waver' (in his own admission) even after he had started to work there. He was nonetheless hired on the spot after he had presented himself at the Rosta offices.[113] Alexander Fevralsky joined Rosta in March 1919 as a member of the cuttings department and became the secretary of the whole organisation and a department head by the end of 1920, still only nineteen years old. The leading staff members were 'old Bolsheviks' but a majority were young men of Fevralsky's own generation.[114] All the work of the collective was shown to Kerzhentsev, as Director of Rosta, for his approval. 'All the material', Kerzhentsev wrote in the late 1920s at an exhibition of Rosta work, 'was edited directly by myself'.[115] In fact, it appears, Kerzhentsev never once withheld his approval from the work that was presented to him, and his supervision appears to have been entirely nominal.[116] It was less easy with Ivan Kogan, head of Rosta's Administrative and Budgetary Department, who sometimes queried the expenditure on Rosta Windows and who also had reservations about some of the more advanced forms that the artists employed. With N. I. Smirnov, who replaced Kerzhentsev in early 1921, relations were still more difficult.[117]

According to the recollections of most participants, the atmosphere at Rosta was a cordial and even familial one. Sometimes this was quite literally true: Mayakovsky's two sisters and his mother, for instance, used to visit the studios and helped to colour the posters and prepare glue; his sisters worked until dawn while his mother went to sleep, her bed often covered with drying posters.[118] Many of the staff lived in the four-storey Rosta building, and many who lived there ended up working for Rosta, so that the 'majority of the building's residents shared common interests'.[119] The Rosta staff used to gather together in the evenings, often in the large and well-lit flat of A. A. Osmerkin, one of the Rosta artists. Malyutin would normally come, but not always Mayakovsky, whose presence tended to turn a social evening into a disputatious one. On one occasion recorded by Nyurenberg, Mayakovsky, being deliberately provocative, began to disparage conventional painting, claiming that he would ban painting if he could and send all those concerned to work in Rosta. Osmerkin, a more traditional artist, became increasingly irate; Mayakovsky agreed that those who specialised in still lifes and landscapes would be 'in no mood for a laugh'. Calm was restored only when Osmerkin's wife brought in a big pot of pale tea brewed from carrots and a dish of thin grey cakes. Munching a cake, Mayakovsky grimaced and remarked 'Very tasty, like your painting'.[120] Others, however, remembered Mayakovsky as a colleague who was always full of good humour, who always took a close but tactful interest in the well-being of Rosta staff, and who was ready to read his verse at Rosta social evenings and other occasions.[121]

Rosta Windows were produced not only in Moscow but also, in many Rosta offices in the localities. Some attempt was made to give central direction of this work: copies of the stencils were distributed widely, then the stencils themselves were sent out for local reproduction, and Malyutin even prepared a short guide to the technique of stencil making. Relatively quickly, however, local artists began to supplement the Windows they received with local material, and Rosta Windows of an entirely independent nature began to appear at about the same time. Visitors to the Rosta studios in Moscow, recalled Cheremnykh, told them that Rosta Windows were appearing everywhere, particularly along the front lines and in railway stations. It was not possible, however, for Rosta in Moscow to keep in touch with, let alone to guide, the work of its local organisations; apart from anything else, communications were poor and there was not even a regular correspondence with most local sections.[122] A comprehensive inventory of civil war posters lists thirty-four local centres in which Rosta Windows were produced; subsequent research has established that by the middle of 1920 independent Rosta Windows were already being produced in more than 30 local sections, and that by the beginning of 1921 almost 50 local sections were engaged in this work. All regional Rosta centres appear to have been involved, including towns and cities as far apart as Smolensk, Kaluga, Rostov on Don, Chita, Ufa, Sebastopol, Baku and Tiflis.[123] As in Moscow, Rosta Win-

dows in the localities tended to follow the establishment of a printed wall-newspaper, which in turn tended to attract local writers and artists to its service. The study of Rosta Windows and of poster production generally outside the major centres is however at a relatively early stage and a full picture of the often varied styles and techniques of local artists will take some time to emerge.[124]

The most important Rosta section outside Moscow, and the first to follow Moscow's lead in the production of a printed wall-newspaper and then in the production of Rosta Windows, was Petrograd. In April 1920 a special poster department was established in the Petrograd Rosta offices, headed by Vladimir Kozlinsky (1891–1967) together with Vladimir Lebedev (1891–1967) and later Lev Brodaty (1889–1954).[125] Kozlinsky at this time directed an engraving studio at the State Free Artistic Studios in Petrograd, and was already known as a newspaper caricaturist. He was also the author of a series of lithographs on revolutionary Petrograd in 1919, including *The Agitator* (Plate 4.18).

4.18 V. I. Kozlinsky, *Agitator* (Agitator), linocut, 1917, 33 × 22 cm.

4.19 I. A. Malyutin, *Svobody zasluzhivaet tol'ko tot, kto ee s vintovskoi otstaivat' idet* (Only He Deserves Freedom, who goes to Defend it with a Rifle), two coloured lithograph, 1920, 52 × 55 cm., BS 1675.

4.20 I. A. Malyutin, *K Rossii s mirom tyanetsya ruka – a polyakam vintovki podaet drugoi* (One Hand Stretches out to Russia with Peace, While the other Gives Rifles to the Poles), coloured lithograph, 1920, 54 × 70 cm., BS 1182.

4.21 I. A. Malyutin, *Na pol'skii front! Krepnet kommuna pod pul' roem. Tovarishchi, pod vintovkoi sily utroim!* (To the Polish Front!), two coloured lithograph, 1920, 62 × 52 cm., BS 1416.

Lebedev had worked as a cartoonist for *Satirikon* and had also taken part in the festive decoration of the city for the anniversary of the revolution. Lev Brodaty was an established *Pravda* cartoonist and had become the editor and publisher of the first satirical journal put out by the Petrograd Soviet, *Krasnyi dyavol* (Red Devil). At this time he was working in the Political Enlightenment Department of the Petrograd military region.[126] Other artists who contributed occasionally to the Petrograd Rosta Windows included Nikolai Radlov, S. A. Pavlov and Aleksei Radakov, who became a prominent poster artist in his own right at about this time.[127] The texts were composed by V. V. Voinov (1891–1938) and A. M. Flit (1892–1954), who had both worked as political satirists in the pre-revolutionary period.[128] Perhaps surprisingly, none of the three leading artists was a member of the Communist Party at this time.[129]

Petrograd Rosta Windows were produced in a rather different way than was the case in Moscow. Instead of using cardboard stencils, the Petrograd artists engraved their drawings on to linoleum and then reproduced offprints in considerable numbers – up to 2,000 copies or more.[130] The engravings were produced in the Academy of Arts workshops, which were directed by Kozlinsky and which became more or less a 'department of Rosta' at this time.[131] The Windows were printed in a single colour and many were then painted by hand in either water colours or aniline dye, often in very different ways. The result was livelier in form and richer in content than the Moscow Rosta Windows, where the stencilling technique placed strict limits on what could be achieved. Hand-drawn and painted posters were also prepared, rather larger in size, which were then reproduced by hand.[132] Once they had been made ready the posters, as in Moscow, were placed in empty shop windows, first of all in four different locations (Nevsky Prospekt, Vassilevsky Island, and the Petrograd and Vyborg districts) and then in many more. In the end up to seventy different display points were being served, in factories and clubs and in military and naval units as well as in windows and on the streets. Some Petrograd Rosta Windows were sent still further afield, to more northerly regions and to parts of the Ukraine.[133] No more than about 300 of the Petrograd Rosta Windows have survived to the present day, although it is known that Lebedev alone produced more than 600 and that the total over two years must have exceeded 1,000 separate items.[134] The text, which was often produced separately and then glued on, is also missing in many of the Petrograd Windows that have survived.[135]

As in Moscow and elsewhere, the Petrograd Rosta artists appear to have worked with great energy and commitment. As the head of the instructional depart-

4.22 Unknown photographer, V. V. Lebedev (from V. Petrov, *Vladimir Vasil'evich Lebedev 1891–1967* [Leningrad: Khudozhnik RSFSR]).

ment of Petrograd Rosta, A. F. Shapov, later recalled, Kozlinsky was the central figure, assisted by Lebedev and Brodaty. This friendly *troika* worked intensively and accepted all the commissions they were given; if the work was 'urgent' or 'essential' they would stay up all night if necessary.[136] Kozlinsky, who had been urged to take on the responsibility for producing Rosta Windows by both Mayakovsky and Kerzhentsev, had already collaborated with Mayakovsky on the illustrations for his *Heroes and Victims of the Revolution*.[137] As in Moscow the work was collective and unsigned, but the individual approaches of the various artists concerned nonetheless emerged clearly. Kozlinsky himself tended towards the colourful, the bold and the heroic (see for instance Plates 4.25 and 27). Lebedev's work was more experimental in style and excited a good deal of controversy both at the time and later. Mayakovsky, on a visit to Petrograd, intervened to change the caption of one of Lebedev's posters from *A Bayonet on the Ground, a Saw in the Hand* to *Work with your Rifle beside you* (Plate 4.26). Lebedev himself acknowledged that this was a better formulation and the poster was issued in this form.[138] Some critics were even sharper. Moor, writing in 1933, reflected the prejudices that were current at the time when he accused Lebedev of applying 'cubist and suprematist' methods to his posters reducing them to the simplest of schemes'.[139] Polonsky, somewhat earlier, accepted that Lebedev was a 'great master of graphics' but argued that he took his work to such a level of abstraction that it was simply incomprehensible to the broad masses for whom it was intended.[140] Despite these differences, the poster artists worked closely together and sometimes even the artists themselves found it hard to tell their work apart.[141]

The fullest retrospective account of the work of the Petrograd Rosta during these years was prepared by the artist Lev Brodaty in a report presented to a commission on the study of the poster which met in 1931. According to this report, which remains unpublished, the places in which the Petrograd Rosta Windows were to be displayed emerged only gradually: to begin with, for instance, they appeared beside ordinary commercial advertising in the same window. Petrograd Rosta

4.23 V. V. Lebedev, *Da zdravstvuet avangard revolyutsii Krasnyi Flot* (Long Live the Vanguard of the Revolution, the Red Fleet), coloured lithograph, 1920, 67 × 50 cm.

Windows were up to four times bigger than those in Moscow, because Petrograd shop windows, especially those on Nevsky Prospekt, were much larger than Moscow ones. The first posters were put up in the windows of a former cafe along this famous thoroughfare. The bigger they were, it turned out, the greater was their impact. Each sequence of pictures was intended to serve a different and regular local audience; there was little in the way of public transport at the time and those who saw a Window on Nevsky Prospekt, for instance, were unlikely to see one in the Petrograd district. On receiving the latest telegram from the front or elsewhere, the theme for each Window would be chosen immediately and verses of up to four lines and a preliminary sketch would be prepared accordingly. The engraving would then be made ready for reproduction. Lebedev was able to produce an engraving in only seven minutes, and the longest time taken was about twenty minutes, otherwise there was a risk that the poster might be out of date by the time it had appeared. The artists, however, had occasional days off to look at the poster work that was being done elsewhere and to sample the public reaction. The illustrations became progressively more schematic, at least in part because of the pressure of time. Lebedev once went so far as to dispense with a nose from the figure of a bourgeois, leading to an indignant public reaction: this was 'some kind of monkey business on the part of the artist, or attempt at some kind of incredible style', it was objected.[142]

Lebedev, in many ways the most interesting and original of the Petrograd Rosta artists, had been born in St Petersburg in May 1891. His father was of peasant origin but had long been resident in the city.[143] Lebedev was little influenced by the events of 1905 and was still a young man when the First World War began. Following the intellectual interests of his father, Lebedev had begun to draw at the age of four or five and had decided to become a professional artist by about the age of fourteen. He soon began to sell his pictures and to publish his work in illustrated journals, although he was for the most part without formal artistic training. He met Tatlin and Shklovsky in 1912 in the private studio of M. D. Bernshtein, who was perhaps his only real teacher, but he joined none of the competing groups or circles in the art world at this time and took little interest in the controversies that were associated with them. Late in 1912 he passed the entrance examination into the St Petersburg Academy of Arts, but he found little of value there apart from the library and continued to frequent Bernshtein's studio. His work extended at this time into the satirical journals, including *Satirikon* and its companion *Novyi Satirikon*; he also contributed a

4.24 V. V. Lebedev, *Krest'yanin, esli ty ne khochesh' kormit' pomeshchika, nakormi front zashchishchayushchii tvoyu zemlyu i tvoyu svobodu* (Peasant, if you don't Want to Feed the Landlord, Feed the Front which is Defending your Land and your Liberty), coloured lithograph, 1920, 61 × 45 cm.

4.25 V. I. Kozlinsky, *Kronshtadtskaya karta bita!* (The Kronstadt Card is Beaten), coloured linocut, 1921, 49 × 31, BS 1320.

4.26 V. V. Lebedev, *Rabotat' nado, vintovka ryadom* (Work with your Rifle beside you), coloured linocut, 1920, 77 × 56 cm., BS 1611.

4.27 V. I. Kozlinsky, *Mertvetsy Parizhskoi Kommuny voskresli pod krasnym znamenem Sovetov!* (The Dead of the Paris Commune have Risen again under the Banner of the Soviets!), coloured linocut, 1921, 76 × 46 cm., BS 323.

sketch to the 'Freedom Loan' competition in the spring of 1917.

Lebedev was among the relatively few artists, particularly in Petrograd, who immediately and unconditionally supported the Bolshevik seizure of power. In 1918 he became a professor at the Petrograd Free Artistic Studios, identifying generally with 'left' artists in the struggle against established institutions and conventions. In the autumn of the same year Lebedev produced a large display placard in honour of the Communist International (not yet formally established) which was displayed on Nevsky Prospekt on the first anniversary of the revolution. From the spring of 1920 onwards Lebedev worked in the Petrograd Rosta offices, becoming its principal artist. Of the 600 or so posters that he produced at this time, however, only about 100 have survived to the present day. Lebedev was mainly occupied in book design and newspaper car-

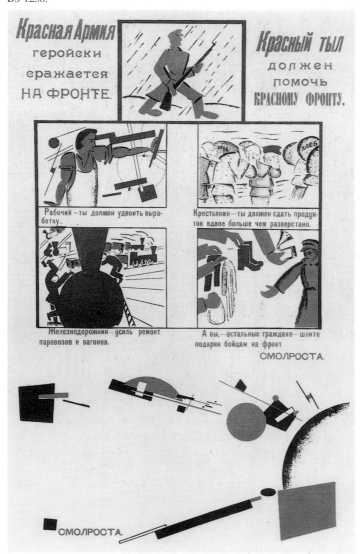

4.28 Anon, *Krasnaya Armiya geroicheski srazhaetsya na fronte* (The Red Army is fighting heroically at the Front), two coloured lithograph, 1920, 48 × 45, BS 1238.

toons in later years, although like others he resumed his poster work during the Second World War. He believed himself, however, that he had done his best work for Rosta and other bodies during the early 1920s.[144]

Of all the other sections of Rosta two more deserve particular consideration: Vitebsk and Odessa. Of all the Rosta sections, that based at Vitebsk was certainly the most innovative and controversial in its work. Every local section of Rosta reflected the influence of the artists who were invited to work there, and the Vitebsk section came naturally to reflect the very distinctive philosophy of the Vitebsk School of Art, headed originally by Marc Chagall and later (after a coup in which Chagall was ousted) by Kazimir Malevich.[145] El Lissitsky was among the artists who came to work at Vitebsk during these years, attracted by its liberal creative regime and (not least) by the relatively good food supply that obtained in the locality.[146] Lissitsky's *Red Wedge* (Plate 3.2), in which colour and design (the active or revolutionary red wedge and the passive or counter-revolutionary white circle) combined to make a political statement at a high level of abstraction, was produced in Vitebsk in 1920. Another poster emanating from Rosta in nearby Smolensk was *The Red Army is fighting heroically at the Front* (Plate 4.28), produced in 1920 by an unknown artist; the lower part of the poster was separately issued with the words 'What have you done for the front?' superimposed upon it.[147]

Teachers were appointed to the Vitebsk Art School without particular formality, Chagall recalled in his autobiography. One of them, whom he had actually appointed as director, spent his whole time sending off food parcels to his family. Another, a female, flirted with the local commissars and accepted their favours freely, claiming that this was for Chagall's benefit and in order to help the school. Some teachers even defected to the other side. Chagall himself, although a native of Vitebsk and an established painter, was hardly an obvious choice as director on political or organisational grounds; his knowledge of Marxism at this time, he later recalled, was 'limited to knowing that Marx was a Jew, and that he had a long white beard'.[148]

The work of the Rosta collective in Vitebsk was certainly distinctive. Chagall's first official function as Commissar of Art and Director of the School of Fine Arts in Vitebsk had been to decorate the town for the anniversary of the revolution, when his multicoloured horses flying through the air met with a mixed response.[149] Two years later, after Chagall had been replaced by Malevich, the film director Sergei Eisenstein passed through the town on the third anniversary of the revolution. The town, he wrote, was 'particularly odd. The red brick of the main streets is covered here with white paint. Green circles, orange squares and blue rectangles swarm over this white background. This is Vitebsk 1920. K. S. Malevich's brush has travelled over its brick walls'.[150] A local journalist who visited Vitebsk in 1920 found that all the fences in the town had been covered with Rosta posters. As there was a lack of glue they had been stuck up with flour paste; in the outskirts of the town the local goats had discovered this and eaten them up. Most Rosta staff in Vitebsk were young and politically immature: they put up posters celebrating the fall of a town in Belorussia which was still under attack, for instance, and were called to account for this by the local army commander. He promised to do what he could to justify their forecast but warned them against any repetitions.[151] In all, the Vitebsk Rosta collective produced about thirty satire windows during the civil was period, as well as decorative displays, painted trams, factory notices and other forms of visual propaganda.[152]

The work that took place at Odessa, on the Black Sea coast, was very different in character but also individual in its inspiration. Poster activity under Rosta auspices began early in 1920 after the interventionist and White armies had retreated.[153] The first posters were put up by a group of artists, among them Boris Efimov, who had come from Kiev and who had brought with them samples of the Moscow Rosta Windows, which they began to copy by hand. In March 1920 a special artistic-agitational department was established in the Odessa branch of Rosta, and more artists and writers became involved in its work. Rosta posters in Odessa were usually painted on to sheets of plywood which were taken down after a few days, washed clean and then repainted. No Odessa Rosta Windows have survived as a result, although the drawings for some of them have been preserved in the local museum. Very occasionally the posters were hand-painted on paper or lithographed, although paper was scarcer than plywood and was usually reserved for the display of telegrams.[154] As elsewhere, the posters were displayed in shop windows in the town, or were stuck up on house walls, crossroads, squares and other public places. The posters were changed twice a day in some cases to keep up with events.

To begin with, the Odessa posters shared the allegorical and symbolic emphases of posters in other parts of Soviet Russia – youths with swords were pitted against hydra-headed monsters, and the ubiquitous St George did battle with the dragon. The influence of local satirical journals and realistic painting was stronger than in Petrograd and Moscow, however, and these earlier approaches were soon discarded. About 800 posters in all were produced between 1920 and early 1921, or about 1,000 over the whole civil war period; this placed Odessa second only to Moscow in terms of total output.[155]

A remarkable range of writers and artists became involved in the work of Rosta in Odessa, reflecting the fertile, cosmopolitan atmosphere that this Black Sea port had always encouraged. Among the writers, Edward Bagritsky, Ilya Ilf, Isaac Babel, Yuri Olesha and Valentin Kataev took a part of some kind in producing texts; among the artists the cartoonist Boris Efimov (born 1900 and still active in the Soviet press in the 1980s) was particularly prominent. Efimov, in his memoirs, recalled that conditions of work at Rosta in Odessa were as informal as anywhere else: artists would make themselves known to him, would be given a trial, and if successful would be taken on.[156] The painters appointed in this way included many cubists and 'decadents'; Efimov considered himself no expert in matters of artistic style and even encouraged techniques of this kind, believing them to be 'terribly revolutionary'. Some of the more abstract designs had however to be rejected as common sense suggested that strangely distorted figures would be unlikely to serve the purposes of popular agitation. There was some resentment among the older artists that a young man, just arrived from Kiev, should presume to take decisions on such matters. To silence his critics Efimov did a poster dealing with Wrangel's retreat from the Crimea, which was hung up in front of the Rosta offices. A departing White Guard, pausing before it momentarily, was heard to remark: 'Bastard! Like it or not, you have to laugh!'. Efimov later moved to Kharkov and Kiev before, in the early 1920s, becoming one of *Pravda*'s most regular cartoonists.[157] In all more than fifty writers, artists and other personnel appear to have been active at some time in the Odessa branch of Rosta, not including copyists and stencillers.[158] As elsewhere, the work reached a peak of intensity in 1920 and then petered out gradually over the following two years.

БУДЬ НА СТРАЖЕ!

Польша выбросила на нашу территорию несколько новых значительных банд под руководством того самого петлюровского бандита Тютюника, который подлежал высылке за пределы Польши. Неслыханно провокационный характер этого нового нападения заставил всю армию встрепенуться и спросить себя: "доколе же?".

Каждый красноармеец должен уяснить себе действительное положение дел. В Польше не одно правительство, а два. Одно — официальное, гласное, выступающее в парламенте, ведущее переговоры, подписывающее договоры. Другое — негласное, опирающееся на значительную часть офицерства, с так называемым начальником государства Пилсудским во главе. За спиной тайного правительства стоят крайние империалисты Франции. В то время как официальное польское правительство под давлением не только трудящихся, но и широких буржуазных кругов, вынуждено стремиться к миру с советской Россией, провокаторы Польского штаба изо всех сил стремятся вызвать войну.

Мы не знаем, победят ли в Польше этой зимой или ближайшей весной сторонники мира или преступные поджигатели. Мы должны быть готовы к худшему.

Красная армия снова раздавит Петлюровские банды, выброшенные к нам польскими авантюристами. Красная армия удвоит свою работу по боевой подготовке. Никакой поворот событий не застигнет красную армию врасплох.

Л. Троцкий.

5.1 D. S. Moor, *Bud' na strazhe!* (Be on Guard), coloured lithograph, 1920/1, 107 × 70 cm., courtesy of the Musée d'histoire contemporaine, Paris.

CHAPTER FIVE
Themes and Impact

Over the early post-revolutionary years and beyond them the issues that were treated in Soviet political posters broadly paralleled the major developments in the country's political, economic and social life. A total of well over 3,600 posters of different kinds appeared between 1918 and 1921; the majority (57.5 per cent) were printed, and the remainder (42.5 per cent) were produced by hand.[1] As Table 1 makes clear, there were considerable variations in both quantity and subject matter over these years. As far as numbers are concerned, the output of posters rose sharply over the post-revolutionary years up to a peak in 1920, the year of the Russo-Polish war and the final stages of the struggle against domestic oppositionists. At the same time the proportion of posters that were hand-produced rather than printed, a reasonable indicator of the urgency of their appearance, rose from 1.2 per cent in 1918 and 8.5 per cent in 1919 up to a massive 55.5 per cent in 1920. The following year, however, the output of posters dropped sharply, and the proportion that were printed rose to 62.9 per cent. In subsequent years the output of posters continued to decline still further, and some categories of production (such as the Rosta Windows, in 1922) disappeared entirely.[2]

Table 1: Soviet Poster Production, 1918–21

Type of poster	1918	1919	1920	1921	Total
Political	42	86	532	175	835
(%)	(32.8)	(23.4)	(30.5)	(19.1)	(26.7)
Military	21	170	718	106	1015
(%)	(16.4)	(46.4)	(42.0)	(11.6)	(32.4)
Economic	43	58	313	458	872
(%)	(34.4)	(15.8)	(18.3)	(50.2)	(27.9)
Cultural	21	53	156	174	404
(%)	(16.4)	(14.4)	(9.2)	(19.1)	(13.0)
Total	127	367	1719	913	3126
(%)	100	100	100	100	100

Adapted from V. S. Butnik-Siversky, *Sovetskii plakat epokhi grazhdanskoi voiny 1918–21* (Moscow: Izd. Vsesoyuznoi knizhnoi palaty, 1960), p. 23.

In terms of subject matter the clearest trend that emerges from Table 1 is the sharp rise in the proportion of posters of a military character, up to a peak in 1920 when nearly half of all posters were war-related, followed by a gentle and then a precipitous decline in the more peaceful circumstances of 1921. The output of political posters broadly corresponds to this trend. In contrast, the output of posters on economic themes, a relatively small proportion of the total in 1919 and 1920, rose sharply in 1921 to account for more than half of all the posters produced in that year. The output of posters on cultural and educational themes, similarly, registered its highest level in the same year of the civil war period. The output of posters over the post-revolutionary years in fact corresponds fairly closely to the major developments in Soviet life over the same period. The regime first of all establishes itself (political and economic posters receive priority), is then challenged from within and without (military posters become predominant), and then, having secured its own position, turns to problems of peaceful social and economic development (economic and cultural themes move rapidly to the fore). The importance of posters, as a means of mass communication and persuasion, first rises and then falls over the same period.

Considered more closely, the changing subject matter of Soviet political posters over the post-revolutionary period represents, as Mayakovsky somewhat grandiloquently put it, a 'protocol record of a most difficult three year period of revolutionary struggle, conveyed by means of spots of paint and the echoing sound of slogans'.[3] The earliest Soviet posters were, as we have noted, produced largely under the auspices of VTSIK in Moscow, beginning with the publication of *The Tsar, the Priest and the Kulak* and *The Price of Blood* in August 1918 (see above, pp. 23–4). Although its poster output was relatively speaking not a large one, even in these early months VTSIK produced a new poster on average every five days.[4] Among the poster themes initiated at this time was the revolutionary-historical, exemplified in Apsit's posters of Pugachev, Stepan Razin and Ivan Bolotnikov (see above, p. 29). The first satirical posters were produced by Cheremnykh under the auspices of VTSIK at about the same time, their representations of the foreign capitalist, the interventionist soldier, the White Guard general, the deserter and the kulak being further developed in the poster work of subsequent years, particularly in the Rosta Windows. Cheremnykh's *How the English oppress the Peasants in their Dominions* (Plate 5.2), its text adapted from a brochure by Kerzhentsev with the same title, made its appearance at the end of 1918 and gave some indication of the way in which the stylistic conventions of a multi-frame poster could be adapted for use on a larger scale. The commemorative poster also originated in the latter part of 1918, particularly in connection with the first anniversary of the revolution (which was also the occasion for the first full-scale exercises in the decoration of public buildings and street theatre). Apsit's poster *A Year of the Proletarian Dictatorship* (Plate 2.12) and his *First of May* (Plate 2.18) were representative early examples of this genre.

5.2 M. M. Cheremnykh, *Kak anglichan'e pritesnyayut krest'yan v svoikh vladeniyakh* (How the English Oppress the Peasants in their Dominions), three coloured lithograph, 1918, 71 × 53 cm., BS 230.

Much of the poster work of 1918 and early 1919, as we have noted, was allegorical or symbolic in character. Apsit's *To the Deceived Brothers* (Plate 2.21), for instance, was a notable early example of this kind of work; so also was *The Master of the World is Capital, the Golden Idol* (Plate 5.6), which was based upon a satirical drawing, *Freedom*, by the Czech artist Frantisek Kupka.[5] Other types of poster which made their appearance in these early months were posters which were close to *lubki* or pictures in content, for instance *The Nightmare of the Deserter* (Plate 5.7), which appeared in early 1919, or *How the Tsars deceived the People* (Plate 5.3), produced in late 1918 by N. Krylov with an accompanying text by Demyan Bedny. This showed the misfortunes that attended a peasant who responded to the call to arms, fought bravely, and was then abandoned when he returned from the front as a cripple (the pile of skulls in the lower part of the picture was a reference to V. V. Vereshchagin's anti-militaristic *Apotheosis of War*, painted in 1871–2).[6] The poster *The Peoples of the Whole World welcome the Red Army of Labour* (Plate 5.5) was issued by VTSIK in the early summer of 1919 and was similarly

5.3 N. Krylov, *Kak tsari izdevalis' nad narodom* (How the Tsars deceived the People), coloured lithograph, 1918, 71 × 51 cm., BS 235.

5.4 Anon, *Narody vsego mira privetstvuyut Krasnuyu Armiyu truda* (The People of the whole World welcome the Red Army of Labour), coloured lithograph, 1919, 71 × 53 cm., BS 1431.

5.5 Anon, *Zdanie sotsializma* (The Building of Socialism), black and white lithograph, 1919, 71 × 104 cm., BS 207.

pictorial in style. Instructional and educational posters were also issued during these first post-revolutionary months, among them *The Building of Socialism* (Plate 5.5), produced by VTSIK at the beginning of 1919, which sought to depict the development of the labour and socialist movement from the middle ages up to the October revolution.

The latter part of 1919 saw these early poster themes largely superseded by subjects of a more military or revolutionary character, produced for the most part under the auspices of the Political Directorate of Revvoensovet and more particularly by its publishing agency Litizdat. Some of the earliest military-revolutionary posters were again the work of Apsit, for instance his *Forward, to the Defence of the Urals*, his *Stand up for the Defence of Petrograd* and his *Day of the wounded Red Armyman* (Plates 2.14, 15 and 16), all of which were produced for Litizdat. With the arrival of Moor and Deni in the summer of 1919, however, the work of Litizdat took on its classic form: simple, bold, appealing directly to the viewer, and more often seeking action (enrolment in the Red Army, contributions to the war effort, or the unmasking of saboteurs) than passive contemplation. Altogether 123 separate and consecutively numbered posters were issued by Litizdat between the middle of 1919 and the beginning of 1921; as some numbers were repeated two or three times, the real total is in fact at least 137.[7] Moor's first poster for Litizdat was *We shall not Surrender Petrograd* (Plate 3.7), which at once attracted attention by its original, fresh

ВЛАДЫКА МИРА-КАПИТАЛ, ЗОЛОТОЙ КУМИР.

Недавно еще он грозно восседал на троне, окруженный вооруженными наемниками, а безоружные рабы его шли для него работать... Но заря сознания осветила ум рабочего класса, он берет в руки оружие и Кумир будет низвергнут во всем мире.

5.6 Anon, *Vladyka mira – kapital, zolotoi kumir* (The Master of the World is Capital, the Golden Idol), three coloured lithograph, 1919, 54 × 35 cm., BS 54.

manner of execution. The year 1919 was nonetheless for Moor a year of experiment and development in his approach to the military-revolutionary poster, and he did not immediately find the bold and direct graphic language that was so characteristic of his work in 1920. Other Moor posters of the latter part of 1919, such as *Death to World Imperialism* and *Soviet Russia is an Armed Camp* (Plates 3.6 and 8), were for the most part of a narrative and symbolic rather than directly agitational character. His *People's Court* (Plate 5.8), for instance, issued in a very large edition in October 1919, was ostensibly devoted to the expulsion of the Tsar and his entourage from Russia by the force of worker-peasant power; the individual figures were drawn satirically, but the composition as a whole recalled traditional folk pictures of the 'mice bury the cat' type, and the atmosphere of festival and procession suggested a voluntary departure rather than a forcible expulsion.[8]

Deni was more fully formed as an artist when he came to work for Litizdat and his poster work during

this period shows less variation and evidence of experiment than that of Moor. His first posters for Litizdat included *Either Death to Capital, or else Death under the Heel of Capital* (Plate 5.10), issued in the late summer of 1919, as well as *The League of Nations, The Entente under the Mask of Peace, Capital, The Spider and the Flies* and others.[9] These and Deni's other military-revolutionary posters tended to share the same common features, above all a sharply satirical treatment of their subject, which was normally located prominently in the foreground. Other poster artists who worked for Litizdat during the latter part of 1919 included Nikolai Kochergin, Vladimir Fidman, Konstantin Spassky and Vassily Spassky.

The autumn of 1919 saw the most decisive military encounters of the whole of the civil war. Admiral Kolchak still held most of Siberia in the east; Denikin advanced to within 200 miles of Moscow in October; and Yudenich, who had been advancing on Petrograd since May 1919, reached the outskirts of the city later the same month. The poster work of Litizdat, as well as of the Rosta Windows which were coming into existence at about the same time, was devoted to these various challenges. Deni's "*Liberators*" and Apsit's

5.7 Anon, *Koshmar dezertira* (The Nightmare of the Deserter), coloured lithograph, 1919, 71 × 53 cm., BS 1234.

5.8 D. S. Moor, *Sud narodnyi* (People's Court), coloured lithograph, 1919, 36 × 51 cm., BS 620.

5.10 V. N. Deni, *Ili smert' kapitalu, ili smert' pod pyatoi kapitala* (Either Death to Capital, or Death under the Heel of Capital), three coloured lithograph, 1919, 72 × 106 cm., BS 219.

5.9 V. N. Deni, *Nezabyvaemaya krepost'* (Unshakeable Fortress), coloured lithograph, 1919, 44 × 27 cm., BS 1463.

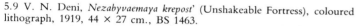

Retreating before the Red Army (Plate 3.24 and 2.17), for instance, showed the fate that would supposedly be meted out to those who fell under Denikin's control in the south. Deni's *Denikin's Band* (Plate 3.23) sought to represent the social nature of Denikin and his supporters; his *Unshakeable Fortress* (Plate 5.9) suggested that Denikin's campaign – represented as a boat labelled 'counter-revolution' – would never overcome the resistance of the Soviet republic. Nikolai Pomansky's *Only the Red Army will give us Bread* (Plate 5.12) sought more positively to suggest that the more successful the advance of the Red Army against Denikin the grain areas of the Ukraine, the better would be the food supply in Moscow and Petrograd.

The struggle against Kolchak on the eastern front was the theme of posters such as Apsit's *Forward to the Defence of the Urals* (Plate 2.14) and Deni's *The Rich Man and the Paunchy Priest* (Plate 5.11), which showed Kolchak advancing on a carriage pulled by a capitalist, a priest and a kulak under a banner reading 'The land and factories to the landlords and capitalists'. Yudenich's advance on Petrograd in the autumn of 1919 evoked, for

5.11 V. N. Deni, *Bogatei s popom bryukhatym i s pomeshchikom bogatym . . .* (The Rich Man and the Paunchy Priest), coloured lithograph, 1919, 73 × 91 cm., BS 882.

5.12 N. Pomansky, *Khleb nam dast tol'ko Krasnaya Armiya* (Only the Red Army will give us Bread), two coloured lithograph, 1919, 53 × 71 cm., BS 1846.

instance, Kochergin's *The Enemy is at the Gates* (Plate 3.32); such was the urgency of the situation that the poster was prepared within twenty-four hours and 'thrown out on the street with telegraph-like rapidity', as Polonsky later described it. Apsit's *The Enemy wants to Capture Tula*, Vladimir Fidman's *The Enemy wants to take Moscow, the Heart of Soviet Russia* and Dmitri Moor's *The Enemy is at the Gates* (Plates 3.5) appeared within the following few days.[10] For some time, in the latter part of 1919, the fate of the newly-established Soviet regime hung in the balance. In the end, however, the Red Army successfully counter-attacked: Kolchak was pressed back into Siberia and, in February 1920, captured and executed; Denikin was forced back into the Crimea; and by November Yudenich's forces had been forced to retreat from Petrograd. This brought to an end what has traditionally been known to Soviet historiography as the Entente's 'second offensive' (the first had been Kolchak's initially successful advance in Siberia in the earlier part of 1919).

The following year, 1920, saw the Entente's 'third offensive', and it was also the year in which the Soviet political poster reached the peak of its development. More posters were issued in 1920 than in any other post-revolutionary year; more of them were devoted to military-revolutionary subjects; and more of them were of the bold, simple and agitational character that has secured for many of them an enduring place in poster history as well as in the iconography of the Russian civil war. The military situation, again, was of compelling importance. In May 1920 Russo-Polish hostilities broke out when the Poles launched an offensive and captured Kiev. They were eventually beaten back and the Red Army itself went on to the offensive, pressing forward into what they thought would soon become a Soviet

Poland. In August 1920, in the 'miracle of the Vistula', the Poles defeated the Red Army in sight of Warsaw, with the whole of the post-war settlement hanging to the balance. In October 1920 an armistice was signed, and in March 1921 a formal peace treaty was concluded. Meanwhile Baron P. N. Wrangel, leading the remnants of Denikin's army, had advanced again in southern Russia, and the latter part of the year was occupied with the military struggle against this latest threat to the survival of Soviet rule. The Red Army again prevailed, and by November 1920 Wrangel had been defeated in the Crimea and forced to evacuate his remaining troops. Influenced particularly by the advance into Poland, 1920 saw some of the most remarkable posters devoted to the Communist International and world revolution; it also saw the first posters devoted to reconstruction on the domestic front, which rapidly became the chief priority once the civil war had ended.

Many of the posters of 1920 were devoted, in general rather than specific terms, to the Red Army itself and to the assistance it required from the civilian population.

5.13 P. Kiselis, *Belogvardeiskii khishchnik terzaet telo rabochikh i krest'yan* (The White Guard Beast of Prey is tearing the Body of Workers and Peasants to pieces), three coloured lithograph, 1920, 106 × 70 cm., BS 869.

Moor's outstanding *Have You Volunteered?* (Plate 3.12), for instance, was devoted to recruitment into the armed forces; his *Red Soldier at the Front* (Plate 3.16), produced by Litizdat in October 1920, urged greater support for the forces in the front line. Deni's *Every Blow of the Hammer is a Blow to the Enemy*, issued in July 1920, sought to associate industrial output and military success; so too did Moor's *Red Present to the White Pan* (Plate 5.15), which depicted a worker passing ammunition to the Red Army then engaged in the struggle against Poland. Moor's *Soviet Turnip* (Plate 3.8), issued in May 1920, dealt with the Red Army in more general terms; so too did the series of posters that was devoted to the theme of desertion. Moor's *Give me your Hand, Deserter* (Plate 5.17), for instance, went on: 'You are as much a destroyer of the worker-peasant state as I am, a capitalist; you are now my only hope'. A poster of about the same period although rather different in style, Petr Kiselis's *The White Guard Beast of Prey is tearing the Body of Workers and Peasants to Pieces* (Plate 5.13), called

for assistance to be given to the wounded. Nikolai Kogout's *Happy New Year* (Plate 5.16), produced rather later, dealt with the Red Army as the victor in successive years of civil war and intervention.

The posters devoted to the Polish campaign included some of Moor and Deni's best-known work. Deni, for instance, devoted his *Sow, dressed in Paris* (Plate 3.27) to the idea that Polish expansionism rested upon Allied support; his *Noble Poland – the last Dog of the Entente* depicted that country as a slavering mastiff whose advance into Russia in the spring of 1920 was intended to put an end to 'worker-peasant Russia'.[11] *Peasant! The Polish Landlord wants to make you a Slave* (Plate 3.28) was also issued in the late spring of 1920 when the Polish army was advancing rapidly into Soviet territory. S. Mukharsky's *How the Polish Enterprise will End* (Plate 5.14), issued in the summer of 1920 as the Red Army was advancing on Warsaw, showed the last reactionaries being finished off while workers and peasants held up a banner reading 'Long live Soviet Poland' to welcome

5.14 S. Mukharsky, *Chem konchitsya panskaya zateya* (How the Polish Enterprise will End), coloured lithograph, 1920, 71 × 89 cm., BS 1865.

5.15 D. S. Moor, *Krasnyi podarok belomu panu* (A Red Present to the White Pan), two coloured lithograph, 1920, 70 × 52 cm., BS 1295.

the Red cavalry. Some posters of this period were issued in Polish, for instance *Out of the Way* (Plate 5.17), which showed the Red cavalry advancing successfully into Poland and towards a new dawn of peace and prosperity.

Moor's posters on the Polish campaign placed less emphasis upon the Red Army's advance into Poland and rather more upon the need to keep them out of Soviet territory. His poster *The Departing Gentry* (Plate 5.18),

5.16 N. Kogout, *S novym godom* (Happy New Year), three coloured lithograph, 1921, 70 × 107 cm., BS 1668.

5.17 D. S. Moor, *Ruku, dezertir. Ty takoi zhe razrushitel' raboche-krest'yanskogo gosudarstva, kak ya kapitalist* (Give me your Hand, Deserter!), two coloured lithograph, 1920, 52 × 67 cm., BS 1666.

for instance, produced in July 1920 under the auspices of Litizdat, warned that the departing Polish forces were destroying cities and slaughtering the civilian population as they left (Kiev was specifically identified in the

5.18 D. S. Moor, *Ukhodyashchaya shlyakhta v bessil'noi zlobe dinamitom Antanty vzryvaet goroda, istreblyaet naselenie* (The Departing Gentry), two coloured lithograph, 1920, 106 × 71 cm., BS 1831.

„Z DROGI"

5.19 Anon, *Z drogi!* (Out of the way!), coloured lithograph, 1920, 71 × 98 cm., text in Polish.

illustration). One of his most dramatic posters, which for obvious reasons is rarely referred to in Soviet publications, appeared rather later in the year: entitled *Be on Guard* (Plate 5.1), it showed Trotsky, dressed as a Red Armyman, standing with his bayonet at the Russo-Polish frontier. The text warned that while the official Polish government might have signed an armistice there were still powerful forces with high-level backing in that country which might seek, with French support, to invade the territory of the USSR once again if a suitable opportunity presented itself.[12] Many Rosta Windows, particularly the single-frame posters produced in the earlier part of 1920, also drew attention to various aspects of the struggle with Poland (see for instance Plates 4.17–20).

Later in the year Wrangel, with indirect Allied support, began to advance in the south and to present a serious danger to vital energy resources such as the coal mines of the Donbass. A series of posters, issued in sometimes very large numbers, drew attention to the unexpected danger that now threatened from this quarter. *Wrangel is still Alive! Finish him off without Mercy* (Plate 5.23), one of Moor's best-known posters,

was issued in 50,000 copies in July 1920; it showed Wrangel, assisted by Kolchak, Denikin and Yudenich, stretching out his hand towards the Donetsk basin. Kochergin's colourful and dynamic *Wrangel is coming! To Arms, Proletarians!* (Plate 3.35) was issued slightly later in still larger numbers – 75,000 copies were printed.[13] Moor's *Devil Doll* (Plate 5.24), issued in October 1920, sought to suggest that Wrangel, despite appearances, was no more powerful than the timorous Entente who supported him. Deni's *At the Grave of the Counter-Revolution* (Plate 3.25) depicted a priest and a capitalist weeping bitterly beside a cemetery in which Wrangel as well as other White leaders had been interred. A poster by an anonymous artist, *Where Wrangel sends his Bread* (Plate 5.22), issued in October 1920, showed Wrangel shipping off sacks of grain to the Entente in return for arms and ammunition. Nikolai Kogout's *RSFSR: Workers of all Countries, Unite!* (Plate 5.25), with a text in Russian and Crimean Tatar, called for a joint effort to defeat Wrangel, the bourgeoisie and the Entente in the interests of liberty and peace. Rosta Windows on the campaign against Wrangel were meanwhile appearing on a very frequent, all but daily basis.[14]

5.20 Anon, *Kuda devaet khleb Vrangel'* (Where Wrangel sends his Bread), two coloured lithograph, 1920, 46 × 69 cm., BS 1338.

At least two other types of poster emerged with particular prominence during 1920: posters devoted to the Communist International, and posters commemorating anniversaries such as the third year of Soviet power. The Communist International or Comintern had been founded at a small and somewhat irregularly constituted congress in March 1919; in the summer of 1920, however, as Soviet forces were moving rapidly into Poland, it held a much larger and more representative second congress. Moor's *Long Live the Communist International* (Plate 5.26), with its text in several western languages, was issued in honour of the second congress; so too was Sergei Ivanov's *Long Live the Communist International* (Plate 5.27), with an accompanying text in English, Italian, French and German. More innovative in style were the posters produced by VKHUTEMAS (the Higher Artistic-Technical Studios) the following year: *Long Live the Communist International* (Plate 5.28), *We Destroy the Boundaries between Countries* (Plate 5.29), and more particularly *Red Moscow is the Heart of the World Revolution* (Plate 5.30), which appeared in June 1920.

A more allegorical poster on the same subject, *On the*

5.22 Anon, *Rabochie zavoevali vlast' v Rossii* (The Workers have Conquered Power in Russia), two coloured lithograph, 1920, 66 × 98 cm., BS 539.

Eve of the World Revolution (Plate 5.38), has been attributed to Dmitri Moor, although this seems unlikely on stylistic grounds.[15] Moor was however the author of several other posters on revolutionary anniversaries, among them *October 1917 – October 1920: Long Live the Worldwide Red October* (Plate 3.19). Other posters issued on the third anniversary of the revolution included *Labour will be the Master of the World!* (Plate 5.21), by an unknown artist, and *The Workers have Conquered Power in Russia* (Plate 5.22), also by an unknown artist. A more attractive representation of the same theme was Dmitri Melnikov's *Down with Capital, Long Live the Dictatorship of the Proletariat* (Plate 5.40), issued in just 5,000 copies in October 1920. May Day was also an occasion for commemorative posters (see for instance Plates 2.18, 3.20, 34 and 36). Moor's *1 May – An all-Russian Voluntary Workday* (Plate 5.39) appeared in April 1920. Lighter and more festive in character was Sergei Ivanov's *1st of May – Long Live the Festival of the Workers of all Countries* (Plate 5.42), which also appeared in April 1920.

The following year, 1921, brought further changes in the themes that were treated in Soviet posters. With the final defeat of the anti-Bolshevik forces and, in the spring, the conclusion of treaties with Britain, Poland, Turkey and several other border states, military matters lost their previous priority and military-related posters quickly dropped to a a very small proportion of total poster output (see Table 1). In contrast, the needs of economic development and social change became much greater, and approaching three-quarters of all posters issued in 1921 were devoted to such purposes. A poster issued in early 1921, *Red Armyman! Attack Disorder!* (Plate 5.31) pointed directly to the very different tasks that now had to be accomplished. On the military front,

5.21 Anon, *Vladykoi mira budet trud!* (Labour will be the Master of the World), two coloured lithograph, 1920, 106 × 71 cm., BS 2038.

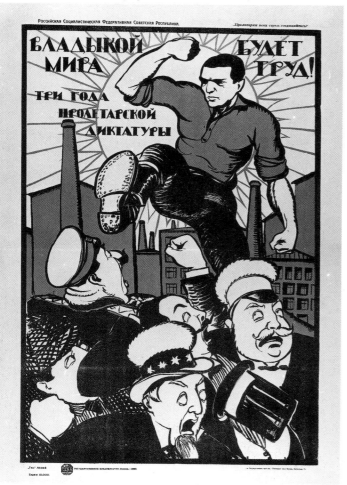

Facing page

5.23 (*above left*) D. S. Moor, *Vrangel' eshche zhiv. Dobei ego bez poshchadi* (Wrangel is still Alive! Finish him off without Mercy), two coloured lithograph, 1920, 69 × 50 cm., BS 960.

5.24 (*above right*) D. S. Moor, *Chortova Kukla* (Devil Doll), coloured lithograph, 1920, 70 × 44 cm., BS 1873.

5.25 (*below left*) N. Kogout, *Proletarii vsekh stran, soedinyaites'!* (Workers of all Countries, Unite!), three coloured lithograph, no date [1920?], 71 × 53 cm., text in Russian and Tatar.

5.26 (*below right*) D. S. Moor, *Da zdravstvuet III Internatsional!* (Long Live the 3rd International!), coloured lithograph, 1920, 107 × 69 cm., BS 138.

This page

5.27 (*above left*) S. Ivanov, *Da zdravstvuet III-i Kommunisticheskii Internatsional!* (Long Live the 3rd Communist International), coloured lithograph, 1920, 66 × 88 cm., BS 309.

5.28 (*above right*) vkhutemas, *Da zdravstvuet Kommunisticheskii Internatsional!* (Long Live the Communist International!), coloured lithograph, 1921, 71 × 53 cm., BS 110.

5.29 (*below left*) vkhutemas, *My razrushaem granitsy mezhdu stranami* (We Destroy the Boundaries between Countries), coloured lithograph, 1921, 54 × 71 cm., BS 340.

5.30 (*below right*) vkhutemas, *Krasnaya Moskva – serdtse proletarskoi mirovoi revolyutsii* (Red Moscow is the Heart of the World Revolution), coloured lithograph, 1920, 71 × 53 cm., BS 274.

5.31 Anon, *Krasnoarmeets. Na fronte voennom ty s shtykom v ruke pobezhdal vraga* ... (Red Armyman! Attack disorder!), coloured lithograph, 1921, 53 × 64 cm., BS 1262.

it began, the enemy had been defeated with the bayonet. Now the labour front was the one that faced them, and their weapons were the plough and the hammer. Another poster, *Four Years* (Plate 5.41), produced in Tsaritsyn (now Volgograd) in just 1,000 copies, made the same point in a different way. Moor's *The Bloody Path of Struggle is Over* (Plate 5.32) promised that 1921 would be a peaceful year but warned that there was still a need for vigilance in the face of hypocritical professions of peace from the Western powers. The major national priorities in these new circumstances included not only the recovery of industry and agriculture, to which Moor's poster had drawn attention, but also a series of more general tasks in the areas of education, female emancipation and public health.

Strenuous efforts were made, for instance, to encourage literacy and reading. Knowledge, declared a poster by Aleksei Radakov, one of the most prominent artists of posters of this kind, would 'tear apart the chains of

5.33 A. A. Radakov, *Znanie razorvet tsepi rabstva* (Knowledge will Tear apart the Chains of Slavery), coloured lithograph, 1920, 89 × 61 cm., BS 3295.

slavery' (Plate 5.33). Another well-known poster by the same artist warned that the illiterate was like a blind man who would always encounter unpleasant surprises (Plate 5.40). Radakov's *Children!* (Plate 5.34) warned that those who neglected their education would live the fearful and ignorant life of the illiterate. A poster by

5.32 D. S. Moor, *Konchen bitvy put' krovavyi* ... (The Bloody Path of Struggle is Over), three coloured lithograph, 1921, 35 × 105, BS 2201.

5.34 A. A. Radakov, *Deti! Strashno zhit' negramotnomu, zhivet on, kak v temnom lesu* (Children!), coloured lithograph, 1920, 51 × 58 cm., BS 3273.

5.36 S. I. Ivanov, *Chtenie – odna iz obyazannostei cheloveka* (Reading is one of a Person's Duties), two coloured lithograph, 1920, 48 × 65 cm., BS 3408.

Sergei Ivanov announced that a book was 'nothing but a person talking publicly' (knowledge, in this instance, appeared to come from the heavens) (Plate 5.35). Another, *Day of Soviet Propaganda: Knowledge – to All* (Plate 5.47), issued in 1919, showed scientific and cultural works as well as Marx's *Capital* being distributed freely to the population. A poster on the same subject in a more allegorical style (Plate 5.49) announced that literacy was the 'path to communism'; it appeared in a print run of 75,000 copies, with further editions in Hebrew, Polish and Tatar.[16] Other posters (Plates 5.36 and 37) declared that knowledge was one of the basic necessities

5.35 S.I. Ivanov, *Kniga nichto inoe kak chelovek, govoryashchii publicho* (A Book is Nothing but a Person talking Publicly), two coloured lithograph, 1920, 64 × 47 cm., BS 3317.

5.37 A. Zelinsky, *Chtoby bol'she imet' – nado bol'she proizvodit'* (In order to have More, you must produce More), coloured lithograph, 1920, 65 × 47 cm., BS 3412.

5.38 Anon,
*Nakanune mirovoi
revolyutsii* (On
the Eve of the
World
Revolution),
coloured
lithograph, 1920,
72 × 100 cm.

5.39 D. S.
Moor, *I-oe Maya
vserossiiskii
subbotnik* (I
May – an all-
Russian
Voluntary
Workday),
coloured
lithograph, 1920,
71 × 53 cm., BS
437.

5.40 (*below*)
D. I. Mel'nikov,
*Doloi kapital, da
zdravstvuet
diktatura
proletariata!*
(Down with
Capital, Long
Live the
Dictatorship of
the Proletariat!),
three coloured
lithograph, 1920,
102 × 68 cm., BS
181

5.41 (*below*)
Anon, *Cherye
goda* (Four
Years), coloured
lithograph, 1921,
72 × 44, BS 730

5.42 S. I. Ivanov, *1-e maya. Da zdravstvuet prazdnik trudyashchikhsya vsekh stran!* (1st of May. Long Live the Festival of the Workers of all Countries), coloured lithograph, 1920, 106 × 65 cm., BS 427.

5.51 A. A. Radakov, *Zhizn' bezgramotnogo … Zhizn' gramotnogo …* (The Life of the Illiterate; the Life of the Literate), coloured lithograph, 1920, 51 × 69 cm., BS 3288.

able food supply. Most painters, Kandinsky told a French interviewer in 1921, worked to make a living, and it was for this reason that they engaged in poster work, for which the pay was often extremely good.[105] Edward Bagritsky, who had been involved in the preparation of paintings as well as texts in Odessa, recalled in his autobiography that his daily work at this time consisted of writing poems for posters and jingles for wall and oral newspapers, but this was 'only a duty, only a means of making a living'.[106] Those who directed poster work during the civil war years in turn appear to have felt an obligation to extend an offer of work to their colleagues so as to afford them at least a minimal existence: Kochergin, for instance, found that artists in Kiev were hungry when he went there in the spring of 1919 and managed to obtain permission for about 200 of them to decorate a Red Army barracks, in return for which all were given army rations. By no means all of them had 'declared for Soviet power'.[107] Viktor Shklovsky, similarly, was invited to work in Rosta by Mayakovsky as he was in a difficult material situation at the time.[108] Even Mayakovsky himself, as his correspondence with Lili Brik suggests, was not unaware of the material advantages in terms of food and accommodation that they were able to obtain by working for a state institution such as Rosta.[109] Given the involvement of such a heterogeneous groups of artists, nearly all of whom had acquired their skills under a very different regime, it is perhaps surprising that 'mistakes' in their work were not more frequent.

ИЗ РОССИИ
НЭПОВСКОЙ
БУДЕТ РОССИЯ
СОЦИАЛИСТИЧЕСКАЯ
(ЛЕНИН)

6.1 G. G. Klutsis, *K leninskim dnaym* (Towards the Leninist Days), photomontage, 1930, 120 × 82 cm.

CHAPTER SIX
The Bolshevik Political Poster and After

Contemporaries were well aware that the civil war years had marked the highest point in the creative development of the Soviet poster. 'Many of our agitational posters', wrote a contributor to *Vestnik agitatsii i propagandy* in early 1921, agreeing with Sosnovsky's strictures quoted in the previous chapter, 'are bad, unsuccessful [and] do not achieve their intended purpose'. The problem was not simply their poor or inappropriate content, bad draftsmanship or clumsy text; it was also a matter of their overall appearance. Comparing current Soviet posters with those that were produced in bourgeois Europe or with those that had appeared in Tsarist Russia or in connection with the 'Freedom Loan' or the Constituent Assembly elections, it was obvious they had not just lagged behind but had gone 'significantly backwards'. Too many posters were either colourless or too highly coloured, and some drawings were unduly complicated and took some time to work out even after careful studying. All this, he declared, was a serious waste of valuable paper and human effort. In future, the

6.2 A. I. Strakhov, *V. I. Ul'yanov (Lenin). 1870–1924*, coloured lithograph, 1924, 108 × 68 cm.

contributor suggested, the content of the poster should be entirely comprehensible without reference to the text; the subject of the drawing should be concrete and unambiguous; the drawing itself should be simple and prominent; and the text should be short, convincing and easily memorisable. This in turn required that the production of posters should be centralised, and that the best artists should be selected for this work and provided with the necessary materials.[1] Mayakovsky, also in 1921, expressed his dissatisfaction with the economic posters that were being produced: they were far too general, and were having not the slightest effect upon those for whom they were intended.[2] Mayakovsky's own proposal was for the establishment of a 'scientific bureau for research into the effectiveness of different forms of agitation'.[3]

Other writers agreed, In fact since about 1922, wrote a commentator in *Krasnaya niva* a few years later, 'there had been a sharp decline in the political poster – both qualitatively and quantitatively'. The 'daily life' poster had begun to develop, on health, hygiene, anti–religious and other themes, but it was 'significantly weaker than its heroic predecessor'.[4] The art critic Yakov Tukhendkhold, writing in 1926, felt there was scarcely any doubt that the Soviet poster was 'presently experiencing a deep crisis'. The streets were still decorated with posters and proclamations as before, but this could not obscure the 'undoubted fact' that Soviet public art of this kind was 'in transition, at a cross–roads'. A closer analysis would show a sharp decline in political and cultural themes, and a rise in simple advertising. If five years before there had not been a single publishing house that did not issue hundreds of posters, publishers like Glavpolitprosvet and Gosizdat now only produced twenty or so and Litizdat had completely stopped, while economic, cinema and other forms of poster publishing had greatly increased. Having gone through a heroic period during the civil war, pointing the way forward for the revolution, the poster had 'almost degenerated into a form of advertising'. It was perhaps symptomatic of this situation that when a commission had been formed by VTSIK in 1925 to hold a competition for the best poster to celebrate the 1905 revolution, not a single entry had been found worthy of the first prize.[5]

The decline of the political poster after the civil war years was remarked upon by the poster artists themselves as well as by art historians of the period. Dmitri Moor, writing in the early 1930s, conceded that in the reconstruction period of the 1920s poster life had 'quietened down a bit', although it had not, as some had suggested, expired completely.[6] Adolf Strakhov, also writing in the 1930s, explained his own abandonment of the political poster by his belief that it had now been superseded by monumental art.[7] Viktor Koretsky, who became prominent in poster art in later years, recalled that during the latter part of the 1920s a 'definite decline' had taken place in the development of the political poster; too many organisations were publishing them, too many of the artists concerned lacked creative talent or originality, and too much of the work that was done was hack–work or pure sensation–seeking.[8] Tukhendkhold, in a book published in 1926, remembered wistfully the 'poster fever' of earlier years – the

years when, despite the difficult situation of the civil war and in particular the exceedingly difficult printing situation, posters poured out literally as from the horn of plenty, when there was no region, town, station, railway carriage, Red Army or workers' club that was not decorated with these brilliant sheets of paper, proclaiming the appeals of the revolution.

6.3 A. I. Strakhov, *8 marta – den' raskreposhcheniya zhenshchin* (8th of March – Day of the Liberation of Women), coloured lithograph, 1926, 108 × 68 cm.

These had been years of an 'unprecedented flourishing of the poster', unprecedented in Russia or even in the capitalist West. With the coming of an era of peaceful reconstruction, however, the wave of poster production fell, and the Soviet political poster entered a 'new and still critical phase of its development'.[9] Other writers remarked upon the 'dangerous' repetition of the foreign, bourgeois commercial poster, or drew attention to the 'alien figures of foreign trade' that had appeared in Soviet posters;[10] *Krasnaya niva* went so far as to declare in 1923 that Soviet poster work had 'ended a year ago'.[11]

It would, however, be an exaggeration to suggest that the Soviet poster went into a slow and unrelieved decline after the heroic civil war years. Adolf Strakhov's *Lenin* (Plate 6.2), originally a cover for the Russian edition of John Reed's *Ten Days that Shook the World*, won a gold medal in a Paris world exhibition in 1925 and is still a powerful and expressive image.[12] Strakhov's *Eighth of March* (Plate 6.3), produced in connection with International Women's Day, appeared two years later. Cheremnykh, Deni, Moor and other artists continued to produce posters on a more occasional basis of which some retain their interest today (see for instance Plate 6.4). Commercial, educational, theatre and posters developed vigorously, with Alexander Rodchenko, the Stenberg brothers and other artists involved in their production; work of this kind owed much to constructivism and yet suffered no loss of intelligibility. During the early 1930s in particular there were innovative developments associated with the photomontage posters of Gustav Klutsis (1895–1944), whose work in many ways parallelled that of the German John Heartfield, itself exhibited in the USSR in the early 1930s. Klutsis insisted that the photomontage had in effect superseded all other forms of representational art, a position which gave rise to lively academic exchanges and which had a considerable influence upon younger artists.[13] Klutsis's own work varied in quality but at its best was capable of a striking juxtaposition of images, particularly apparent in his posters dealing with the first Five Year Plan (see for instance Plate 6.1). El Lissitsky and Rodchenko also did outstanding work in this idiom.[14]

A further and more remarkable revival occurred during the Second World War, or the Great Fatherland War as it is known in the USSR. Many of the poster artists of the civil was year were still alive and active, and after Hitler's invasion in June 1941 they and their younger colleagues soon resumed or increased their efforts. Within a week of the invasion five posters had been produced and more than fifty were in preparation.[15] Over the course of the war the Iskusstvo publishing house in Moscow alone produced 800 posters in a total of 34 million copies; about 700 were produced in Leningrad.[16] In some cases the motifs of the civil war years were simply repeated, for instance in Moor's *How have You Helped the Front* (Plate 6.5), which was clearly based upon his 'Have you volunteered' poster of 1920, or Deni's posters of 1943 and 1945 showing Red Armymen sweeping Nazis off the surface of the world much as Lenin had been depicted in 1920 sweeping away priests, bankers and monarchs.[17] Mikhail Cheremnykh was personally responsible for the very first of the 'Tass Windows', a form of visual commentary upon the war effort which took its origins directly from the Rosta

6.4 D. S. Moor, *Chernye vorony gotovyat razboinichii nabeg na SSSR. Proletarii – bud' na cheku!* (Black ravens are preparing a robber's raid on the USSR. Proletarians – be on guard!), coloured lithograph, 1930, 104 × 63 cm.

ТЫ

ЧЕМ ПОМОГ ФРОНТУ?

6.5 D. S, Moor, *Ty chem pomog frontu?* (How have you Helped the Front?), coloured lithograph, 1941, 102 × 69 cm.

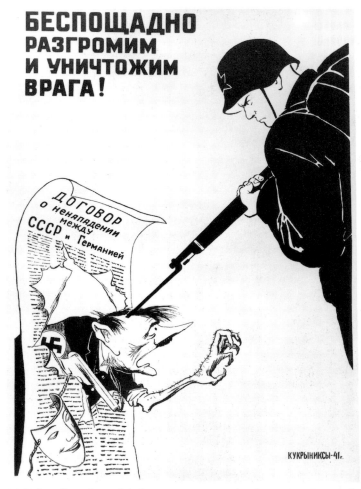

БЕСПОЩАДНО
РАЗГРОМИМ
И УНИЧТОЖИМ
ВРАГА!

6.6 Kukryniksy, *Bezposhchadno razgromim i unichtozhim vraga!* (We shall mercilessly Defeat and Destroy the Enemy), coloured lithograph, 1941, 87 × 60 cm.

poster *We shall Mercilessly Defeat and Destroy the Enemy* (Plate 6.6) was among the first to appear within a few days of Hitler's invasion in 1941.[20] Other younger poster artists who became prominent during the Second World War included Irakly Toidze (born in 1902), Viktor Ivanov (born in 1909) and Viktor Koretsky (born in the same year). Some of their work, for instance Toidze's *The Motherland Calls* of 1941 (Plate 6.7), has earned an enduring place in the iconography of the war and can be placed on the same level as the best work of the civil war period.

The Second World War, as we have already noted, also saw the revival of Rosta Windows, this time as 'Tass Windows', named after the news agency which had been established in 1925 and which had taken over most of Rosta's functions. The decision to launch a series of Tass Windows was taken at a meeting organised by the Union of Artists within two days of Hitler's invasion, and an organising committee was elected to undertake their production. The first Tass Windows appeared just three days later, on 27 July 1941, on Kuznetsky Bridge in central Moscow. Over seventy

6.7 I. M. Toidze, *Rodina-mat' zovet!* (The motherland-mother calls), coloured lithograph, 1941, 102 × 69 cm.

РОДИНА-МАТЬ
ЗОВЕТ!

Windows of the civil war years with which he had been closely associated. Vladimir Lebedev, another established artist, personally contributed about forty Tass Windows.[18]

On the whole, however, the leading poster artists of the Second World War were those who had come to professional maturity in the years after the revolution. One of the most notable of their number was the collective known as the Kukryniksy, a group of three artists who worked together (as well as separately) from the late 1920s and who became particularly prominent during the war. The three were Mikhail Kupriyanov (born in the Volga area in 1903), Porfiry Krylov (born in Tula in 1902) and Nikolai Sokolov (born in Moscow in 1903).[19] The Kukryniksy had all studied together in VKHUTEMAS in the 1920s and began to collaborate in student publications at this time, first of all as the 'Kukryniks' and then from 1927 as the Kukryniksy. Their first joint work appeared in December 1925, and from 1933 their cartoons began to appear regularly in *Pravda*. They were also the joint authors of book illustrations, and of conventional easel paintings. Their

artists were involved at some time in the production of Tass Windows, including older artists like Cheremnykh, Lebedev and Radakov as well as younger ones. Comparable arrangements were made in other Soviet towns and cities, just as had been the case with Rosta Windows. Tass Windows were stencilled, as their predecessors had been, and were then reproduced in up to 1,000 copies in three or more colours. The Windows were based, as the Rosta Windows had been, on the files of telegrams which reached Tass offices twice daily; suitable themes were selected for poster illustration, and the corresponding Windows were completed within a day or less and then displayed in public places. To begin with there were fifteen or twenty new Tass Windows monthly; later there were up to twenty-four.[21] An analogous series of posters was issued in Leningrad under the title of *Militant Pencil*.[22]

Nonetheless, and in spite of an occasional outstanding poster from later years (for instance Viktor Ivanov's contribution to the Lenin anniversary in 1970 [Plate 6.8] or a related work of 1965 [Plate 6.9]), it would be difficult to argue that Soviet poster art of any subsequent period has come close to matching the vigour, forcefulness and imagination of the best work of the civil war years. Difficult and possibly presumptuous though is may be to try to explain the sources of artistic endeavour, there would seem to be at least four major causes of the decline of the Soviet poster from the heights of 1918, 1919 and 1920. The first of these is organisational change, in particular the transition from the flexible, responsive and largely self-managing arrangements of the civil war years to the centralised and much more prescriptive system that developed in the years that followed. During the civil war years, Polonsky wrote in 1922, both posters and *lubok* pictures were composed from occasion to occasion, as the need arose. There was no systematically worked-out plan, nor indeed could there be; the work, on the contrary, was dictated by the changing needs of the current moment. In this sense one could say that 'life itself spoke in the language of colours and lithographic machines'. Every morning, and often every hour brought forward new tasks; posters, in response to this, reflected the most difficult stages, the concerns and demands, of each successive stage of the civil war.[23]

Delays, as we have seen, could be fatal, and posters had had sometimes to be prepared at very short notice indeed. During Yudenich's advance on Petrograd in October 1919, for instance, Kochergin's *Enemy at the Gates* (Plate 3.32) was prepared within twenty-four hours; so too was Apsit's *Stand up for the Defence of Petrograd* (Plate 2.15). Moor's *Volunteer* poster was another that we know to have been prepared overnight

6.8 V. S. Ivanov, *Lenin – zhil, Lenin – zhiv, Lenin – budet zhit'*, (Lenin lived. Lenin is living, Lenin will live!), (V. Mayakovsky), coloured lithograph. 1970, 118 × 79 cm.

to meet the needs of a particular energency.[24] The need for speed dictated even the colours that were used. Every extra colour meant an extra period of time on the lithographic machine. Sometimes posters had to be produced in one colour only, such was the urgency of the situation; whenever possible two colours were employed; but only exceptionally, when a week or two was available, was it possible to consider using three or more colours. In the provinces, which, as Polonsky noted, received no directives or general plan from the centre, matters developed quite independently.[25] In Odessa, for example, themes for posters were generally provided by the agitprop section of the local party committee, but the conception of the poster itself could belong either to the artist or to the writer who prepared the accompanying text.[26]

Arrangements within Rosta were similar to this not simply in their urgency but also in their informality. The themes treated in the Rosta Windows, Cheremnykh recalled, were very varied, and drew upon many different sources – the telegrams that arrived at Rosta offices, party and government decrees, important anni-

6.9 V. S. Ivanov, *Lenin – vozhd'* (Lenin – leader!), coloured lithograph, 1965, 67 × 97 cm.

versaries and so forth. There were no 'directives' of any kind, however; 'we were so caught up in the work that we understood ourselves what had to be done'.[27] The writer and translator Rita Rait, in her memoirs, explained how the selection of themes had in fact taken place. Mayakovsky himself prepared almost all of the texts, though some were given occasionally to others to compose (Rait was herself given what Mayakovsky called 'women's themes', such as sanitation and hygiene, children, illiteracy and so forth). Apart from commissions of this kind, all the staff had to scan the newspapers looking for items that might form suitable themes for new Windows. On Fridays all such suggestions were handed to Mayakovsky. If he smiled and read the text aloud it was accepted; less successful proposals he merely glanced through, silently tore in two and threw under the table. To begin with Rait achieved no more than two or three successes out of every ten suggestions she put forward; after a while, however, she developed a better instinct for what was required and was successful with five or six.[28] In Gosizdat, similarly, 'themes for broadsheets and posters

were not planned, as they were supposed to react in a lively way to the developments of the day, changing their content according to the situation and current party requirements'. Gosizdat's own lack of staff, the printing situation and difficulties of communication indeed left no alternative.[29]

With the ending of the civil war these somewhat improvised arrangements came to an end, as they did in most other areas of Soviet life. In the Moscow Rosta offices the changes began with the departure of Kerzhentsev to diplomatic work early in 1921. His successor Nikolai Smirnov, formerly editor of the railwaymen's newspaper *Gudok* (Siren), was a man of narrower sympathies who was generally much stricter and more formal than Kerzhentsev had been. One of his first decisions was to end the production of Rosta Windows; they did in the end continue, but under the auspices of Glavpolitprosvet (a part of the People's Commissariat of Enlightenment) rather than those of Rosta. Many staff left at the same time, to Narkompros or elsewhere. Posters, however, were peripheral to the activities of Narkompros, and continued there for no more than a further year or so. Mayakovsky himself had much less to do with the Windows that were issued by Glavpolit-prosvet and indeed, according to at least one memoir source, was not regarded within Narkompros with much sympathy or understanding.[30] Glavpolitprosvet itself found its political educational efforts gradually curtailed, and in 1930 it was would up as an organisation. Its separate Art Section had ceased to exist in 1922.[31]

Poster production did continue under other auspices, but here too there were organisational changes and, often, difficulties. In the area of military publishing, which had been primarily responsible for the political poster of the civil war years, Litizdat was abolished in 1921 and replaced by a Department for Military Litera-ture under the Revolutionary Military Council, whose purpose was to centralise and plan all publishing of this kind throughout the country. No military publication, indeed, was supposed to see the light of day without the explicit authorisation of the Department.[32] Military publishing, however, found itself affected by the general harshness of the RSFSR budget in the 1920s, and local military publishing in particular was obliged to seek additional funding from local sources. The Department of Military Literature itself was compelled in the sum-mer of 1922 to make significant reductions in the scale of its activities; staff were reduced in number and some periodicals had to be closed down. Posters and other publications approved by the Department were formally issued in the name of Gosizdat, and at this point further difficulties arose.[33] In short, a combination of centrali-sation and financial stringency, together with some in-sensitive personnel appointments, had brought about a situation by the later 1920s in which the political poster could no longer react, promptly and with adequate resources, to the issues of the day as they presented themselves.

A second reason for the decline of the civil war poster, as these publishing difficulties may already have suggested, was the complex of social and economic changes associated with the transition from wartime conditions to those of peaceful reconstruction. The flowering of the civil war poster had in fact occurred under a very specific set of circumstances. Levels of literacy were low, so there was a premium upon the graphic representation of political issues. Supplies of newsprint were very limited, so there was little com-petition from newspapers and journals, and in any case it was felt that scarce resources of this kind should be devoted to forms of production that would receive the widest possible public exposure. Newspapers them-selves often bore a heading during these years urging those who read them to pass them on when they had finished, and consisted of no more than a single sheet of poorly printed paper. A political poster, placed in a shop window, on a wall or in a railway station, could service a much larger number of people page for page, and it could often respond more quickly to current develop-ments since it often had no need to rely upon a backward and debilitated printing industry. As we have noted, Rosta Windows could appear within forty minu-tes or an hour of the receipt of an important telegram from the front; so rapidly could the Windows be produced that they became almost the 'monopolists' of several campaigns, responding much more quickly to changing circumstances than printed publications were able to do.[34] The urgency and immediacy of posters at this time was indeed one of the secrets of their very broad appeal.

The economic circumstances of the time contributed to the success of political posters in other ways as well. The shops, for instance, were mostly closed or empty during the civil war period, and there was little competition for the use of window space or the attention of the passing public. H. G. Wells, on his visit to Pet-rograd in September 1920, found that there were at most half a dozen shops still open, a government crock-ery shop and, much to his delight, some flower shops where for 'five thousand roubles . . . one can get a very pleasing bunch of big chrysanthemums'.[35] Other im-pressions were similar: Colonel Malone, for instance, found the shops on Nevsky Prospekt 'for the most part bare' in September 1919, and H. N. Brailsford, a year later, reported that Petrograd looked 'like a dead city', with grass and even wild flowers growing in its streets, and with its shops and avenues empty.[36] The German economist Alfons Goldschmidt, who was in Moscow at about the same time, found its shops mostly closed or even boarded up.[37] The transport system was still in a poor state so that the central press, when it appeared, had difficulty in circulating, and there was a premium on local informational arrangements of all kinds. These were circumstances in which political posters, quickly prepared and often representing the only available source of news of its kind, could be assured of the warmest public welcome.

With the transition from the civil war to peaceful reconstruction from about the end of 1920, formalised at the highest level with the adoption of the New Economic Policy by the 10th Party Congress in March 1921, a very different set of circumstances began to prevail. Levels of literacy, for instance, began to rise (the Red Army itself played a considerable part in this achievement through the literacy classes that were conducted under its auspices; an estimated two million soldiers were instructed in this way during the civil war).[38] The New Economic Policy, which involved a partial retreat into capitalist conditions including the reintroduction of small-scale private trading, also had serious implications for state-sponsored activities such as poster production. Attempts were made to introduce firm budgetary discipline and a stable currency, and state bodies of all kinds found it necessary to reduce their staffing levels and range of activities in order to balance their accounts. Posters, newspapers and other forms of propaganda had previously been issued, as a rule, free of charge or at a nominal rate;[39] now they had to be paid for and to justify their existence in cost-accounting terms. This signalled the end for the Petrograd Rosta Windows, as Lev Brodaty recalled: they had previously been given out free, but this could not continue when Rosta went on to a self-financing basis under NEP.[40]

The revival in economic activity and particularly in private trading had other implications for poster work. In the first place, shops began to have something to sell again and were less willing to allow their windows to be used to display propaganda posters. Mayakovsky, writing some years later, well remembered the dying out of this work. The bill poster, a fattish man called Mikhailov, had approached him and announced: 'Eliseev's [a famous grocery store on Tverskaya, now Gorky street] won't let me hang them up – the shop's opening up there now.' Soon Moscow was covered with posters of women's hats and cinema performances, prepared by former Rosta stencillers.[41] The political poster had to compete, not just for window space, but for public attention with these other kinds of posters, and it was generally the loser. The printing houses revived, the fronts were liquidated, Mayakovsky wrote elsewhere, and now all that was left of their work was the stencilled cinema posters that were being produced in great quantities.[42] Cinema posters in particular had appeared like 'mushrooms after the rain', wrote the critic Tukhendkhold in 1926; they had 'almost squeezed out all other kinds of poster, almost monopolised lithographic resources, [and] seized almost exclusive control of the streets'.[43]

A further consequence was that newsprint became more freely available, allowing established newspapers and journals to increase their circulation and new ones to come into existence. The major newspapers themselves began to publish cartoons, *Pravda*, for instance, from about 1921 onwards, which were then often republished in the local press. 'The cartoon'. Boris Efimov recalled, 'became a desirable and even a necessary component of the newspaper page', and the demand for cartoonists increased considerably.[44] Of particular importance in this connection was the establishment of a large number of satirical journals in the early 1920s to

which, almost without exception, the civil war artists transferred their various talents. In Petrograd satirical journals had begun to appear as early as 1918 and 1919 (*Krasnyi dyavol* and *Gilotina* (Guillotine)); now they were joined by *Begemot* (Hippopotamus), from 1922, *Kipyatok* (Boiling Water), from 1927, and many others. In Moscow Mayakovsky brought out *Bov* in a single issue in 1921; *Krasnyi perets* began to appear in 1922, *Bich* in 1924, and *Lapot* (Bast Sandal) in the same year. Much the most important of these new periodicals was *Krokodil*, founded in 1922 and still in vigorous existence, which drew directly upon the poster artists (the core of Rosta, as *Krokodil*'s historian has written, became the 'soul of *Krokodil*').[45] For the poster artists themselves not the least of the attractions of the new journals was that, with their bouyant, paid subscriptions, they could offer far greater monetary incentives than the remaining poster publishers were able to do. Some poster artists, as Tukhendkhold noted, simply became too 'expensive' for their previous employers.[46]

A third factor involved in the decline of the civil war poster was the political pressures that were increasingly brought to bear upon it and upon those who worked for it. Very few of the early poster artists, as we have noted, were members of the Communist Party at least during the civil war period; most were of non-proletarian or even privileged background; and in the case of the futurists their association with the new regime was almost an accidental one, as it alone seemed to offer the opportunity to escape the dominance of the established artists of the Academy of Arts which had previously declined to favour them.[47] The new futurist artists quickly became dominant within the Visual Arts Department of Narkompros, and although the Department was closed in 1921, avant-garde artists continued to wield considerable influence in other locations such as, in particular, INKHUK (the Institute of Artistic Culture) and VKHUTEMAS (the Higher State Artistic-Technical Studios). The Commissar for Enlightenment, Anatoly Lunacharsky, took exception to the futurists' attacks upon the art of earlier periods, but he seems to have been an important influence within the leadership as a whole in preventing or at least moderating direct attacks upon avant-garde art and literature in the early post-revolutionary years.[48] With Lunacharsky's retirement as Commissar in 1929 and his early death in 1930 artistic innovation had lost one of its most important patrons.

Despite the influence of figures such as Lunacharsky, the first two post-revolutionary decades saw the gradual establishment of firm and increasingly detailed regime control over all aspects of artistic endeavour. Literature and publishing had, for the most part, been brought under central control by the middle of the 1920s. Poster production came under central party scrutiny at about the same time and in 1931 a Central Committee resolution, 'On poster literature', enunciated the policies that would henceforward have to be followed. The resolution criticised the 'disgraceful' attitude to poster production of a number of publishing houses, which had allowed themselves to publish a 'significant percentage of anti-Soviet posters and pictures' (presumably those in which Western commercial influences had been greatest). Control by Glavlit, the censorship body, over such activities has been 'completely unsatisfactory'. Those responsible for anti-Soviet poster work would be brought to justice; all poster work would be centralised in Izogiz (the artistic department of Gosizdat), which would itself be purged of unacceptable elements; and overall supervision of poster work was given to the Department of Agitation and Mass Campaigns of the Central Committee apparatus, which was instructed to bring forward further recommendations for improvement. A special society of poster artists was meanwhile to be organised to raise the 'ideological and artistic level' of such work.[49] A body of this kind, the Union of Workers of the Revolutionary Poster, was formed later the same year; it pledged itself to base 'all its socio-political and artistic work' on the Central Committee resolution, whose fulfilment would be its 'basic task'.[50] The following year a more general resolution, 'On the reconstruction of literary and artistic organisations', set down directives for all other areas of the creative arts.[51]

The tasks that stood before Soviet poster artists were reviewed in more detail at a special meeting held under the auspices of the Communist Academy in 1932. The Central Commitee resolution, it was declared, meant a

> cultural rearming of fellow-travelling and allied cadres, the strengthening of the further struggle for a dialectical-materialist creative method, the consolidation of communist and proletarian forces on the representational front, merciless struggle with the class enemy in the field of culture, the creation of Magnitostrois of art, art worthy of the demands of the period of transition into socialism.

With the defeat of the left and right oppositions, it was argued, the field of art was being used for the 'contraband infiltration' of anti-Soviet ideology. In the light of Stalin's letter to the editor of the journal *Proletarskaya revolyutsiya* (Proletarian Revolution), in which the party leader had emphasised Lenin's 'ruthless struggle with opportunism of every kind', the struggle with such 'falsifiers' and 'contrabandists' acquired particular significance. The discussion that followed saw sharp attacks upon the 'bourgeois tendencies' which had appeared in recent Soviet posters and the 'theatricalisation' of Lenin; 'painterly', 'passive' and 'formal' approaches were also condemned, together with 'mysticism and symbolism'. Deni was among those whose work was criticised for being insufficiently agitational, and even Moor was found wanting in his failure to develop heroic figures appropriate to the tasks of the current period. Poster artists should not, indeed could not be allowed to be passive onlookers at the sites of socialist construction; they and their organisations must rather play a constructive part, helping to establish 'Magnitostrois of art' to parallel advances in other fields.[52]

These harsh, unambiguous and more highly politicised demands could not fail to affect all Soviet poster artists to some degree. Those whose work was most obviously experimental or who had lived or studied most extensively abroad were likely, under Stalinist conditions, to suffer the most harshly. Gustav Klutsis, a non-Russian and a conspicuous innovator, was arrested in 1938 and died in a prison camp six years later.[53] Alexander Deineka, a pupil of Moor's whose work included book illustrations, sculpture and easel painting as well as posters, was denounced in the 1940s by Andrei Zhdanov.[54] Malevich, admittedly a figure largely peripheral to the political poster, was arrested in 1930 on his return from Berlin and came under attack as a 'subjectivist', although he continued to teach at art school until his death in 1935.[55] Vladimir Lebedev, perhaps the most innovative of the Petrograd Rosta artists, came under still more open and repeated attack; he was criticised at a conference on children's literature held under Central Committee auspices in the mid-1930s (he had undertaken some illustrations for books of this kind), and was attacked in *Pravda* for the 'formalism' and 'deeply reactionary' nature of his work.[56] Lebedev's 'suprematist stylisation' was 'incomprehensible to the masses', an academic symposium complained in 1948; two years later the unfortunate Lebedev was taken to task for his 'Renoirist tendencies' in the leading Soviet art journal.[57] El Lissitsky's work was no more acceptable: 'who could really need an abstract resolution of the bitter political struggle with Whiteguardism in the form of a red wedge, cutting into a white circle?', the same academic symposium complained.[58]

Even established poster artists who remained in official favour found themselves under the same intense pressures. Deni, for instance, who became an 'honoured art worker of the RSFSR' in 1932 with a number of other poster artists, had to adapt his *Third International* (Plate 3.31) to a variety of other purposes: instead of striking down the capitalist class, the bolt of lightning now struck down, in different versions, the *Counterrevolutionary Wrecker* (1932) or the *Trotskyist-Bukharinist*

6.10 V. N. Deni, *Trubka Stalina* (Stalin's pipe), *Pravda*, 25 February 1930, p. 1.

Swine (1937) (it was adapted again during the Second World War to strike down the German general staff at Stalingrad).[59] His other work of the 1930s dealt with themes such as *Stalin's Pipe* (Plate 6.10) – carried out with 'great warmth', wrote a contemporary scholar – and the downfall of 'Judas-Trotsky', who was shown leading cloven-hoofed and heavily armed fascist powers towards the Soviet border.[60] Nikolai Kochergin found himself at about the same time undertaking sketches of Magnitostroi and of the Moscow-Volga canal.[61] Radakov was obliged to study the work of tea planters in Batumi, and then to go to the railway workshops at Tiflis and Baku.[62] Klutsis made a 'creative journey' to the Donbass in the early 1930s, travelling down to the coalface with the 10 p.m. shift.[63] Boris Efimov turned, in cartoons rather than posters, to a particularly unpleasant series of sketches seeking to identify Trotsky

and his associates with the Nazi menace to which they had in fact more consistently than Stalin drawn attention.[64] Viktor Koretsky's poster, 'Beloved Stalin – the people's joy' appeared in 1949, the year of the dictator's seventieth birthday; the poster, declared the leading art journal of the time, had successfully conveyed the 'great idea of the unshakable link between the leader and his people, expressing the essence of Soviet democracy'.[65]

Dmitri Moor, though in a prominent and exposed position during these years, appears to have been able almost entirely to avoid hack-work of this kind. His illustrations in anti-religious journals, although they alienated, for instance, Ivan Malyutin, were attacked by others for their much too kindly depiction of the supernatural enemy, and were at all events very popular with readers.[66] Nonetheless he too had to turn his hand to Stalinist political purposes, preparing a series of drawings on 'The path of the kulak', for instance, after Stalin's address to a Central committee conference in 1933 on party work in the countryside.[67] Cheremnykh, it appears, was one of the poster artists who had more difficulties than most during these years. After the same speech by Stalin he was obliged to travel to a village in the Moscow region to 'familiarise himself more closely with the practice of collective farm construction'; an album of illustrations that he produced at about the same time was based largely on Stalin's speech to the first Congress of Collective Farm Shockworkers in 1933. He subsequently went with a *Krokodil* brigade to work on the Omsk railway, and the following year he organised a studio on the site of the Moscow-Volga canal where political prisoners were working.[68] Despite a number of civic distinctions including the joint award of a Stalin prize, Cheremnykh had further difficulties with the authorities in later years: in 1950, for instance, he had to add 'As comrade Stalin has correctly stated' to the wording of one of his posters, as the original version had quite impermissibly paraphrased what the leader had said ('His every word is sacred', Cheremnykh was told).[69]

It would, however, be a mistake to regard organisational changes, socio-economic circumstances or even political pressures as sufficient in themselves to account for the demise of the political poster of the civil war years. Posters continued to be produced, and in substantial numbers, despite these difficulties, and circumstances alone can hardly be held responsible for a failure which was, in the end, one of creative energies and artistic imagination. It is perhaps simplest and most satisfactory to conclude that it was above all the nature of the times which brought forth the creative upsurge of the civil war poster, an upsurge which was paralleled in other countries during both world wars and in the USSR itself during the struggle with Nazi Germany. The successes of the Bolshevik poster during the civil war years were not simply those of superior technique (in this the Whites were hardly inferior), nor even a greater freedom of artistic endeavour. Central to their success, it would appear, were the themes that the Bolshevik poster artists had at their disposal, themes such as social justice, education and female emancipation, and above all the theme of the motherland in danger (in this case from foreign interventionist forces with their domestic allies). The Bolsheviks were able to rally substantial popular support, even from those who did not share their political philosophy, because it appeared that they alone stood for withdrawal from a war in which Russia's treaty partners appeared to have most to gain. After the revolution, it was again the Bolsheviks who appeared most consistently to stand for a Russia that would be socialist but also totally independent of outside economic and political control (it was of course the Bolsheviks' thesis that these two were inextricably connected).

It is surely more than a coincidence that the acknowledged peak of Soviet poster art, in 1919 and 1920, was precisely the period when the new regime appeared most likely to be toppled by its domestic and foreign opponents; again, it seems more than a coincidence that the best or at any rate most influential Soviet posters of later years, such as Toidze's 'Motherland calls', were produced at a time when the threat of conquest by external forces (this time those of Nazi Germany) were also at their greatest. It is acknowledged by Soviet poster artists themselves that their work became less effective, aesthetically and in other ways, when the Red Army moved on to the offensive from 1943 onwards and began no longer to defend Russia's historic territories but to extend the boundaries of Soviet rule.[70] The association between art and war, or art and its social context more generally, is obviously a complex and indirect one; but the greatest achievements, at least in Soviet poster art, do seem to be clearly associated with times of transcendent national need. The themes of economic and social reconstruction, of public health and the formation of cooperatives, worthy though they were, could hardly hope to call up a popular resonance comparable with that of *la patrie en danger*; the poster artists of these later years, perhaps in consequence, did not succeed in rivalling the still unequalled achievement of their predecessors of the civil war years.

Notes

Chapter One

1. G. Demosfenova et al., *Sovetskii politicheskii plakat* (Moscow: Iskusstvo, 1962), p. 7; similarly M. F. Savelev, 'Sovetskii politicheskii plakat 1917–20 godov', in *Ocherki po russkomu i sovetskomu iskusstvu. Sbornik statei* (Moscow: Sovetskii khudozhnik, 1965), pp. 23–4.

2. Ya. Tukhendkhol'd, 'Sovremennyi plakat', *Pechat' i revolyutsiya*, 1926, no. 8, pp. 56–74, at p. 59; similarly V. Okhochinsky, *Plakat: razvitie i primenenie* (Leningrad: Izdatel'stvo Akademii khudozhestv, 1926), p.92.

3. O. Yu. Shmidt et al., eds., *Bol'shaya sovetskaya entsiklopediya*, 1st ed., 65 vols. (Moscow: Sovetskaya entsiklopediya, 1926–48), vol. 37, col. 446.

4. Yu. Ovsyannikov, comp., *Lubok: russkie narodnye kartinki XVII–XVIII vv.* (Moscow: Sovetskii khudozhnik, 1968), pp. 5–6.

5. V. Bakhtin and D. Moldavsky, comps., *Russkii lubok XVII–XIX vv.* (Moscow-Leningrad: Gosudarstvennoe izdatel'stvo izobrazitel'nogo iskusstva, 1962), p. 1; N. A. Kozhin and I. S. Abramov, *Narodnyi lubok vtoroi poloviny XIX veka i sovremennyi* (Leningrad: Izdatel'stvo Obshchestva pooshchreniya khudozhnikov, 1929), p. 35.

6. Ovsyannikov, *Lubok*, p. 10.

7. O. D. Baldina, *Russkie narodnye kartinki* (Moscow: Molodaya gvardiya, 1972), p. 155.

8. Ibid., p. 3.

9. Bakhtin and Moldasky, *Russkii lubok*, p. 4; Baldina, *Russkie narodnye kartinki*, pp. 191–2.

10. Baldina, *Russkie narodnye kartinki*, pp. 4–7. Sytin's production figures are mentioned in I. D. Sytin, *Zhizn' dlya knigi* (Moscow: Gospolitizdat, 1962), p.43.

11. Baldina, *Russkie narodnye kartinki*, ch. 3; Alla Sytova, comp., *The Lubok: Russian Folk Pictures* (Leningrad: Aurora, 1984), pp. 7–8.

12. Baldina, *Russkie narodnye kartinki*, p. 140; Ovsyannikov, *Lubok*, p. 26.

13. Kozhin and Abramov, *Narodnyi lubok*, p. 36; *Bol'shaya sovetskaya entsiklopediya*, vol. 37, col. 446.

14. Baldina, *Russkie narodnye kartinki*, p. 196; Nikolai Tarabukin, 'Lubochnyi plakat'. *Sovetskoe iskusstvo*, 1925, no. 3, pp. 63–6, at p. 63.

15. Ovsyannikov, *Lubok*, p. 14.

16. Baldina, *Russkie narodnye kartinki*, pp. 193, 195.

17. Bakhtin and Moldavsky, *Russkii lubok*, pp. 4–5; Sytova, *The Lubok*, p. 12 (decrees of 1839 and 1851 were particularly important).

18. Sytova, *The Lubok*. p. 15.

19. V. V. Kandinsky to N. I. Kul'bin, 12 December 1911, in *Pamyatniki kul'tury: novye otkritiya. Ezhegodnik 1980* (Leningrad: Nauka, 1981), p. 407; a further letter of 28 March 1912 is on p. 408.

20. Bakhtin and Moldavsky, *Russkii lubok*, p. 11.

21. Sytova, *The Lubok*, p. 15.

22. Bakhtin and Moldavsky, *Russkii lubok*, p. 11.

23. Ibid., p. 12. Rovinsky's collection is in D. A. Rovinsky, *Russkie narodnye kartinki*, 5 vols. (St Petersburg: Imperatorskaya Akademiya nauk, 1881–93).

24. See Baldina, *Russkie narodnye kartinki*, ch. 4.

25. Okhochinsky, *Plakat*, ch. 8. A selection of work of this kind is reproduced in Angelica Z. Rudenstine, ed., *The George Costakis Collection: Russian Avant-Garde Art* (London: Thames and Hudson, 1981), pp. 421–9. V. Denisov, *Voina i lubok* (Petrograd: Izdatel'stvo novogo zhurnala dlya vsekh, 1916), suggests that 'Contemporary Lubok' was founded by a group of 'Moscow youth' (col. 31); he notes also that many were reproduced in postcard format (col. 33).

26. Denisov, *Voina i lubok*, ills. 32, 39. Parallels between this work and (for instance) Nikolai Kochergin's 'It's Wrangel's turn' (1920) are noted in V. Matafonov, 'Revolyutsionnye plakaty N. M. Kochergina', *Iskusstvo*, 1972, no. 6, pp. 34–8, at p. 37.

27. General studies of icon painting include Kurt Weitzmann et al., *The Icon* (New York: Knopf, 1983); on Russian icon painting more particularly see George H. Hamilton, *The Art and Architecture of Russia*, 3rd ed. (New York: Penguin, 1982), part 2. Good recent surveys in Russian include M. V. Alpatov, *Drevnerusskaya ikonopis'*, 2nd ed. (Moscow: Iskusstvo, 1978), and V. N. Lazarev, *Russaya ikonopis'. Ot istokov do nachala XVI veka*, 6 parts (Moscow: Iskusstvo, 1983).

28. Lazarev, *Russkaya ikonopis'*, part 1, pp. 159–60, and part 5, *Moskovskaya shkola*, pp. 366–7 (with extensive bibliography). Further discussions are in Robin Milner-Gulland, 'Art and architecture of old Russia, 988–1700', in Robert Auty and Dimitri Obolensky, eds., *An Introduction to Russian Art and Architecture: Companion to Russian Studies*, vol. 3 (Cambridge: Cambridge University Press, 1980), p. 43, and in Konrad Onasch, *Russian Icons* (Oxford: Phaidon, 1973), p. 10. V. A. Plugin has recently and controversially argued that the 'Trinity' may not have been created for the Trinity-St Sergius monastery at Zagorsk but may have been a gift to the monastery by Ivan the Terrible ('O proizkhozhdenii "Troitsy" Rubleva', *Istoriya SSSR*, 1987, no. 2, pp. 64–79).

29. A. A. Sidorov, 'Iskusstvo plakata', *Gorn*, 1922, no. 2, pp. 122–7, was unusual in defining the poster as a 'contemporary icon' (p. 125); in his memoirs, however, he took the view that the Soviet poitical poster was 'absolutely new [and] revolutionary' in Soviet representational art ('Iskusstvo 1920-kh godov i ego mastera', *Iskusstvo*, 1977, no. 11, pp. 67–77, at p. 74).

30. M. V. Alpatov, *Kraski drevnerusskoi ikonopisi* (Moscow: Izobrazitel'noe iskusstvo, 1974), p. 94.

31. See below, p. 80.

32. *Vsemirnaya illyustratsiya*, 1923, no. 10, p. 13. The 'Virgin Hodigitria' is in Alpatov, *Drevnerusskaya ikonopis'*, plate 86.

33. Lev Kopelev, *The Education of a True Believer* (London: Wildwood House, 1981), pp. 37–8.

34. *Petrogradskie 'Okna Rosta'. Svodnyi katalog* (Leningrad: Gosudarstvennaya Publicheskaya Biblioteka im. Saltykova-Shchedrina, 1964), p. 16.

35. Marc Jansen, *A Show Trial under Lenin* (The Hague: Nijhoff, 1982). p. 145.

36. S. Bojko, 'Agitprop Art: the Streets were their Theater', in

Stephanie Barron and Maurice Tuchman, eds., *The Avant-Garde in Russia, 1920–1930: New Perspectives* (Cambridge, Mass.: MIT Press, 1980), p.74.

37. Ulf Abel, 'Icons and Soviet art', in Claes Arvidsson and Lars Erik Blomqvist, eds., *Symbols of Power: The Esthetics of Political Legitimation in the Soviet Union and Eastern Europe* (Stockholm: Almqvist and Wiksell, 1987), pp. 144–5.

38. On the Lenin cult see particularly Nina Tumarkin, *Lenin Lives! The Lenin Cult in Soviet Russia* (Cambridge, Mass.: Harvard University Press, 1983). On 'red corners, see Bojko, 'Agitprop Art', p. 74.

39. This wording (article 18 of the 1918 Constitution) was retained in the 1936 Constitution (art. 12) but was dropped in the present 1977 Constitution. Lunacharsky's remarks were in his 'Svoboda knigi i revolyutsiya', *Pechat' i revolyutsiya*, kn. 1 (May-June 1921), pp. 3–9, at pp. 7–8.

40. A. Platonov, *Izbrannoe* (Moscow: Moskovskii rabochii, 1966), p. 49 (this passage is omitted in some Soviet editions).

41. 'Lektsii D. S. Moora o plakatnom iskusstve i ego istroii' (n. d.), TsGALI f. 1988 op. 1 ed. khr. 68.

42. 'Avtobiografiya' (1934), TsGALI f. 1988 op. 2 ed. khr. 13.

43. Ibid.

44. See for instance P. I. Lebedev, *Sovetskoe iskusstvo v period inostrannoi interventsii i grazhdanskoi voiny* (Moscow-Leningrad: Iskusstvo, 1949), p. 76; Demosfenova et al., *Sovetskii politicheskii plakat*, p. 12.

45. A. A. Sidorov, *Russkaya grafika nachala XX veka* (Moscow: Iskusstvo, 1969), p. 60.

46. John Bowlt, *The Silver Age: Russian Art in the Early Twentieth Century and the 'World of Art' Group* (Newtonville, Mass.: Oriental Research Rartners, 1979), p. 111.

47. I. P. Abramsky, *Smekh sil'nykh. O khudozhnikakh zhurnala 'Krokodil'* (Moscow: Iskusstvo, 1977), pp. 24–6. *Simplicissimus* itself took a close interest in Russian affairs: see Lennart Kjellberg, 'Der *Simplicissimus* und die Slawen, 1896–1914', *Scando-Slavica*, vol. 28 (1982), pp. 69–90.

48. Z. A. Pokrovskaya, comp., *Russkaya satiricheskaya periodika 1905–7gg. : Svodnyi katalog* (Moscow: Gosudarstvennaya biblioteka im. Lenina, 1980), pp. 10–1. The same source notes (p. 8) that satirical periodicals were produced in more than 30 different towns, and that many more were suppressed before they could bring out a single issue.

49. See respectively A. A. Timonich, *Russkie satiriko-yumoristicheskie zhurnaly* (Moscow: mimeo., 1930), p. 136; V. F. Botsianovsky and E. Gollerbakh, *Russkaya satira pervoi russkoi revolyutsii* (Leningrad: Giz, 1925), p. 222.

50. Sidorov, *Russkaya grafika*, p. 117.

51. G. Yu. Sternin, *Ocherki russkoi satiricheskoi grafiki* (Moscow: Iskusstvo, 1964), p. 240.

52. Sidorov, *Russkaya grafika*, pp. 117, 119.

53. B. S. Butnik-Siversky, *Sovetskii plakat epokhi grazhdanskoi voiny 1918–21* (Moscow: Izdatel'stvo Vsesoyuznoi knizhnoi palaty, 1960), p. 14. The fullest survey of the satirical graphics of this period is V. V. Shleev et al., eds., *Revolyutsiya 1905–7 godov i izobrazitel'noe iskusstvo*, 3 parts (Moscow: izobrazitel'noe iskusstvo, 1977–81); a useful selection is in David King and Cathy Porter, *Blood and Laughter: Caricatures from the 1905 Revolution* (London: Cape, 1983), which includes the modified Manifesto on p. 89.

54. Okhochinsky, *Plakat*, p. 5.

55. Sidorov, *Russkaya grafika*, p. 122.

56. *Kommunist*, 1982, no 1, pp. 63–6. On Chemodanov, see Sidorov, *Russkaya grafika*, p. 130, and I. M. Maisky, *Vospominaniya sovetskogo posla*, 2 vols (Moscow: Nauka, 1964), vol. 1, pp. 73–82.

57. Shleev, *Revolyutsiya 1905–7 godov*, vyp. 1, p. 8.

58. A further example was A. A. Radakov's 'Pyramid of classes', published by 'Parus' in March 1917 (*Literaturnoe nasledstvo*, vol. 65 [Moscow: Nauka, 1958], p. 552).

59. Shleev, *Revolyutsiya 1905–1907 godov*, vyp. 2, p. 5.

60. Ibid., p. 6.

61. Ibid., vyp. 1. pp. 10–11.

62. Ibid., pp. 13–14; Sidorov, *Russkaya grafika*, p. 119.

63. Sidorov, *Russkaya grafika*, pp. 119–22; Bilibin's arrest is noted in his 'Professional'noe zhizneopisanie khudozhnika I. Ya. Bilibina', *V mire knig*, 1976, no. 8, pp. 26–7, at p. 26. See also Sergei Golynets, *Ivan Bilibin* (London: Pan, 1981), pp. 185–6 and elsewhere. Sidorov describes Bilibin's 'Donkey' as the 'most powerful graphic attach on tsarism' at this time (*Russkaya grafika*, p. 122).

64. Sidorov, *Russkaya grafika*, p. 119.

65. Abramsky, *Smekh sil'nykh*, p. 28.

66. Moor's work in 1905–7 is recorded in Pokrovskaya, *Russkaya satiricheskaya periodika*, and in S. Roshchupkin, 'Pervye risunki D. S. Moora', *Khudozhnik*, 1972, no. 4, pp. 26–7; his later career is considered in Chapter 3 below.

67. On Radakov, see N. V. Kuz'min, *Davno i nedavno* (Moscow: Sovetskii khudozhnik, 1982), p. 240, who notes that Nikolai Radlov and Viktor Lebedev also began their graphic careers in *Novyi Satirikon* (see also below, p. 138 n.127); on Chekhonin, see Sidorov, *Russkaya grafika*, p. 118. On Deni and Malyutin, see below, Chaps. 3 and 4.

68. *Periodicheskaya pechat' SSSR 1917–49*, vyp. 8 (Moscow: Izdatel'stvo Vsesoyuznoi knizhnoi palaty, 1958), no. 1388. The journal is discussed briefly in Sidorov, 'Iskusstvo 1920–kh godov i ego mastera', p. 71.

69. Butnik-Siversky, *Sovetskii plakat*, p. 42.

70. B. Zemenkov, 'Karikatura v sovetskoi obshchestvennosti', *Sovetskoe iskusstvo*, 1925, no, 6, pp. 66–70, at p. 66.

71. *Niva*, 1907, no 1, p. 13 (illustration), 16 (discussion).

72. Butnik-Siversky, *Sovetskii plakat*, no. 471, p. 188.

73. Ibid. This version is illustrated in G. Garritano, intr., *Manifesti della rivoluzione russa* (Rome: Riuniti, *c*. 1966), plate 22.

74. Quoted in Butnik-Siversky, *Sovetskii plakat*, p. 4. General histories of the poster include Harold F. Hutchinson, *The Poster: An Illustrated History from 1860* (London: Studio Vista, 1968); Bevis Hillier, *Posters* (London: Weidenfeld and Nicolson, 1969); John Barnicott, *A Concise History of Posters* (London: Weidenfeld and Nicolson, 1972); Max Gallo, *The Poster in History* (London: Hamlyn, 1974); Dawn Ades, ed., *The Twentieth Century Poster* (New York: Abbeville Press, 1984); and Alain Weill, *The Poster: A Worldwide Survey and History* (London: Sotheby's, 1985). Several useful illustrated volumes have been produced by Maurice Rickards including *The Rise and Fall of the Poster* (Newton Abbot: David and charles, 1971). Robert Philippe, *Political Graphics: Art as a Weapon* (Oxford: Phaidon, 1982), is also helpful.

75. Butnik-Siversky, *Sovetskii plakat*, pp. 9–11. See further Nina Baburina, 'Dorevolyutsionnyi russkii plakat', *Tvorchestvo*, 1975, no. 10, pp. 10–13, and Yurii Makunin, 'Byla li afisha v Rossii?', *Tvorchestvo*, 1986, no. 10, pp. 31–2. When it appears, the fullest available account will be Nina Baburina, *Russkii plakat vtoroi poloviny XIX-nachala XX veka* (Leningrad: Khudozhnik RSFSR, forthcoming).

76. Baburina, 'Dorevolyutsionnyi russkii plakat', pp. 11–12; see also Okhochinsky, *Plakat*, ch. 7.

77. Okhochinsky, *Plakat*, p. 64. Makunin, 'Byla li afisha', argues that Russian posters were in fact significantly under-represented at the exhibition (p. 32).

78. Baburina, 'Dorevolyutsionnyi russkii plakat', p. 13.

79. Efforts of this kind are recorded in Joseph Darracott and Belinda Loftus, *First World War Posters* (London: Imperial War

Museum, 1972); Joseph Darracott, *The First World War in Posters* (New York; Dover, 1974); Maurice Rickards, *Posters of the First World War* (London: Evelyn, Adams and Mackay, 1968); and more generally Cate Haste, *Keep the Home Fires Burning: Propaganda in the First World War* (London: Allen Lane, 1978).

80. Okhochinsky, *Plakat*, p. 72.

81. Butnik-Siversky, *Sovetskii plakat*, p. 11; other examples are given in Rickards, *Posters*, ills. 64 and 65.

82. Illustrated in *Affiches et imageries russes 1914–21* (Paris: Musée des deux guerres mondiales, 1982), nos. 5, 13 and 17.

83. Butnik-Siversky, *Sovetskii plakat*, p. 12.

84. L. O. Pasternak, *Zapisi raznykh let* (Moscow: Sovetskii Khudozhnik, 1975), p. 84. His 'Help for war victims' is illustrated in ibid., p. 83; the adapted version, 'The price of blood', appears in *Literaturnaya gazeta*, 30 May 1957, p. 1.

85. See *Graficheskoe iskusstvo v SSSR 1917–1927. Sbornik statei* (Leningrad: Gosizdat, 1927), pp. 152–3. Soviet scholars hold that Kustodiev made a 'genuine mistake' by participating in an official competition of this kind, but that he later overcame his 'illusions' in this respect (see B. Kapralov, 'Russkii khudozhnik Boris Kustodiev', *Iskusstvo*, 1970, no. 1, pp. 22–32, at p. 28). According to more recent oral testimony, Kustodiev's original was 'crudely and unceremoniously "corrected"' for poster reproduction, leading the artist to write to the newspapers to complain (A. M. Turkov, *Boris Mikhailovich Kustodiev* [Moscow: Iskusstvo, 1986], p. 112n.)

86. Okhochinsky, *Plakat*, p. 72.

87. Vyacheslav Polonsky, *Russkii revolyutsionnyi plakat* (Moscow: Gosizdat, 1925), p. 21. Okhochinsky, writing in *Graficheskoe iskusstvo v SSSR 1917–1927*, argued that the Cadets should rather be placed first for the variety and vividness of their posters at this time, with the Socialist Revolutionaries in second place, but added that none of these posters had had much popular impact at the time (p. 154).

88. Butnik-Siversky, *Sovetskii plakat*, p. 22. Vera Slavenson, 'Sotsial'nyi plakat', *Kniga i revolyutsiya*, 1920, no. 6, pp. 11–15, noted however that 'despite its extreme modesty, this poster attracted universal attention' (pp. 11–12).

89. Butnik-Siversky, *Sovetskii plakat*, p. 15.

91. Polonsky, *Russkii revolyutsionnyi plakat*, p. 21.

Chapter Two

1. A. A. Lipatov and N. T. Savenkov, eds, *Istoriya sovetskoi konstitutsii (v dokumentakh) 1917–56* (Moscow: Gosudarstvennoe izdatel'stvo yuridicheskoi literatury, 1957), pp. 143–4.

2. *Vos'moi s"ezd RKP(b) mart 1919 goda. Protokoly* (Moscow: Gosudarstvennoe izdatel'stvo politicheskoi literatury, 1959), pp. 390–411, at pp. 390, 394.

3. Ibid., p. 395.

4. *Itogi Vsesoyuznoi perepisi naseleniya 1970 goda*, tom III (Moscow: Statistika, 1972), pp. 570–1. Somewhat lower figures for 1920 are reported in *Gramotnost' v Rossii* (Moscow: TsSU, 1922): according to this source, only 31.4 per cent of males and females in the RSFSR were literate, or 39.9 per cent of those over eight years old (pp. 9, 10). On this question and its implications for Bolshevik propaganda generally see Roger Pethybridge, *The Social Prelude to Stalinism* (London: Macmillan, 1974), ch. 4, and Peter Kenez, *The Birth of the Propaganda State. Soviet Methods of Mass Mobilization, 1917–29* (Cambridge: Cambridge University Press, 1985).

5. A. I. Nazarov, *Oktyabr' i kniga* (Moscow: Nauka, 1968), p. 167.

6. E. L. Nemirovsky and V. I. Kharlamov, eds., *Istoriya knigi v SSSR, 1917–21*, 3 vols. (Moscow: Kniga, 1983–6), vol. 1, p. 65.

7. Ibid., vol. 2, pp. 152–3.

8. S. I. Stykalin, *Okna satiry ROSTA* (Moscow: Izdatel'stvo Moskovskogo Universiteta, 1976), pp. 7–8.

9. Nazarov, *Oktyabri i kniga*, p. 189; Nemirovsky and Kharlamov, *Istoriya knigi*, vol. 1, p. 71.

10. A good general study of this question is available in Jeffrey Brooks, 'The breakdown in production and distribution of printed material, 1917–27', in Abbott Gleason et al., eds., *Bolshevik Culture* (Bloomington: University of Indiana Press, 1985), pp. 151–74.

11. See A. Strigalev, 'K istorii vozniknoveniya leninskogo plana "monumental'noi propagandy"', in *Voprosy sovetskogo izobrazitel'nogo iskusstva i arkhitektury* (Moscow: Sovetskii khudozhnik, 1976), pp. 213–51, and more recently V. P. Tolstoi, *U istokov sovetskogo monumental'nogo iskusstva 1917–23* (Moscow: Izobrazitel'noe iskusstvo, 1983). Good accounts in English include John Bowlt, 'Russian sculpture and Lenin's plan of monumental propaganda', in Henry A. Millon and Linda Nochlin, eds., *Art and Architecture in the Service of Politics* (Cambridge, Mass.: MIT Press, 1978), and Christina Lodder, 'Lenin's plan of monumental propaganda', *Sbornik*, no. 3 (1980), pp. 67–84.

12. L. D. Trotsky, *Moya zhizn'*, 2 vols. (Berlin: Granat, 1930), vol. 2, pp. 65–6.

13. *Dekrety sovetskoi vlasti*, vol. 2 (Moscow: Gosudarstvennoe izdatel'stvo politicheskoi literatury, 1959), pp. 95–7, and vol. 3 (1964), pp. 118–19.

14. *Agitatsionno-massovoe iskusstvo pervykh let Oktyabr'skoi revolyutsii. Katalog vystavki* (Moscow: Sovetskii khudozhnik, 1967), p. 8. The bas relief is now in the Russian Museum in Leningrad.

15. I. E. Grabar' et al., eds., *Istoriya russkogo iskusstva*, 16 vols. (Moscow: Izdatel'stvo Akademii nauk SSSR, 1953–69), vol. 9, p. 33.

16. *Agitatsionno-massovoe iskusstvo pervykh let Oktyabr'skoi revolyutsii*, p. 14. The demonstrations of the period are considered in detail in A. Raikhenstein, 'I maya i 7 noyabrya 1918 goda v Moskve', in E. A. Speranskaya, ed., *Agitatsionno-massovoe iskusstov pervykh let Oktyabrya: materialy i issledovaniya* (Moscow: Iskusstvo, 1971), pp. 67–109.

17. *Agitatsionno-massovoe iskusstvo pervykh let Oktyabr'skoi revolyutsii*, p. 14.

18. René Fülöp-Miller, *The Mind and Face of Bolshevism* (London and New York: Putnam, 1927), p. 96.

19. *Agitatsionno-massovoe iskusstvo pervykh let Oktyabr'skoi revolyutsii*, p. 15.

20. Ibid., p. 22; see also below, pp. 88–9. The demonstrations of the period in Petrograd are considered further in *Massovye prazdnestva. Sbornik komiteta sotsiologicheskogo izucheniya iskusstv* (Leningrad: Academia, 1926), pp. 55–84; A. Gushchin, *Oformlenie massovykh prazdnestv za 15 let diktatury proletariata* (Moscow: Ogiz-Izogiz, 1932); and Speranskaya, ed., *Agitatsion-no-massovoe iskusstvo pervykh let Oktyabrya*, pp. 9–66 (which also deals with Saratov and Nizhnyi Novgorod [now Gorky], pp. 134–61). An extensive collection of documents and photographs is available in V. P. Tolstoi, ed., *Agitatsionno-massovoe iskusstvo. Oformlenie prazdnestv*, 2 vols. (Moscow: Iskusstvo, 1984).

21. Fülöp-Miller, *Mind and Face*, pp. 138–40, 147–8, 183–4. On street theatre particularly see Robert Russell, 'People's theatre and the October revolution', *Irish Slavonic Studies*, no. 7 (1986), pp. 65–84.

22. V. A. Karpinsky, ed., *Agitparpoezda VTsIK. Ikh istoriya,*

apparat, metody i formy raboty. Sbornik statei (Moscow: Gosizdat, 1920), p. 5.

23. Vyacheslav Polonsky, *Russkii revolyutsionnyi plakat* (Moscow: Gosizdat, 1925), pp. 59–60; Karpinsky, *Agitparpoezda*, p. 10; Arthur Ransome, *The Crisis in Russia* (London: Allen and Unwin, 1921), pp. 86–7. Front pages of some of the train newspapers are in *Krasnyi zhurnalist* no. 1 (1 August 1920), cols. 15–22.

24. L. Vinogradova, 'Khudozhniki agitpoezdov', *Khudozhnik*, 1959, no. 11, pp. 39–40, at p. 39. The decoration of trains and ships is considered further in I. Bibkova, 'Rospis' agitparakhodov', in Speranskaya, ed., *Agitatsionno–massovoe iskusstvo pervykh let Oktyabrya*, pp. 166–98.

25. Karpinsky, *Agitparpoezda*, pp. 11–12, 6.

26. Polonsky, *Russkii revolyutsionnyi plakat*, pp. 58–9.

27. N. K. Verzhbitsky, *Zapiski starogo zhurnalista* (Moscow: Sovetskii pisatel', 1961), pp. 183–4.

28. Karpinsky, *Agitparpoezda*, p. 13; N. K. Krupskaya, 'Na krasnoi zvezde' (1919), in Krupskaya, *Pedagogicheskie sochineniya v desyati tomakh*, vol. 1 (Moscow: Izdatel'stvo Akademii pedagogicheskikh nauk, 1957), pp. 57–67.

29. Polonsky, *Russkii revolyutsionnyi plakat*, p. 60.

30. Ibid., p. 52.

31. B. S. Butnik-Siversky, *Sovetskii plakat epokhi grazhdanskoi voiny 1918–21* (Moscow: Izdatel'stvo Vsesoyuznoi knizhnoi palaty, 1960), nos. 719 and 720, p. 215; see also above, pp. 14–15, 23.

32. The artist is identified by M. M. Cheremnykh in *Iskusstvo*, 1940, no. 3, p. 39.

33. Butnik-Siversky, *Sovetskii plakat*, nos. 716, 714, p. 215.

34. Ibid., no. 710, pp. 214–15.

35. Ibid., p. 44.

36. Ibid., no. 494, pp. 190–1.

37. Ibid., no. 285, pp. 170–1.

38. Ibid., nos. 1199, 84 and 202 respectively; see also nos 627 and 504.

39. The fullest biographical account, on which most of the following is based, is Arturs Eglitis, 'Aleksandrs Apsitisviens no pirmajiem padomju plakatistiem', in *Latviešu tēlotāja māksla 1957* (Riga: Latgosizdat, 1958), pp. 271–84. See also A. Eglit, 'Pioner sovetskogo plakata', *Daugava*, 1979, no. 11. pp. 121–3.

40. I. N. Pavlov, *Zhizn' russkogo gravera* (Leningrad: Iskusstvo, 1940), p. 162. Some of Apsit's 'patriotic' posters are collected in Sobranie plakatov i lubkov, TsGALI, f. 1931, op. 1, ed. khr. 1.

41. Ibid., p. 162.

42. See O. E. Vol'tsenburg et al., eds., *Khudozhniki narodov SSSR. Biobibliograficheskii slovar' v shesti tomakh*, vol. 1 (Moscow: Iskusstvo, 1970), p. 182.

43. I. N. Pavlov, *Moya zhizn' i vstrechi* (Moscow: Iskusstvo, 1949), pp. 137–40.

44. Pavlov, *Zhizn' russkogo gravera*, p. 160; this incident is missing from the otherwise almost identical account in *Moya zhizn'*, pp. 137–40.

45. Polonsky, *Russkii revolyutsionnyi plakat*, pp. 27–8.

46. D. S. Moor, 'Sovetskii politicheskii plakat, 1917–33', in Moor, *Ya – bol'shevik* (Moscow: Sovetskii khudozhnik, 1967), p. 23.

47. E. Povolotskaya and M. Ioffe, *Tridtsat' let sovetskogo plakata* (Moscow-Leningrad: Iskusstvo, 1948), p. 5.

48. See for instance Eglit, 'Pioner sovetskogo plakata', and Viktor Koretsky, *Zametki plakatista* (Moscow: Sovetskii khudozhnik, 1958), p. 23.

49. Butnik-Siversky, *Sovetskii plakat*, p. 45.

50. Eglit, 'Pioner sovetskogo plakata', p. 123. Serov's poster is illustrated in G. Demosfenova et al., *Sovetskii politicheskii plakat* (Moscow: Iskusstvo, 1962), p. 337.

51. *Programma partii kommunistov (bol'shevikov)* (Ekaterinburg: Agenstvo Tsentropechati, 1920).

52. Eglit, 'Pioner sovetskogo plakata', p. 122.

53. 'Mshchenie tsaryam', in Butnik-Siversky, *Sovetskii plakat*, no. 355. On the 'Varshavyanka', see P. F. Lebedev, 'Revolyutsionnye pesni rossiiskogo proletariata', *Voprosy istorii*, 1967, no. 11, pp. 214–18, at pp. 216–17.

54. *Sovetskii entsiklopedicheskii slovar'* (Moscow: Sovetskaya entsiklopediya, 1979), p. 502.

55. Eglit, 'Pioner sovetskogo plakata', p. 122. Butnik-Siversky, *Sovetskii plakat*, lists 35 posters by 'A. Petrov' and two by 'I. Osinin', but does not include, for instance, Apsit's 'To horse, proletarian!'

56. M. L. Etkind, intr., *Boris Kustodiev* (Moscow: Sovetskii khudozhnik, 1982), pp. 343, 345 (illustration).

57. *Agitatsionno-massovoe iskusstvo pervykh let Oktyabr'skoi revolyutsii*, p. 19. Speranskaya, *Agitatsionno-massovoe iskusstvo pervykh let Oktyabrya*, pp.67–8, dates the first appearance of the hammer and sickle to 1918 but illustrates the Saratov symbol of 1917 on p. 145.

58. Lipatov and Savenkov, eds., *Istoriya sovetskoi konstitutsii*, pp. 157–8, 546. The respective positions of hammer and sickle were not specified and they were often placed the wrong way round, even on Moscow tram cars (K. I. Dunin-Borkovsky, *O gerbe i flagakh RSFSR* [Moscow: NKID, 1922], p. 13). A full discussion of the development of these and other new symbols is in V. V. Pokhlebkin, 'Iz istorii sovetskoi emblematiki', *Voprosy istorii*, 1978, no. 3, pp. 81–97; he argues (p. 93) for Sergei Chekhonin as the author of the new Soviet state emblem.

59. Richard Stites, 'The origins of Soviet ritual style: symbol and festival in the Russian revolution', in Claes Arvidsson and Lars Erik Blomqvist, eds., *Symbols of Power: The Esthetics of Political Legitimation in the Soviet Union and Eastern Europe* (Stockholm: Almqvist and Wiksell, 1987), pp. 23–42, at p. 37.

60. Illustrated in V. V. Shleev, ed., *Revolyutsiya 1905–7 godov i izobrazitel'noe iskusstvo*, 3 parts (Moscow: Izobrazitel'noe iskusstvo, 1977–81), vyp. 1, p. 69.

61. Demosfenova et al., *Sovetskii politicheskii plakat*, p. 28.

62. Ibid., p. 38; E. V. Litvinenko, comp., *Plakaty, vypushchennye k godovshchine Velikoi Oktyabrskoi sotsialisticheskoi revolyutsii v Sovetskom Soyuze i za rubezhom* (Moscow: Gosudarstvennyi muzei revolyutsii SSSR, 1958), p. 9.

63. Demosfenova et al., *Sovetskii politicheskii plakat*, p. 38.

64. M. F. Savelev, 'Sovetskii politicheskii plakat 1917–20 godov', in *Ocherki po russkomu i sovetskomu iskusstvu, Sbornik statei* (Moscow: Sovetskii khudozhnik, 1965), pp. 20–36, at p. 26.

65. A. G. Budrina, comp., *Ural'skii plakat vremen grazhdanskoi voiny* (Perm': Permskoe knizhnoe izdatel'stvo, 1968), p. 33.

66. Butnik-Siversky, *Sovetskii plakat*, p. 59.

67. Moor, *Ya – bol'shevik*, p. 144.

68. Richard Stites, 'Adorning the Russian Revolution: the primary symbols of Bolshevism, 1917–1918', *Sbornik*, no. 10 (1984), pp. 39–42, at p. 40.

69. Demosfenova et al., *Sovetskii politicheskii plakat*, p. 39.

70. *Pechat' i revolyutsiya*, kn. 1 (1921), p. 190.

71. Pokhlebkin, 'Iz istorii sovetskoi emblematiki', p. 88.

72. A. A. Sidorov, 'Iskusstvo plakata', *Gorn*, 1922, no. 2, pp. 122–7, at p. 126.

73. Demosfenova et al., *Sovetskii politicheskii plakat* p. 39.

74. A full listing is available in Butnik-Siversky, *Sovetskii plakat*.

Chapter Three

1. E. L. Nemirovsky and V. I. Kharlamov, eds., *Istoriya kniqi v SSSR, 1917–21,* 3 vols. (Moscow: Kniga, 1983–6), vol, 2, p. 13.
2. Ibid., vol. 2, pp. 7, 8, 9–10, 12–13.
3. Ibid., vol. 1, p. 176.
4. E. A. Dinershtein and T. P. Yavorskaya, comps., *Izdatel'skoe delo v pervye gody sovetskoi vlasti (1917–22). Sbornik dokumentov i materialov* (Moscow: Kniga, 1972), pp. 63–5.
5. Nemirovsky and Kharlamov, *Istoriya knigi,* vol. 2, p. 14.
6. *Otchet o deyatel'nosti Otdela voennoi literatury pri RVSR i Vysshego voennogo redaktsionnogo soveta s 1 yan. 1921g. po 31 dek. 1922g.* (Moscow: Vysshii voennyi redaktsionnyi sovet, 1923), p. 5. On military publishing see more generally N. F. Katkov, *Agitatsionno-propagandistskaya rabota bol'shevikov v voiskakh i tylu belogvardeitsev v period 1918–20 gg.* (Leningrad: Izdatel'stvo Leningradskogo universiteta, 1977) and A. A. Marinov, *V stroyu zashchitnikov Oktyabrya. Voenno-politicheskaya kniga 1918–25* (Moscow: Nauka, 1982).
7. *Otchet o deyatel'nosti,* pp. 10, 221. El Lissitsky's composition is described as the 'first metaphysical poster in the whole history of art' in Larissa A. Zhadova, *Malevich: Suprematism and Revolution in Russian Art 1910–1930* (London: Thames and Hudson, 1982), p. 80. Lissitsky records in an autobiographical account that this was one of several posters he produced for the same authorities at this time: see his 'Avtobiografiya' (1941), TsGALI, f. 2361, op. 1, ed. khr. 58.
8. 'Avtobiografiya' (1929), TsGALI, f. 1328, op. 3, ed. khr. 56. A brief biographical account is presented in the introduction to Vyach. P. Polonsky, *Na literaturnye temy. Izbrannye stat'i* (Moscow: Sovetskii pisatel', 1968), pp. 5–39.
9. *Izvestiya,* 29 February 1932, p. 4.
10. Cited in Polonsky, *Na literaturnye temy,* p. 7n.
11. Vyach. Polonsky, 'Russkii revolyutsionnyi plakat', *Pechat' i revolyutsiya,* kn. 5 (1922), pp. 56–77; Polonsky, *Russkii revolyutsionnyi plakat* (Moscow: Gosizdat, 1925).
12. The following is based upon Moor's 'Avtobiograficheskii ocherk', in D. S. Moor, *Ya – bol'shevik. Sbornik statei,* ed. Yu. Khalaminsky (Moscow: Sovetskii khudozhnik, 1967), pp. 7–14; see also p. 109.
13. Rafuil S. Kaufman, *D. S. Moor* (Moscow: Izogiz, 1937), p. 5.
14. D. S. Moor, 'Khudozhniki o revolyutsii 1905 goda', *Iskusstvo,* 1935, pp. 39–40; 'Avtobiografiya' (1934), TsGALI, f. 1988. op. 2, ed. khr. 13.
15. R. S. Kaufman, personal communication, December 1981.
16. Moor, *Ya – bol'shevik,* p. 116.
17. Kaufman, *Moor,* p. 6; S. Roshchupkin, 'Pervye risunki Moora', *Khudozhnik,* 1972, no. 4, pp. 26–7.
18. Moor, *Ya – bol'shevik,* p. 118, On his pseudonym, see Boris Efimov, *Na moi vzglyad* (Moscow: Iskusstvo, 1987), p.25.
19. Ibid., p. 8 (illustrated in Kaufman, *Moor,* p. 15).
20. Moor, *Ya – bol'shevik,* p. 8; Kaufman, *Moor,* p. 16.
21. Moor, *Ya – bol'shevik,* pp. 8–9.
22. Ibid., pp. 118–19. A collection of these *lubki* is in 'Sobranie plakatov i lubkov', TsGALI, f. 1931, op. 1, ed. khr. 9. The comparison with Tommy Atkins is in V. Okhochinsky, *Plakat: razvitie i primenenie* (Leningrad: Izdatel'stvo Akademii khudozhestv, 1926), ch. 8.
23. S. R-ii [Raevsky], 'Pervaya russkaya gazetnaya karikatura na tsarya', *Zhurnalist,* 1925, no. 3, pp. 33–4.
24. Moor, *Ya – bol'shevik,* p. 122.
25. Ibid., p. 9.
26. Ibid., p. 142; according to *Plakat i reklama posle Oktyabrya* (Leningrad: Izdanie vystavochnogo komiteta, 1926), in three years since the beginning of 1919 Moor had done about 150 pictures and posters for the Red Army (pp. 14–15).
27. Cited from Soviet archives in Moor, *Ya – bol'shevik,* p. 142, n. 76.
28. Polonsky, 'Russkii revolyutsionnyi plakat', p. 66.
29. V. D. Duvakin, *Radost', masterom kovannaya. Ocherki tvorchestva V. V. Mayakovskogo* (Moscow: Sovetskii pisatel', 1964), p. 157.
30. Moor, *Ya – bol'shevik,* p. 11.
31. I. N. Pavlov, *Moya zhizn' i vstrechi* (Moscow: Iskusstvo, 1949), p. 260.
32. Ibid.
33. Moor, *Ya – bol'shevik,* pp. 108, 232, 146. 108. Moor's later career is considered in Chapter 6.
34. A. A. Sidorov, 'Russkaya grafika v gody revolyutsii', *Pechat' i revolyutsiya,* kn. 7 (1922), pp. 100–39, at p. 110.
35. See above, pp. 6–7.
36. N. M. Cheremnykh, *Khochetsya, chtoby znali i drugie* (Moscow: Sovetskii khudozhnik, 1965), p. 43.
37. Moor, *Ya – bol'shevik,* p. 129; illustrated in Angelica Z. Rudenstine, ed., *The George Costakis Collection: Russian Avant-Garde Art* (London: Thames and Hudson, 1981), plate 965. Another early poster, 'Solemn vow' (1918), is reproduced in G. Garritano, intr., *Manifesti della rivoluzione russa,* (Rome: Riuniti, *c.* 1966), plate 1.
38. B. S. Butnik-Siversky, *Sovetskii plakat epokhi grazhdanskoi voiny 1918–21* (Moscow: Izdatel'stvo Vsesoyuznoi knizhnoi palaty, 1960), p. 55 (the same view is put forward in *Affiches et imageries russes 1914–21* (Paris: Musée des deux guerres mondiales, 1982), p. ix); Kaufman, *Moor,* p. 21.
39. An earlier unpublished variant is illustrated in G. Demosfenova et al., *Sovetskii politicheskii plakat* (Moscow: Iskusstvo, 1962), p. 246.
40. Moor, *Ya – bol'shevik,* p. 148. Moor himself noted that the poster took only one night to complete in 'Moskovskie mastery satiry', *Iskusstvo,* 1938, no. 2, pp. 1–28, at p. 3.
41. Soviet archives, cited in Moor, *Ya – bol'shevik,* p. 151; the print run is given in ibid., p. 152.
42. Valentin Kataev, *Sobranie sochinenii v devyati tomakh,* vol. 8 (Moscow: Khndozhestvennaya literatura 1971), p. 24.
43. *Obrazotvorche mistetstvo,* 1940, no. 8, pp. 3–6, at p. 4.
44. These and other versions of the Kitchener poster are reproduced in Joseph Darracott and Belinda Loftus, *First World War Posters* (London: Imperial War Museum, 1972), pp. 63–4.
45. Illustrated in *Das Plakat,* January 1920, p. 24. The author has recently been identified as Sandor Konya (see N. Faminskaya, 'Plakat vengerskoi sovetskoi respubliki (1919 god)', *Iskusstvo,* 1985, n. 4, pp. 56–9); it is however unlikely (to say the least) that it shows the 'unmistakable influence' of Moor's better-known work as Moor's poster appeared a year earlier.
46. Moor, *Ya – bol'shevik,* p. 149; this poster is reproduced in Maurice Rickards, *Posters of the First World War* (London: Evelyn, Adams and Mackay, 1968), plate 11.
47. Kaufman, *Moor,* p. 26. Frank Kämpfer notes that both this poster and Moor's 'Be on guard' (Plate 5.19) have been taken to represent 'crypto-portraits' of Leon Trotsky: a more considered verdict, including Moor's preliminary sketches as well as both poster, suggests this is unlikely ('Der rote Keil'. *Das politische Plakat: Theorie und Geschichte* [Berlin: Mann, 1985], pp. 264–6).
48. Okhochinsky, *Plakat,* p. 81.
49. *EKO,* 1986, no. 5, front cover; also 'Have you become a volunteer of *perestroika*?', *Sobesednik,* no. 16, April 1987, front cover.
50. Moor, *Ya – bol'shevik,* p. 108; similarly p. 160. 'Help' has been called the 'peak of the Soviet agitational psychological poster'

(Butnik-Siversky, *Sovetskii plakat*, p. 125).

51. Moor, *Ya – bol'shevik*, pp. 10–11, 69. The art critic and contemporary A. A. Sidorov recalled being 'genuinely stunned' by the poster when it appeared ('Iskusstov 1920-kh godov i ego mastera', *Iskusstvo*, 1977, no. 11, pp. 57–77, at p. 74).

52. Boris Efimov, *Rasskazy o khudozhnikakh-satirikakh* (Moscow: Sovetskii khudozhnik, 1963), pp. 12–13. Very similar accounts have appeared in Efimov's other volumes of memoirs.

53. Pavlov, *Moya zhizn'*, p. 260. Efimov refers to the cartoon in his *Sorok let. Zapiski khudozhnika-satirista* (Moscow: Sovetskii khudozhnik, 1961), pp. 94–5, but slightly misdates it; the British protest about this 'grossly insulting and mendacious cartoon' was contained in Sir Austen Chamberlain to M. Rozengolz, 23 February 1927, House of Commons Command Paper Cmd 2822 (1927), at p. 5.

54. Pavlov, *Moya zhizn'*, p. 261.

55. N. Dolgorukov, *Stranitsy zhizni* (Leningrad: Khudozhnik RSFSR, 1963), p. 17; the court decision is cited from the archives in Moor, *Ya – bol'shevik*, p. 225.

56. Moor, *Ya – bol'shevik*, p. 225; Dolgorukov, *Stranitsy*, p. 19.

57. Dolgorukov, *Stranitsy*, p. 19; Moor, *Ya – bol'shevik*, p. 225.

58. Moor, *Ya – bol'shevik*, pp. 225, 227; Dolgorukov, *Stranitsy*, p. 18.

59. Pavlov, *Moya zhizn'*, p. 261.

60. Dolgorukov, *Stranitsy*, p. 17.

61. Ibid., pp. 17–18; Moor, *Ya – bol'shevik*, p. 226.

62. Dolgorukov, *Stranitsy*, p. 17.

63. Ibid., pp. 18–19.

64. Ibid., p. 17; similarly Moor, *Ya – bol'shevik*, p. 227.

65. Moor, *Ya – bol'shevik*, p. 92.

66. The following is based upon I. A. Sviridova, *Viktor Nikolaevich Deni* (Moscow: Iskusstvo, 1978), p. 9 and elsewhere.

67. Efimov, *Rasskazy*, pp. 15–16.

68. Sviridova, *Deni*, pp. 20–6.

69. See A. Raskin, *Shalyapin i russkie khudozhniki* (Moscow-Leningrad: Iskusstvo, 1963), p. 103.

70. Sviridova, *Deni*, p. 37; Efimov agrees that Deni made a 'big mistake' in failing to understand that he could no longer work in *Bich* under such an editorship (*Rasskazy*, p. 20).

71. *My, nashi druz'ya i nashi vragi v risunkakh Deni* (Moscow-Leningrad: Gosizdat, 1930), p. 7.

72. Illustrated in Georg Piltz, *Russland wird rot. Satirische Plakate 1918–22* (Berlin: Eulenspiegel, 1977), plate 39.

73. Sviridova, *Deni*, p. 52; similarly A. Novikov, *Leniniana v plakate* (Moscow: Sovetskii khudozhnik, 1970), p. 9. Polonsky, *Russkii revolyutsionnyi plakat*, p. 14, describes it as by an 'unknown artist'. The poster was also reproduced as a postcard (Yu. Malinin, 'Leniniana V. N. Deni', *Iskusstvo*, 1985, no. 6, pp. 26–9, at p. 27).

74. *Pravda*, 3 June 1923, p. 8.

75. Ibid.

76. *Vsemirnaya illyustratsiya*, 1923, no. 10, p. 11.

77. Illustrated in Polonsky, *Russkii revolyutsionnyi plakat*, p. 50.

78. Sviridova, *Deni*, p. 74.

79. Illustrated in Polonsky, *Russkii revolyutsionnyi plakat*, p. 88.

80. Butnik-Siversky, *Sovetskii plakat*, lists 47; Sviridova, *Deni*, lists 45 for the period 1918–21 inclusive.

81. Sviridova, *Deni*; see further below, pp. 000–000.

82. Polonsky, 'Russkii revolyutsionnyi plakat', p. 69.

83. D. S. Moor, 'Moskovskie mastery satiry', *Iskusstvo*, 1938, no 2, pp. 1–28, at pp. 8–12.

84. *My, nashi druz'ya i nashi vragi*, pp. 7–8.

85. 'Pis'ma A. V. Lunacharskogo', 17 and 27 March 1920, *Novyi mir*, 1965, no. 4, pp. 244–6.

86. V. V. Shleev, ed., *V. I. Lenin i izobrazitel'noe iskusstvo: dokumenty, pis'ma, vospominaniya* (Moscow: Izobrazitel'noe iskusstvo, 1977), pp. 490–1, 513 n. 5.

87. Efimov, *Rasskazy*, pp. 26–7.

88. Dolgorukov, *Stranitsy*, pp. 29–32.

89. The following is based upon V. Matafonov, 'Revolyutsionnye plakaty N. M. Kochergina', *Iskusstvo*, 1972, no. 6, pp. 34–8, and upon the same author's much fuller account, *Nikolai Mikhailovich Kochergin* (Leningrad: Khudozhnik RSFSR, 1978).

90. Illustrated in L. V. Vladich, *Ukrain'skii politichnii plakat* (Kiev: Politvidav Ukraini, 1981), plates 10 and 9.

91. Matafonov, 'Revolyutsionnye plakaty', p. 36.

92. Polonsky, *Russkii revolyutsionnyi plakat*, p. 92.

93. Matafonov, *Kochergin*.

94. Polonsky, 'Russkii revolyutsonnyi plakat', p. 64.

95. Sidorov, 'Iskusstvo 1920-kh godov', p. 75.

Chapter Four

1. P. M. Kerzhentsev, *Gazeta: Organizatsiya i tekhnika gazetnogo dela*, 4th ed. (Moscow Leningrad: Gosizdat, 1925), p. 129. See also P. M. Kerzhentsev, 'Ros. T. A. Dva goda', *Krasnyi zhurnalist*, nos. 4–6 (30 December 1920), cols. 289–94.

2. *Deyateli SSSR i Oktyabr'skoi revolyutsii*, part 1 (Moscow: Granat, 1929), cols. 185–6.

3. Kerzhentsev, *Gazeta*, p. 129. Useful secondary accounts are available in N. A. Brylyakov, *Rossiiskoe telegrafnoe . . .* (Moscow: Mysl', 1976), and S. I. Stykalin, *Okna satiry ROSTA* (Moscow: Izdatel'stvo Moskovskogo universiteta, 1976), esp. pp. 12–16.

4. Kerzhentsev, *Gazeta*, pp. 129–33.

5. Viktor Duvakin, introduction to V. V. Mayakovsky, *Groznyi smekh. Okna satiry ROSTA* (Moscow-Leningrad: Iskusstvo, 1938), p. v.

6. V. Duvakin, *Radost', masterom kovannaya. Ocherki tvorchestva V. V. Mayakovskogo* (Moscow: Sovetskii pisatel', 1964), p. 151.

7. K. N. Suvorova, comp., *V. V. Mayakovsky. Opisanie dokumental'nykh materialov*, vyp. 1: '*Okna' ROSTA i Glavpolitprosveta, 1919–22* (Moscow: TsGALI, 1964), p. 7.

8. V. V. Mayakovsky, *Polnoe sobranie sochinenii*, 13 vols. (Moscow: Khudozhestvennaya literatura, 1955–61), vol. 12, p. 34.

9. M. M. Cheremnykh, 'Mayakovsky v ROSTA', *Iskusstvo*, 1940, no. 3, pp. 39–44, at p. 39; similarly Boris Zemenkov, *Udarnoe iskusstvo Okon satiry* (Moscow: Khudozhestvennoe izdatel'skoe aktsionernoe obshchestvo AKhR, 1930), p. 18, and Duvakin, *Radost'*, p. 151. It has been suggested by less authoritative sources that the first Rosta Window in fact appeared on Petrovka in central Moscow: see B. V. Veimarn, ed., *Istoriya iskusstva narodov SSSR*, vol. 7 (Moscow: Izobrazitel'noe iskusskva, 1972), p. 24, and I. E. Grabar' et al., eds., *Istoriya russkogo iskusstva*, 13 vols. (Moscow: Izdatel'stvo Akademii nauk SSSR, 1953–69), vol. 9, p. 71.

10. Suvorova, *Mayakovsky*, pp. 7–8; Duvakin, *Radost'*, p. 152.

11. Suvorova, *Mayakovsky*, p. 8.

12. Ibid.

13. Ibid., p. 9; Duvakin, *Radost'*, pp. 162–3.

14. 'Proshu slova' (1930), in Mayakovsky, *Polnoe sobranie sochinenii*, vol. 12, pp. 205–9.

15. Duvakin, *Radost'*, p. 169.

16. Suvorova, *Mayakovsky*, p. 10; N. M. Cheremnykh, *Khochetsya, chtoby znali i drugie* (Moscow: Sovetskii khudozhnik, 1965), p. 21.

17. Duvakin, *Radost'*, pp. 179–80; A. I. Eventov, *Mayakovsky – plakatist* (Moscow-Leningrad: Iskusstvo, 1940), p. 44.

18. Suvorova, *Mayakovsky*, p. 11; Samuel and Ann Charters, *I Love* (London: Deutsch, 1979), pp. 148, 161.

19. Suvorova, *Mayakovsky*, pp. 13–14.

20. Ibid., p. 4.
21. Duvakin, *Radost*, p. 153.
22. Ibid., pp. 165–6; Suvorova, *Mayakovsky*, p. 9.
23. Duvakin, *Radost'*, p. 152.
24. Ibid., p. 155.
25. Ibid., p. 152.
26. The fullest biographical account is provided by Cheremnykh's second wife, a poetess who collaborated with him in much of his work: see Cheremnykh, *Khochetsya*. Cheremnykh's personal file in the School of Painting, Sculpture and Architecture records his social status as 'gentry' (*dvoryan's*): see TsGALI, f. 680, op. 2, ed. khr. 2347.
27. Cheremnykh, *Khochetsya*, pp. 67.
28. Ibid., pp. 8–9.
29. Ibid., p.8; TsGALI, f. 680, op. 2, ed. khr. 2347.
30. O. Savostyuk and B. Uspensky, intr., *Mikhail Mikhailovich Cheremnykh* (Moscow: Sovetskii Khudozhnik, 1970), p. 5.
31. TsGALI, f. 680, op 2, ed. khr. 2347.
32. N. K. Verzhbitsky, *Zapiski starogo zhurnalista* (Moscow: Sovetskii pisatel', 1961), p. 181, which records a conversation with Cheremnykh in December 1918.
33. B. S. Butnik-Siversky, *Sovetskii plakat epokhi grazhdanskoi voiny 1918–21* (Moscow: Izdatel'stvo Vsesoyuznoi knizhnoi palaty, 1960), no. 202. Although not in this instance, Cheremnykh normally dated his posters 'I', 'II' and so forth, numbering them not from the birth of Christ but from the revolution (I. P. Abramsky, *Smekh sil'nykh. O khudozhikakh zhurnala 'Krokodil'* [Moscow: Iskusstvo, 1977], p. 48).
34. For other work of the same period see Butnik-Siversky, *Sovetskii plakat*, nos. 504, 627 and 1199.
35. M. Ioffe, *Mikhail Mikhailovich Cheremnykh* (Moscow-Leningrad: Iskusstvo, 1949), p. 5.
36. M. L. Ioffe, intr., *Mikhail Mikhailovich Cheremnykh* (Moscow-Leningrad: Sovetskii khudozhnik, 1950), unpaginated.
37. Ioffe, *Cheremnykh* (1949), p. 5.
38. Savostyuk and Uspensky, *Cheremnykh*, p. 14.
39. Abramsky, *Smekh sil'nykh*, p. 53.
40. Cheremnykh, *Khochetsya*, pp. 90, 97.
41. V. I. Kostin, comp., *Mikhail Mikhailovich Cheremnykh* (Moscow: Sovetskii khudozhnik, 1957). p. 8.
42. This illustration appears in O. Savostyuk and B. Uspensky, intr., *Mastera sovetskoi karikatury: M. Cheremnykh* (Moscow: Sovetskii khudozhnik, 1984), unpaginated.
43. Kostin, *Cheremnykh*, p. 8.
44. Cheremnykh, *Khochetsya*, p. 17.
45. This account follows Verzhbitsky, *Zapiski*, pp. 179–80, which is based upon a conversation with Cheremnykh in December 1918; Ioffe, *Cheremnykh* (1949), pp. 8–9; and Cheremnykh, *Khochetsya*, pp. 13–15. Somewhat different versions appear in V. V. Shleev, ed., *V. I. Lenin i izobrazitel'noe iskusstvo: dokumenty, pis'ma, vospominaniya* (Moscow: Izobrazitel'noe iskusstvo, 1977), pp. 222–8, and other sources.
46. L. D. Trotsky, *Moya zhizn'*, 2 vols. (Berlin: Granat, 1930), vol, 2, pp. 75–6.
47. Verzhbitsky, *Zapiski*, pp. 180–1. Lunacharsky reportedly suggested that the same operation should be carried out on the Peter and Paul fortress in Leningrad (Cheremnykh, *Khochetsya*, p. 15).
48. Cheremnykh, *Khochetsya*, p. 14. An historically unfounded account of this incident is given in N. F. Pogodin's play, *The Kremlin Chimes* (*Kremlevskie kuranty*), first performed in 1942.
49. B. Efimov, *Mne khochetsya rasskazat'* (Moscow: Sovetskii khudozhnik, 1970), p. 32.
50. Ibid., p. 29; a similar view is taken in Cheremnykh, *Khochetsya*, pp. 28–9.
51. B. Efimov, *Rasskazy o khudozhnikakh-satirikakh* (Moscow: Sovetskii khudozhnik, 1963), p. 35.
52. Abramsky, *Smekh sil'nykh*, p. 53.
53. Cheremnykh, *Khochetsya*, pp. 27, 36.
54. Ioffe, *Cheremnykh* (1949), p. 11; Duvakin, *Radost'*, p. 166.
55. Cheremnykh, *Khochetsya*, p. 21.
56. Ibid., pp. 27–8.
57. Wiktor Woroszylski, *The Life of Mayakovsky*, tr. Boleslaw Taborski (London: Gollancz, 1972), p. 262.
58. Cheremnykh, *Khochetsya*, p. 31; Vyacheslav Polonsky, *Russkii revolyutsionnyi plakat* (Moscow: Gosizdat, 1925), p. 100; Cheremnykh, 'Mayakovsky v ROSTA', p. 39 (on Malyutin).
59. I. N. Pavlov, *Moya zhizn' i vstrechi* (Moscow: Iskusstvo, 1949), p. 330.
60. Ibid.
61. Abramsky. *Smekh sil'nykh*, p. 57.
62. *Iskusstvo*, 1940, no. 3, pp. 45, 41.
63. Abramsky, *Smekh sil'nykh*, pp. 57–8.
64. Ibid.; Pavlov, *Moya zhizn'*, p. 323.
65. The fullest biographical account in English is Edward J. Brown, *Mayakovsky: a Poet in the Revolution* (Princeton, NJ: Princeton University Press, 1973); in Russian, V. Pertsov, *Mayakovsky: zhizn' i tvorchestvo*, new ed., 3 vols. (Moscow: Nauka, 1969–72) is comprehensive.
66. 'Ya sam' (1922, 1928), in Mayakovsky, *Polnoe sobranie sochinenii*, vol. 1, pp. 7–29, at p. 13.
67. Ibid., p. 8.
68. Ibid., p. 11.
69. Ibid., p. 14.
70. Ibid., p. 16; Brown, *Mayakovsky*, p. 46.
71. 'Ya sam', p. 22; Brown, *Mayakovsky*, p. 110.
72. Illustrated in Angelica Z. Rudenstine, ed., *The George Costakis Collection: Russian Avant-Garde Art* (London: Thames and Hudson, 1981), plate 958.
73. Text in Mayakovsky, *Polnoe sobranie sochinenii*, vol. 1, p. 359. All Mayakovsky's compositions of this kind are printed in ibid., pp. 355–60 (twenty-two items), together with the texts of thirty-two *lubki*-postcards (ibid., pp. 360–4). Some of this work is illustrated in V. A. Katanyan, comp., *Mayakovsky – khudozhnik* (Moscow: Izobrazitel'noe iskusstvo, 1963).
74. Brown, *Mayakovsky*, p. 146.
75. The fullest account of this period is E. A. Dinershtein, 'Mayakovsky v fevrale-oktyabre 1917g.', *Literaturnoe nasledstvo*, vol. 65 (Moscow: Nauka, 1968), pp. 541–76.
76. 'Ya sam', p. 25.
77. Z. S. Paperny, intr., *V. Mayakovsky v vospominaniyakh sovremennikov* (Moscow: Gosudarstvennoe izdatel'stvo khudozhestvennoi literatury, 1963), p. 151.
78. 'Ya sam', p. 25.
79. Ibid., pp. 25–6; 'Mystery-bouffe' in its original version is in Mayakovsky, *Polnoe sobranie sochinenii*, vol. 2, pp. 167–241.
80. Duvakin, *Radost'*, p. 132.
81. Mayakovsky, *Polnoe sobranie sochinenii*, vol. 12, pp. 8–9.
82. Ibid., vol. 2, pp. 89–91 (Heroes), 92–4 (Soviet alphabet). On the production and distribution of the 'Soviet alphabet' see Pertsov, *Mayakovsky*, vol. 2, pp. 124–6. The original is held in the Mayakovsky papers (TsGALI f. 336, op. 5, ed. khr. 92).
83. 'Tol'ko ne vospominaniya' (1972), in Mayakovsky, *Polnoe sobranie sochinenii*, vol. 12, pp. 149–58, at p. 153.
84. 'Ya sam', p. 26.
85. Eventov, *Mayakovsky – plakatist*, p. 25.
86. Cited from Soviet archives in D. S. Moor, *Ya – bol'shevik* (Moscow: Sovetskii khudozhnik, 1967), p. 139.
87. G. Demosfenova et al., *Sovetskii politicheskii plakat* (Moscow: Iskusstvo, 1962), pp. 19, 21, 23.
88. P. I. Lebedev, *Sovetskoe iskusstvo v period inostrannoi interventsii*

i grazhdanskoi voiny (Moscow-Leningrad: Iskusstvo, 1949), p. 96.

89. On Mayakovsky's poster work more generally see Eventov, *Mayakovsky – plakatist*; V. Duvakin, *ROSTA-Fenster. Majakowski als Dichter und bildender Künstler*, 2nd ed. (Dresden: Verlag der Kunst, 1975); and Georgii Sokolov, 'Vladimir Mayakovsky kak plakatist', *Iskusstvo*, 1983, no. 7, pp. 39–46.
90. Cheremnykh, 'Mayakovsky v ROSTA', p. 44.
91. See Butnik-Siversky, *Sovetskii plakat*, no. 1413, pp. 284–5.
92. A. V. Fevral'sky, *Vstrechi s Mayakovskim* (Moscow: Sovetskaya Rossiya, 1971), pp. 11–12.
93. Viktor Shklovsky, *Zhili-byli* (Moscow: Sovetskii pisatel', 1966), p. 364.
94. Ibid., pp. 365–6.
95. Duvakin, *Radost'*, p. 159.
96. Ibid., p. 158.
97. A. M. Nyurenberg, 'Mayakosky s khudozhnikami', *Iskusstvo*, 1940, no. 3, pp. 45–9, at p. 45.
98. Cheremnykh, 'Mayakovsky v ROSTA', p. 40.
99. Ibid. Mayakovsky himself recalled these races in his 'Tol'ko ne vospominaniya' and added that they had astonished foreign visitors such as John Reed (*Polnoe sobranie sochinenii*, vol. 12, p. 207).
100. Nyurenberg, 'Mayakovsky s khudozhnikami', p. 46–7.
101. Eventov, *Mayakovsky – plakatist*, pp.66.
102. Mayakovsky, *Polnoe sobranie sochinenii*, vol, 12, pp. 33–5 and 207–8.
103. Semenkov, *Udarnoe iskusstvo*, p. 74.
104. Roberta Reeder, 'The Interrelationship of Codes in Maiakovskii's ROSTA Posters', *Soviet Union*, vol. 7, parts 1 and 2 (1980), pp. 28–52, at p. 32.
105. Cheremnykh, 'Mayakovsky v ROSTA', p. 41 (Butnik-Siversky, *Sovetskii plakat*, p. 80, credits Nyurenberg).
106. Cheremnykh, 'Mayakovsky v ROSTA', p. 41.
107. Ibid.; Butnik-Siversky, *Sovetskii plakat*, p. 80.
108. Paperny, *Mayakovsky v vospominaniyakh*, pp. 256–7.
109. Mayakovsky, *Polnoe sobranie sochinenii*, vol. 12, p. 207.
110. Nyurenberg, 'Mayakovsky s khudozhnikami', p. 47.
111. Charters, *I Love*, p. 150.
112. Cheremnykh, *Khochetsya*, pp. 29–30.
113. Verzhbitsky, *Zapiski*, pp. 161–2.
114. Fevral'sky, *Vstrechi*, p. 11.
115. P. M. Kerzhentsev, intr., *Vystavka 'Okna satiry ROSTA'* (Moscow: Gosudarstvennaya Tret'yakovskaya galereya, 1929), p. 4.
116. Cheremnykh, 'Mayakovsky v ROSTA', p. 39.
117. Fevral'sky, *Vstrechi*, pp. 14–15.
118. L. V. Mayakovskaya and A. I. Koloskov, eds., *Mayakovsky v vospominaniyakh rodnykh i druzei* (Moscow: Moskovskii rabochii, 1968), p. 46.
119. Fevral'sky, *Vstrechi*, p. 12.
120. Nyurenberg, 'Mayakovsky s khudozhnikami', pp.47–8.
121. Fevral'sky, *Vstrechi*, p. 14; Pertsov, *Mayakovsky*, vol. 2. p. 149. Mayakovsky intervened personally to save Cheremnykh from a charge of 'futurism': see Woroszylski, *Life of Mayakovsky*, p. 262.
122. Cheremnykh, 'Mayakovsky v ROSTA', p. 40.
123. Butnik-Siversky, *Sovetskii plakat*; Stykalin, *Okna satiry ROSTA*, pp. 34–5.
124. Stykalin, *Okna satiry ROSTA*, provides a recent survey.
125. Ibid., p. 27.
126. Ibid., p. 28. On Brodaty see M. Ioffe, *Desyat' ocherkov o khudozhnikakh-satirikakh* (Moscow: Sovetskii khudozhnik, 1971), pp. 86–121.
127. Radakov, according to his autobiographical account, was born the son of a doctor (a member of the *melkoe dvoryan'stvo*) in

1877. He attended the School of Painting, Sculpture and Architecture in Moscow, and before the revolution worked as a caricature artist, a journalist, a theatre organiser, set designer and art teacher. After the revolution he directed the art section of the children's department of Gosizdat in Leningrad; he also took part in the festive decoration in 1918, and later worked in theatre design and journal caricature as well as posters (TsGALI, f. 2041, op 1, ed. khr. 166). Polonsky noted that he was similar to Deni in the 'painterly qualities' of his work but that he lagged behind him in his political sense, and his work (mostly on cultural-education themes) tended to lack 'revolutionary sharpness' (*Russkii revolyutsionnyi plakat*, pp. 88–91). According to *'Okna ROSTA' perioda grazhdanskoi voiny i interventsii v sobranii GPB im. Saltykova-Shchedrina. Katalog* (Leningrad: GPB, 1961), p. 3, he was not a contributor; a fuller inventory indicates that he contributed 'episodically' (*Petrogradskie 'Okna ROSTA'. Svodnyi katalog* [Leningrad: GPB, 1964], p. 11).
128. *'Okna ROSTA' perioda grazhdanskoi voiny*, p. 3.
129. Abramsky, *Smekh sil'nykh*, p. 74.
130. Stykalin, *Okna satiry ROSTA*, p. 28.
131. *Petrogradskie 'Okna ROSTA'*, p. 12; E. Gollerbakh, *Istoriya gravyury i litografii v Rossii* (Moscow-Petrograd: Gosizdat, 1923), p. 107.
132. *Petrogradskie 'Okna ROSTA'. Katalog vystavki* (Leningrad: GPB, 1968), p. 6.
133. Ibid., p. 7.
134. A. V. Chistyakova, 'Petrogradskie "Okna Posta". (Novye materialy)', in *Soobshcheniya Gosudarstvennogo Russkogo Muzeya*, vol. 9 (1968), pp. 13–19, at p. 14.
135. *Okna ROSTA perioda grazhdanskoi voiny*, p. 46.
136. Abramsky, *Smekh sil'nykh*, p. 74.
137. Chistyakova, 'Petrogradskie "Okna ROSTA"', p. 19.
138. Pertsov, *Mayakovsky*, vol. 2, p. 150.
139. Moor, *Ya – bol'shevik*, p. 41.
140. Polonsky, *Russkii revolyutsionnyi plakat*, pp. 102–6.
141. Lev Brodaty, 'Stenogramma komissii po izucheniyu plakata v Gosudarstvennoi Akademii iskusstvovedeniya' (1931), TsGALI, f. 1988, op. 1, ed khr. 31.
142. Ibid.
143. The fullest biography is V. Petrov, *Vladimir Vasil'evich Lebedev 1891–67* (Leningrad: Khudozhnik RSFSR, 1972). See also N. N. Punin, *Russkii plakat 1917–22. Vyp. 1, V. V. Lebedev* (Petrograd: Strelets, 1922), which includes 23 colour illustrations (English and French translations were issued the following year).
144. Petrov, *Lebedev* (for his retrospective assessment of his own work, see p. 248). Lebedev's later career is considered further in Chapter 6, pp. 123–8.
145. Several good background studies are available, including Larissa A. Zhadova, *Malevich: Suprematism and Revolution in Russian Art 1910–30* (London: Thames and Hudson, 1982); Christina Lodder, *Russian Constructivism* (New Haven and London: Yale University Press, 1983); Camilla Gray, *The Russian Experiment in Art, 1863–22*, rev. ed. (London: Thames and Hudson, 1986); and Alan Bird, *A History of Russian Painting* (Oxford: Phaidon, 1987).
146. Sidney Alexander, *Marc Chagall: A Biography* (New York: Putnam, 1978), p. 188.
147. The adapted version is illustrated in Mikhail Guerman, ed., *Art of the October Revolution* (London: Collet's, 1979), plate 62. Other examples of work of this kind are illustrated in Rudenstine, *George Costakis Collection*, plates 972 and 973.
148. Marc Chagall, *Ma vie* (Paris: Stock, 1957), pp. 194–200.
149. Ibid., p. 196.
150. Paperny, *Mayakovsky v vospominaniyakh*, pp. 279–80.

151. *Zhurnalist,* 1968, no. 5, p. 50.
152. A representative selection of this work is in Zhadova, *Malevich,* plates 146–85. A decorated tramcar appears in A. Gushchin, *Oformlenie massovykh prazdnestv za 15 let diktatury proletariata* (Moscow: Ogiz-Izogiz, 1932), p.10; a propaganda board is shown in Sophie Lissitzky-Küppers, *El Lissitzky. Maler. Architekt. Typograf. Fotograf,* 2nd ed. (Dresden: Verlag der Kunst, 1976), plate 42. Butnik-Siversky, *Sovetskii plakat,* lists only eleven Vitebsk posters; Brylyakov, *Rossiiskoe telegrafnoe . . . ,* p. 46, gives a total of thirty.
153. See F. Shaposhnikov, 'Agitatsionnaya grafika YugROSTA', *Iskusstvo,* 1959, no. 1, pp. 66–71, and Vitalii Abramov, 'Khudozhniki YugROSTA', *Obrazotvorche Mistetstvo,* 1979, no. 5, pp. 27–9 (which makes some use of local archives).
154. Boris Efimov, *Sorok let. Zapiski khudozhnika-satirista* (Moscow: Sovetskii khudozhnik, 1961), p. 59.
155. Shaposhnikov, 'Agitsionnaya grafika', pp. 67–8; Brylyakov, *Rossiiskoe telegrafnoe . . . ,* p. 115; Butnik-Siversky, *Sovetskii plakat,* p. 89.
156. Efimov, *Sorok let,* p. 60.
157. Ibid., pp. 60, 63–5. Efimov's own work is considered in M. Ioffe, *Desyat' ocherkov,* pp. 64ff.; a representative selection is in *Mastera sovetskoi karikatury: Boris Efimov* (Moscow: Sovetskii khudozhnik, 1985).
158. Stykalin, *Okna satiry ROSTA,* p. 31; Butnik-Siversky, *Sovetskii plakat,* p. 89.

Chapter Five

1. S. S. Khromov, ed., *Grazhdanskaya voina i voennaya interventsiya v SSSR. Entsiklopediya* (Moscow: Sovetskaya entsiklopediya, 1983), p. 459 (total); B. S. Butnik-Siversky, *Sovetskii plakat epokhi grazhdanskoi voiny 1918–21* (Moscow: Izdatel'stvo Vsesoyuznoi knizhnoi palaty, 1960), p. 23 (proportions).
2. Butnik-Siversky, *Sovetskii plakat,* p. 23
3. 'Proshu slova' (1930), in V. V. Mayakovsky, *Polnoe sobranie sochinenii,* 13 vols. (Moscow: Khudozhestvennaya literatura, 1955–61), vol. 12, p. 205.
4. Butnik-Siversky, *Sovetskii plakat,* p. 44.
5. Ibid., p. 46.
6. Illustrated in I. E. Grabar' et al., eds., *Istoriya russkogo iskusstva,* 13 vols. (Moscow: Izdatel'stvo Akademii nauk SSSR, 1952–69), vol. 11, part 1, p. 279.
7. Butnik-Siversky, *Sovetskii plakat,* p. 53.
8. Ibid., p. 55.
9. See above, Plates 3.29, 1.19, 3.30 and 1.13.
10. Vyach. Polonsky, *Russkii revolyutsionnyi plakat* (Moscow: Gosizdat, 1925), p. 41; Butnik-Siversky, *Sovetskii plakat,* nos. 950–2, p. 240.
11. Illustrated in I. A. Sviridova, *Viktor Nikolaevich Deni* (Moscow: Izobrazitel'noe iskussto, 1978), p. 59.
12. One of the very few recent references to this poster, which at the time was very influential, is in Boris Efimov, *Na moi vzglyad* (Moscow: Iskusstvo, 1987), p. 24. It is not listed in Butnik-Siversky, *Sovetskii plakat,* and is not mentioned in any of the Soviet biographical studies of Moor. Some 25,000 copies were printed, according to Gosizdat archives (TsGAOR, f. 395, op. 1, ed. khr. 147).
13. Butnik-Siversky, *Sovetskii plakat,* no. 961, p. 241.
14. V. Duvakin, *Radost', masterom kovannaya. Ocherki tvorchestva V. V. Mayakovskogo* (Moscow: Sovetskii pisatel', 1964), p. 192.
15. Polonsky, *Russkii revolyutsionhyi plakat,* opposite p. 48.
16. Butnik-Siversky, *Sovetskii plakat,* p. 485.
17. A full account of Mayakovsky and Cheremnykh's work in this idiom is available in E. A. Dinershtein, 'Plakaty V. Mayakovskogo i M. Cheremnykha', *Iskusstvo,* 1960, no. 4, pp. 65–71.
18. Alfons Goldschmidt, *Moskau 1920* (Berlin: Rowohlt, 1920), p. 57.
19. H. N. Brailsford, *The Russian Workers' Republic* (London: Allen and Unwin, 1921), pp. 11, 40.
20. Colonel C. I'E. Malone, *The Russian Republic* (London: Allen and Unwin, 1920), pp. 23–4.
21. Albert Rhys Williams, *Through the Russian Revolution* (London: Labour Publishing Company, 1923), p. 5 (the book was itself richly illustrated with the posters of the period).
22. Theodore Dreiser, *Dreiser looks at Russia* (London: Constable, 1928), p.90.
23. Valentin Kataev, *Sobranie sochinenii v devyati tomakh,* vols. 8 (Moscow: Khudozhestvennaya literatura, 1971), p. 22.
24. Il'ya Erenburg, *Sobranie sochinenii v devyati tomakh,* vol. 8 (Moscow: Khudozhestvennaya literatura, 1966), p. 264.
25. Alexander Barmine, *One who Survived* (New York: Putnam, 1945), p. 38.
26. Alexander Blok, *The Twelve and Other Poems,* tr. Jon Stallworthy and Peter France (London: Eyre and Spottiswoode, 1971), p. 141.
27. Quoted in S. Raevsky, *Plakat A. Strakhova* (Kharkov: Mistetstvo, 1936), p. 14.
28. Duvakin, *Radost',* p. 155.
29. See below, pp. 81, 89.
30. O. Leonidov, 'Voennoe izdatel'stvo za pyat' let', *Politrabotnik,* no. 10–11 (October–November 1921), p. 61. Slightly different figures are given below, p. 109.
31. *Gosudarstvennoe izdatel'stvo RSFSR* (Moscow-Leningrad: Giz, 1925), p. 11.
32. A. I. Nazarov, *Oktyabr' i kniga* (Moscow: Nauka, 1968), p. 197.
33. *Gosudarstvennoe izdatel'stvo v 1922g.* (Moscow-Petrograd: Gosizdat, 'na pravakh rukopisi', 1922), p. 80.
34. *Otchet o deyatel'nosti na 1-oe dekabrya 1920g.* (Moscow: Gosudarstvennoe izdatel'stvo, 1920), p. 8.
35. B. Zemenkov, 'Karikatura v sovetskoi obshchestvennosti', *Sovetskoe iskusstvo,* 1925, no. 6, pp. 66–70, at p. 66.
36. Vyach. Polonsky, 'Russkii revolyutsionnyi plakat', *Pechat' i revolyutsiya,* 1922, no. 5, p. 61.
37. N. Denisovsky, 'Vstrechi s Mayakovskim', *Iskusstvo,* 1940, no, 3, pp. 56–9, at p. 59.
38. Butnik-Siversky, *Sovetskii plakat,* pp. 19 and 572-6 (list of places); a further number cannot be identified by place of origin.
39. *Pravda,* 8 September 1921, p. 1.
40. Mayakovsky, *Polnoe sobranie sochinenii,* vol. 12, pp. 240–1. Lenin's article 'O kharaktere nashikh gazet' (20 September 1918) is in V. I. Lenin, *Polnoe sobranie sochinenii,* 55 vols. (Moscow: Politizdat, 1958–65), vol. 37, pp. 89–91.
41. Polonsky's concern was expressed in *Pechat' i revolyutsiya,* kn. 1 (May-July 1921), p. 14; for Kerzhentsev, see *Krasnyi zhurnalist,* no. 4–6 (30 December 1920), cols. 295–8.
42. Karl Marx and Friedrich Engels, *Sochineniya,* 2nd ed., vol.6 (Moscow: Gospolitizdat, 1957), p. 478.
43. Lenin, *Polnoe sobranie sochinenii,* vol. 34, pp. 255–6.
44. L. D. Trotsky, *Sochineniya,* seriya 6, vol. 21 (Moscow: Giz, 1927), p. 242.
45. *Pravda,* 6 October 1918, cited in Sviridova, *Deni,* p. 46.
46. Boris Efimov, *Rasskazy starogo moskvicha* (Moscow: Moskovskii rabochii, 1981), pp. 40–1.
47. René Fülöp-Miller, *The Mind and Face of Bolshevism* (London and New York: Putnam's, 1927), p. 157.
48. Erenburg, *Sobranie sochinenii,* vol. 8, p. 264.
49. Arthur Ransome, *Russia in 1919* (New York: Huebsch, 1919), pp. 95–6.

50. Blok, *The Twelve and Other Poems,* p. 141.
51. See for instance Boris Efimov, *Sorok let. Zapiski khudozhnika-satirista* (Moscow: Sovetskii khudozhnik, 1961), p. 40.
52. *Vechernye izvestiya,* 1 March 1919, cited in *Graficheskoe iskusstvo v SSSR 1917–27* (Leningrad: Gosizdat, 1927), pp. 157–8.
53. E. A. Speranskaya, ed., *Agitatsionno-massovoe iskusstvo pervykh let Oktyabrya: materialy i issledovaniya* (Moscow: Iskusstvo, 1971), p. 37.
54. V. Astrov, 'Ob agitplakate. (Pis'mo iz Smolenska)', *Pechat' i revolyutsiya,* kn. 1 (1921), p. 190.
55. A. A. Sidorov, 'Dva goda russkogo iskusstva i khudozhestvennoi deyatel'nosti', *Tvorchestvo,* no. 10–11 (October-November 1919), pp. 38–45, at p. 42.
56. Beverly Whitney Kean, *All the Empty Palaces* (London: Barrie and Jenkins, 1983), p. 258.
57. Fülöp-Miller, *Mind and Face,* p. 95.
58. Sidney Alexander, *Marc Chagall: A Biography* (New York: Putnam, 1978), p. 191; *Iskusstvo kommuny,* no. 2 (15 December 1918), cited in Edward J. Brown, *Mayakovsky: a Poet in the Revolution* (Princeton, NJ: Princeton University Press, 1973), p. 194.
59. Marc Chagall, *Ma vie* (Paris: Stock, 1957), p. 196.
60. Sidorov, 'Dva goda', p. 39.
61. Polonsky, *Russkii revolyutsionnyi plakat,* pp. 50–1.
62. Chagall, *Ma vie,* p. 197.
63. Tamara Deutscher, *Not by Politics Alone* (London: Allen and Unwin, 1973), p. 202; the two revolutionaries were also known as the 'bearded bathers': see I. Matsa, ed., *Sovetskoe iskusstvo za 15 let. Materialy i dokumentatsiya* (Moscow-Leningrad: Ogiz-Izogiz, 1933), p. 224.
64. Ransome, *Russia in 1919,* pp. 15–16 (the statue is no longer extant).
65. Matsa, *Sovetskoe iskusstvo,* p. 224.
66. Ibid., pp. 224, 222.
67. Fülöp-Miller, *Mind and Face,* p. 91.
68. Speranskaya, *Agitatsionno-massovoe iskusstvo,* p. 88.
69. Arthur Ransome, *The Crisis in Russia* (London: Allen and Unwin, 1921), pp. 82–4.
70. S. Drobashenko, ed., *Dziga Vertov. Stat'i, dnevniki, zamysli* (Moscow: Iskusstvo, 1966), p. 89.
71. M. M. Cheremnykh, 'Mayakovsky v ROSTA', *Iskusstvo,* 1940, no. 3, p. 39.
72. 'Revolyutsionnyi plakat' (1923), in Mayakovsky, *Polnoe sobranie sochinenii,* vol. 12, p. 34.
73. Boris Zemenkov, *Udarnoe iskusstvo Okon satiry* (Moscow: Khudozhestvennoe izdatel'skoe aktsionernoe obshchestvo AKhR, 1930), pp. 18, 19.
74. P. M. Kerzhentsev, intr., *Vystavka 'Okna satiry ROSTA'* (Moscow: Gosudarstvennaya Tret'yakovskaya gallereya, 1929), p. 4.
75. Lev Brodaty, 'Stenogramma komissii po izucheniyu plakata' (1931), f. 1988, op. 1, ed. khr. 31.
76. A. G. Budrina, comp., *Ural'skii plakat vremen grazhdanskoi voiny* (Perm': Permskoe knizhnoe izdatel'stvo, 1968), p. 23.
77. F. Shaposhnikov, 'Agitatsionnaya grafika YugROSTA', *Iskusstvo,* 1959, no. 1, pp. 67–71, at p. 71.
78. *Krasnyi zhurnalist,* no. 7–9 (1 July 1921), col. 544.
79. F. Roginskaya, 'Deni', *Krasnaya niva,* no. 22 (28 May 1928), p. 10.
80. Soviet archives, cited in V. M. Shcherbak, *Bol'shevistskaya agitatsiya i propaganda (okt. 1917 – mart 1919)* (Moscow: Vysshaya shkola, 1969), p. 134.
81. Sviridova, *Deni,* p. 55 (Plate 5.11).
82. Nikolai Dolgorukov, *Stranitsy zhizni* (Leningrad: Khudozhnik RSFSR, 1963), p. 21.
83. *Yubileinaya vystavka proizvedenii Dmitriya Stakhievicha Moora* (Moscow: Gosudarstvennaya Tret'yakovskaya gallereya, 1936), p. 17.
84. V. Okhochinsky, *Plakat: razvitie i primenenie* (Leningrad: Izdatel'stvo Akademii khudozhestv, 1926), p. 91.
85. Polonsky, *Russkii revolyutsionnyi plakat,* p. 68.
86. *Putevoditel' po vystavke "Plakat i listovka grazhdanskoi voiny"* (Moscow: Musei revolyutsii RKKA, 1926), p. 10.
87. Erenburg, *Sobranie sochinenii,* vol. 8, p. 299; similarly Lev Kopelev, *The Education of a True Believer* (London: Wildwood House, 1981), p. 7.
88. Aleksandr Drozdov, 'Intelligentsiya na Donu', *Arkhiv russkoi revolyutsii,* vol. 2 (1922), pp. 45–58, at p. 53.
89. S. Dobrovol'sky, 'Bor'ba za vozrozhdenie Rossii v severnoi oblasti', *Arkhiv russkoi revolyutsii,* vol. 3 (1921), pp. 5–146, at p. 78.
90. Polonsky, *Russkii revolyutsionnyi plakat,* p. 76.
91. 'Revolyutsionnyi plakat', in Mayakovsky, *Polnoe sobranie sochinenii,* vol. 12, p. 33.
92. *Otchet o deyatel'nosti na 1-oe dekabrya 1920g.,* pp. 21, 13.
93. *Krasnyi zhurnalist,* no. 7–9 (1 July 1921), cols. 533, 477.
94. G. Demosfenova et al., *Sovetskii politicheskii plakat* (Moscow: Iskusstvo, 1962), p. 29.
95. Polonsky, 'Russkii revolyutsionnyi plakat', p. 61.
96. *Kniga i revolyutsiya,* no. 5(17) (1922), p. 68. A rather better review of Moor's *Red Armyman Laughs (Krasnoarmeets smeetsya),* produced for Litizdat the folowing year, appeared in *Kniga i revolyutsiya,* no. 4 (16) (1922), p. 70.
97. Lenin, *Polnoe sobranie sochinenii,* vol. 43, p. 130.
98. 'Obzor agitatsionnogo materiala s mest', *Vestnik agitatsii i propagandy,* no. 1 (21 September 1920), p. 11.
99. 'Plakat o sdache khlebnykh izlishkov', ibid., no. 3 (25 November 1920), p. 28.
100. L. Sosnovsky, 'Plakatnaya agitatsiya', ibid., no. 4 (25 December 1920), p. 17–18.
101. Ibid., p. 18.
102. *Otchet o deyatel'nosti na 1-oe dekabrya 1920g.,* p. 25.
103. *Krasnyi zhurnalist,* no. 7–9 (1 July 1921), col 533.
104. A. M. Rodchenko, *Stat'i. Vospominaniya. Avtobiograficheskie zapiski. Pis'ma* (Moscow: Sovetskii khudozhnik, 1982), p. 57.
105. Wassily Kandinsky, *Complete Writings on Art,* 2 vols. (London: Faber, 1982), vol. 1, p. 477.
106. *Sovetskie pisateli. Avtobiografii,* vol. 3 (Moscow: Gosudarstvennoe izdatel'stvo khudozhestvennoi literatury 1959), p. 35.
107. V. S. Matafonov, *Nikolai Mikhailovich Kochergin* (Leningrad: Khudozhnik RSFSR, 1978), p. 8.
108. Viktor Shklovsky, *Zhili-byli* (Moscow: Sovetskii pisatel', 1966), p. 365.
109. Vladimir Mayakovsky, *Love is the Heart of Everything,* ed. Bengt Jangfeldt (Edinburgh: Polygon, 1986), p. 17.

Chapter Six

1. K. G., 'Eshche o plakatnoi propagande, *Vestnik agitatsii i propagandy,* no. 5–6 (5 February 1921), p. 66.
2. Quoted in F. Senyushkin, 'Formy i metody proizvodstvennoi propagandy', ibid., no. 9–10 (18 April 1921), p. 61.
3. V. V. Mayakovsky, *Polnoe sobranie sochinenii,* 13 vols. (Moscow: Khudozhestvennaya literatura, 1955–61), vol. 12, p. 455.
4. F. R., 'Politicheskii plakat', *Krasnaya niva,* no. 52 (22 December 1929), p. 13.
5. Ya. Tukhendkhol'd, 'Sovremennyi plakat', *Pechat' i revolyutsiya,* kn. 8 (1926), pp. 56–74, at pp. 56–60.
6. D. S. Moor and R. S. Kaufman, 'Sovetskii politicheskii plakat, 1917–33', in Moor, *Ya – bol'shevik* (Moscow: Sovetskii khudozhnik, 1967), p. 30.

7. B. S. Butnik-Siversky, *Sovetskii plakat epokhi grazhdanskoi voiny 1918–21* (Moscow: Izdatel'stvo Vsesoyuznoi knizhnoi palaty, 1960), p. 6.

8. V. Koretsky, *Zametki plakatista* (Moscow: Sovetskii khudozhnik, 1958), p. 45.

9. 'Plakat', in *Gazetnyi i knizhnyi mir*, 2 vols. (Moscow: Ekonomicheskaya zhizn', 1926), vyp. 2, p. 325.

10. V. Okhochinsky, *Plakat: razvitie i primenenie* (Leningrad: Izdatel'stvo Akademii khudozhestv, 1926), p. 85, and in *Graficheskoe iskusstvo v SSSR 1917–27* (Leningrad: Gosizdat, 1927), p. 161.

11. *Krasnaya niva,* no. 8 (23 February 1923), p. 30.

12. R. Raevsky, *Plakat A. Strakhova* (Kharkov: Mistetstvo, 1936), pp. 24–5. Strakhov (1896–79) was born in Ekaterinoslav; his real name was Breslavsky, but he used the pseudonym Strakhov from 1919 onwards (ibid., p. 15).

13. G. Demosfenova et al., *Sovetskii politicheskii plakat* (Moscow: Iskusstvo, 1962), p. 77. Klutsis modestly described himself as the 'founder' of Soviet photomontage in his article 'Fotomontazh' in O. Yu. Shmidt et al., eds., *Bol'shaya sovetskaya entsikopediya*, 65 vols. (Moscow: Sovetskaya entsiklopediya, 1926–48), vol. 58, pp. 322–3. Klutsis' poster work is discussed in L. Yu. Oginskaya, *Gustav Klustsis* (Moscow: Sovetskii khudozhnik, 1981), pp. 100–34. On photomontage more generally, see Aleksandr Zhitomirsky, *Iskusstvo politicheskogo fotomontazha* (Moscow: Plakat, 1983) and Dawn Ades, *Photomontage*, rev. ed. (London: Thames and Hudson, 1986).

14. El Lissitzky's work in this idiom is recorded in Sophie Lissitzky-Küppers, *El Lissitsky. Maler. Architekt. Typograf. Fotograf*, 2nd ed. (Dresden: Verlag der Kunst, 1976), plates 64–188. On Rodchenko, see German Karginov, *Rodchenko* (London: Thames and Hudson, 1979), pp. 121–65, and S. O. Khan-Magomedov, *Rodchenko* (London: Thames and Hudson, 1986).

15. I. E. Grabar' et al., eds., *Istoriya russkogo iskusstva,* vol. 13 (Moscow: Isdatel'stvo Akademii nauk SSSR, 1964), p. 20.

16. Ibid., p. 26.

17. Illustrated in I. A. Sviridova, *Viktor Nikolaevich Deni* (Moscow: Izobrazitel'noe iskusstvo, 1978), pp. 153, 156.

18. V. I. Kostin, comp., *Mikhail Mikhailovich Cheremnykh* (Moscow: Sovetskii khudozhnik, 1957), p. 20; V. Petrov, *Vladimir Vladimirovich Lebedev 1891–67* (Leningrad: Khudozhnik RSFSR, 1972), p. 216.

19. On the Kukryniksy, see M. Ioffe, *Desyat' ocherkov o khudozhnikakh-satirikakh* (Moscow: Sovetskii khudozhnik, 1971), pp. 218–49. Their work is very fully represented in V. S. Kemenov et al., eds., *Kukryniksy. Sobranie proizvedenii v 4-kh tomakh* (Moscow: Izobrazitel'noe iskusstvo, 1982 –).

20. *Istoriya russkogo iskusstva,* vol. 13, p. 20.

21. Ibid., pp. 48–54.

22. Ibid., pp. 56–62. Soviet poster art of the Second World War period is well represented in several collections, among them *Sovetskie plakatisty – frontu* (Moscow: Iskusstvo, 1985).

23. 'Russkii revolyutsionnyi plakat', *Pechat' i revolyutsiya*, 1922, no. 5, p. 72.

24. Vyach. Polonsky, *Russkii revolyutsionnyi plakat* (Moscow: Gosizdat, 1925), p. 41; M. F. Savelev, 'Sovetskii politicheski plakat 1917–20 godov', in *Ocherki po russkomu i sovetskomu iskusstvu. Sbornik statei* (Moscow: Sovetskii khudozhnik, 1965), p. 29. See also above, pp. 46–8.

25. 'Russkii revolyutsionnyi plakat', p. 64; *Russkii revolyutsionnyi plakat*, p. 49.

26. F. Shaposhnikov, 'Agitatsionnaya grafika "YugROSTA"', *Iskusstvo*, 1959, no. 1, p. 67.

27. M. M. Cheremnykh, 'Mayakovsky v ROSTA', *Iskusstvo*, 1940, no. 3, p. 39.

28. Z. S. Paperny, intr., *Mayakovsky v vospominaniyakh sovremennikov* (Moscow: Gosudarstvennoe izdatel'stvo khudozhestvennoi literatury, 1963), p. 245.

29. *Otchet o deyatel'nosti na 1-e dekabrya 1920g.* (Moscow: Gosizdat, 1920), pp. 19, 14.

30. A. Fevral'sky, *Vstrechi s Mayakovskim* (Moscow: Sovetskaya Rossiya, 1971), pp. 26–7.

31. *Agitatsionno-propagandistskaya rabota Glavpolitprosveta* (Moscow: Glavpolitprosvet, 1923), p. 34. On Glavpolitprosvet more generally, see M. B. Keirim-Markus, *Gosudarstvennoe rukovodstvo kul'turoi. Stroitel'stvo Narkomprosa (noyabr' 1917 – seredina 1918g.)* (Moscow: Nauka, 1980); L. F. Morozov, 'Glavpolitprosvet: organ ideologicheskoi raboty v massakh (1920–30 gg.)', *Voprosy istorii KPSS*, 1984, no. 11, pp. 43–56; and A. I. Fomin, 'Razvitie gosudarstvennogo apparata Narodnogo Prosveshcheniya v pervye gody sovetskoi vlasti', *Voprosy istorii*, 1984, no. 12, pp. 3–15.

32. *Otchet o deyatel'nosti Otdela voennoi literatury pri RVSR i Vysshego voennogo redaktsionnogo soveta s 1 yan. 1921g. po 31 dek. 1922g.* (Moscow: Vysshii voennyi redaktsionnyi sovet, 1923), pp. 6–7.

33. Ibid., pp. 14, 16, 20, 233.

34. B. S. Zemenkov, *Udarnoe iskusstvo Okon satiry* (Moscow: Khudozhestvennoe aktsionernoe obshchestvo AKhR, 1930), p. 24.

35. H. G. Wells, *Russia in the Shadows* (London: Hodder and Stoughton, 1921), p. 13.

36. Colonel C. l'E. Malone, *The Russian Republic* (London: Allen and Unwin, 1920), p. 23; H. N. Brailsford, *The Russian Workers' Republic* (London: Allen and Unwin, 1921), p. 24.

37. Alfons Goldschmidt, *Moskau 1920* (Berlin: Rowohlt, 1920), p. 30.

38. Cited in A. A. Sbitneva, 'Izdatel'skaya deyatel'nost' v Krasnoi Armii (1918–20gg.)', *Vestnik Moskovskogo Universiteta: Zhurnalistika*, 1978, no. 6, pp. 27–36, at p. 32.

39. Koretsky. *Zametki plakatista*, p. 24.

40. 'Stenogramma komissii po izucheniyu plakata v Gosudarstvennoi Akademii iskusstvovedeniya' (1931), TsGALI, f. 1988, op. 1, ed. khr. 31.

41. 'Tol'ko ne vospominaniya' (1927) in Mayakovsky, *Polnoe sobranie sochinenii*, vol. 12, p. 153.

42. Ibid., p. 35.

43. Tukhendkhol'd, 'Sovremennyi plakat', pp. 64, 69. A good selection of work of this kind is contained in V. Lyakhov, intr., *Sovetskii reklamnyi plakat 1917–33* (Moscow: Sovetskii khudozhnik,. 1972).

44. Boris Efimov, *Sorok let. Zapiski khudozhnika-satirista* (Moscow: Sovetskii khudozhnik, 1961), p. 70.

45. I. P. Abramsky, *Smekh sil'nykh. O khudozhnikakh zhurnala 'Krokodil'* (Moscow: Iskusstvo, 1977), p. 7.

46. Tukhendkhol'd, 'Sovremennyi plakat', p. 60.

47. Vahan D. Barooshian, *Russian Cubo-Futurism 1910–30* (The Hague: Mouton, 1974), ch. 7, esp. p. 116; similarly S. A. Fedyukin, 'Khudozhestvennaya intelligentsiya v pervye gody sovetskoi vlasti', *Voprosy istorii*, 1969, no. 1, pp. 8–26, at p. 9.

48. See Sheila Fitzpatrick, *The Commissariat of Enlightenment* (Cambridge: Cambridge University Press, 1970).

49. *Sovetskaya pechat' v dokumentakh* (Moscow: Gospolitizdat, 1961), pp. 253–4.

50. See the draft declaration in TsGALI, f. 1988, op. 1, ed. khr. 33.

51. *KPSS v rezolyutsiyakh i resheniyakh s"ezdov, konferentsii i plenumov TsK*, 9th ed., vol. 5 (Moscow: Politizdat, 1984), pp. 407–8.

52. I. Vaisfel'd and A. Mikhailov, eds., *Plakatno–kartiinaya agitatsiya na putyakh perestroiki* (Moscow-Leningrad: Izogiz, 1932), p. 3.

53. Alan Bird, *A History of Russian Painting* (Oxford: Phaidon, 1987), p. 266.
54. Ibid., p. 249.
55. David Karshan, *Malevich: the Graphic Work 1913–30* (Jerusalem: Israel Museum, 1975), p. 18; A. B. Nakov, intr., *Kasimir Malevich* (London: Tate Gallery, 1976), p. 9.
56. Petrov, *Lebedev*, p. 190; *Pravda*, 1 March 1936. p. 3.
57. K. F. Yuon et al., eds., *Tridtsat' let sovetskogo izobrazitel'nogo iskusstva* (Moscow: Iskusstvo, 1948), p. 153; *Iskusstvo*, 1950, no. 1, p. 77.
58. Yuon, *Tridtsat' let,* p. 153.
59. See respectively M. Ioffe, *Viktor Nikolaevich Deni* (Moscow: Iskusstvo, 1947), opposite p. 20; A. Kozlov, *Viktor Nikolaevich Deni* (Moscow-Leningrad: Sovetskii khudozhnik, 1950), unpaginated; and Sviridova, *Deni*, p. 139.
60. Ioffe, *Deni*, p. 25, and 'Shagayut k gibeli svoei' (1937), illustrated in ibid., opposite p. 21.
61. V. S. Matafonov, *Nikolai Mikhailovich Kochergin* (Leningrad: Khudozhnik RSFSR, 1978), p. 41.
62. TsGALI, f. 2041, op. 1, ed. khr. 166.
63. Oginskaya, *Klutsis*, p. 107.
64. See M. Ioffe, *Boris Efimovich Efimov* (Moscow: Iskusstvo, 1952).
65. *Iskusstvo*, 1950, no. 1, p. 46.
66. R. S. Kaufman, *D. S. Moor* (Moscow: Izogiz, 1937), pp. 41–2.
67. M. Ioffe in *Iskusstvo*, 1936, no. 5, p. 158.
68. M. Ioffe, *Mikhail Mikhailovich Cheremnykh* (Moscow-Leningrad: Iskusstvo, 1949), pp. 25–8.
69. N. M. Cheremnykh, *Khochetsya, chtoby znali i drugie* (Moscow: Sovetskii khudozhnik. 1965), pp. 117–18.
70. Koretsky, *Zametki plakatista*, p. 105, and also in Koretsky, *Tovarishch plakat* (Moscow: Plakat, 1978), p. 37; similarly *Istoriya russkogo iskusstva*, vol. 13, p. 46.

Note on Sources

The history of collections of Soviet posters is a subject in itself. As with all ephemeral materials of this kind, particularly those that originated during a civil war, their survival is to a large extent a matter of chance. The Soviet posters with which this book is concerned were not always systematically collected; they were often prepared from poor quality materials which have deteriorated with the passage of time; some of the major collections have suffered from fire and war damage; and they have also suffered from neglect. The fate of the Rosta Windows is perhaps the most conspicuous example of the last of these: left behind in a special room when Rosta moved elsewhere, the new inhabitants used them to wrap up their flour and herrings. Many were saved from destruction only by the swift intervention of N. D. Vinogradov, one of the stencillers, and of Cheremnykh himself.[1] Later still many Rosta Windows were badly damaged when the Central State Archive of Literature and Art, in which many of them had been kept, arranged for them to be cut into their constituent frames for convenience of storage and consultation and then for the edges (sometimes with fragments of text) to be cut straight. This has made it difficult to reconstruct the original Windows, still more so to be certain of their heights and widths.[2]

The largest collection of Soviet posters is presently held by the Lenin Library in Moscow, which has enjoyed the right since 1862 to at least a single copy of all printed material issued on Russian or Soviet territory. The Lenin Library's collection is however not systematically recorded in a catalogue to which outsiders have access; posters which are politically sensitive are not normally available for consultation; and the library's holdings are seriously deficient so far as the Rosta Windows are concerned (those issued in Petrograd are for the most part to be found in the Saltykov-Shchedrin Public Library and the Russian Museum in Leningrad.) Some of the Library's gaps have been filled in more recent years by the purchase of private collections or the transfer of material from other institutions, such as the Tretyakov Gallery.[3] A number of significant collections remain in private hands in the USSR, although they have tended to suffer the fate of other private collections and have often been sold or dispersed on the owner's death. As recently as 1983 a very significant private collection of early revolutionary posters formed by the economist Ya. E. Rubinshtein was disposed of by a relative after the collector died intestate.[4]

Poster collections outside the USSR have obviously been deprived of the advantage of copyright privileges and have for the most part stemmed from the enthusiasm and resources of private collectors, reinforced by institutional purchases. The posters of the wartime years in the George Costakis collection, for instance, were acquired from the private collector Evgeny Platonovich Ivanov.[5] The collection in the British Library, a small but interesting one, is based upon items obtained by the British Labour Party delegation which visited Russia in 1920. The much more extensive collection at the Musée d'histoire contemporaine (formerly the Musée des deux guerres mondiales) in Paris derives from the visits of several French officials and private citizens to Russia in the early post-revolutionary years; a large part of the collection was destroyed during the Second World War, but most of the gaps were filled by Anatole de Monzie, a French diplomat who had visited Russia in 1924 in connection with the resumption of Franco-Soviet diplomatic relations.[6]

The collection at Uppsala, also a large and important one, has perhaps the most interesting history. It was presented to the University Library by Torsten Lundell (1889–1970), a Swedish Red Cross official who visited Russia extensively between 1918 and 1921 and who was authorised to acquire two copies of all published and other material that interested him by Anatoly Lunacharsky, the People's Commissar for Enlightenment. Lundell collected 239 posters, placards and proclamations, as well as much larger holdings of newspapers, books, photographs and gramophone records;[7] the material is in a particularly good state of preservation.

Rather smaller but often interesting collections have also been examined at a number of other institutions as listed in the Bibliography.

1. *Iskusstvo*, 1940, no. 3, p. 44.
2. V. N. Duvakin, *Radost', masterom kovannaya* (Moscow: Sovetskii pisatel', 1964), pp. 146–7, note 3.
3. Nina Baburina, 'Istoriya kollektsii', in *Sovetskii politicheskii plakat*, 3 parts (Moscow: Sovetskii khudozohnik, 1984), part 1, pp. 9–10.
4. Il'ya Zilbershtein in *Literaturnaya gazeta*, 23 January 1985, p. 13.
5. Angelica Z. Rudenstine, ed., *The George Costakis Collection: Russian Avant-Garde Art* (London: Thames and Hudson, 1981), p. 421.
6. *Affiches et imageries russes 1914–1921* (Paris: Musée des deux guerres mondiales, 1982), p. iv.
7. Lennart Kjellberg, 'The collection of prints from the Russian revolution in the Uppsala University Library', in Folke Sandgren, ed., *Otium et Negotium* (Stockholm: Acta Bibliothecae Stockholmiensis, vol. 16, 1973). pp. 181–7.

Bibliography

Archival sources

Central State Archive of Literature and Art (TSGALI), Moscow:
V. N. Deni archive (*fond* 2007)
Gosudarstvennaya Akademiya Iskusstvovedeniya archive (*fond* 984)
El' Lissitsky archive (*fond* 2361)
V. V. Mayakovsky archive (*fond* 336)
D. S. Moor archive (*fond* 1988)
Moskovskoe obshchestvo lyubitelei khudozhestv archive (*fond* 660)
V. P. Polonsky archive (*fond* 1382)
A. A. Radakov archive (*fond* 2041)
Uchilishche zhivopisi, vayaniya i zodchestva archive (*fond* 680)
Central State Archive of the October Revolution (TSGAOR), Moscow:
Gosizdat RSFSR archive (*fond* 395)
Central State Archive of the Soviet Army (TsGASA), Moscow:
Upravlenie Privolzhskogo voennogo okruga archive (*fond* 25889)

Collections of Posters

Bibliothèque Nationale, Paris
British Library, London
Central State Archive of Literature and Art, Moscow (*fond* 1931)
Imperial War Museum, London
Lenin Library, Moscow
Library of Congress, Washington DC
Musée d'histoire contemporaine, Paris
National Library of Scotland, Edinburgh
New York Public Library
Saltykov-Shchedrin Public Library, Leningrad
Stedelijk Museum, Amsterdam
Uppsala University Library, Stockholm
Victoria and Albert Museum, London

Catalogues of Exhibitions

Affiches et imageries russes 1914–1921 (Paris: Musée des deux guerres mondiales, 1982)
Agitatsionno-massovoe iskusstvo pervykh let Oktyabr'skoi revolyutsii. Katalog vystavki (Moscow: Sovetskii khudozhnik, 1967)
Mikhail Mikhailovich Cheremnykh. Vystavka proizvedenii k 70-letiyu so dnya rozhdeniya. Katalog, sost. R. Glukhovskaya (Moscow: Sovetskii khudozhnik, 1966)
V. N. Deni. Vystavka politicheskogo plakata i grafiki. K 80-letiyu so dnya rozhdeniya, sost. N. I. Baburina (Moscow: GBL, 1973)
Gosudarstvennaya Tret'yakovskaya galereya. *Vsytavka 'Okna satiry ROSTA'*, intr. P. M. Kerzhentsev (Moscow: GTG, 1929)
V. Lebedev. Katalog vystavki (Leningrad 1928)
Petrogradskie 'Okna ROSTA'. Katalog vystavki (Leningrad: GRB, 1968)
Putevoditel' po vystavke 'Plakat i listovka grazhdanskoi voiny' (Moscow: Muzei RKKA, 1926)
Ryska Affischer 1917–1922 (Uppsala: Universitetsbibliotek, 1984)

Vystavka proizvedenii Mikhaila Mikhailovicha Cheremnykha k 60-letiyu so dnya rozhdeniya, intr. A. A. Sidorov (Moscow 1950)
Vystavka risunkov V. V. Lebedeva (Leningrad 1928)
Yubileinaya vystavka proizvedenii Dmitriya Stakhievicha Moora (Moscow: GTG, 1936)

Collection of Reproductions

A. V. Chistyakova, intr., *Okna ROSTA* (Leningrad: Avrora, 1981)
Grafika pervogo 10-letiya 1917–1927. Risunok. Estamp. Kniga, intr. A. A. Sidorov (Moscow: Iskusstvo, 1967)
Mikhail Guerman, intr., *Art of the October Revolution* (London: Collet's 1979; Russian edition *Serdtsem slushaya revolyutsiyu* [Leningrad: Aurora, 1980])
Lenin, Oktyabr'. Sovetskii politicheskii plakat, sost. S. Petrova (Moscow 1977)
Manifesti della rivoluzione russa, intr. G. Garritano (Rome: Riuniti, c. 1966; German, French and English editions were also issued)
G. Piltz, ed., *Russland wird rot: satirische Plakate 1918–1922* (Berlin: Eulenspiegel, 1977)
Plakaty strany sovetov, sost. S. Petrova (Moscow: Plakat, 1977)
Plakaty strany sovetov, sost. V. Burdina (Moscow: Plakat, 1982)
Revolyutsionnyi prazdnichnyi plakat 1917–1927 (Leningrad: Khudozhik RSFSR, 1982)
Sovetskii politicheskii plakat, 1917–1980, 3 parts (Moscow: Sovetskii khudozhnik, 1984; an English edition was issued by Penguin Books in 1985)
The Soviet Political Poster, intr. G. N. Pavlov (Leningrad: Aurora, 1973)
The Soviet Political Poster, vyp. 2, intr. G. N. Pavlov (Leningrad: Aurora, 1976)
A. Strakhov, *Azbuka revolyutsii 1917–1921. Seriya plakatov* (Ekaterinoslav: Izd. PUR Khar'kovskogo voennogo okruga, 1921; repr. Kiev, 1969)
Klaus Waschik, intr., *Seht her, Genossen! Plakate aus der Sowjetunion* (Dortmund: Harenberg, 1982)

Guides to Collections and Inventories

A. G. Budrina, comp., *Ural'skii plakat vremen grazhdanskoi voiny* (Perm': Permskoe knizhnoe izdatel'stvo, 1968)
B. S. Butnik-Siversky, comp., *Sovetskii plakat epokhi grazhdanskoi voiny 1918–1921* (Moscow: Izdatel'stvo Vsesoyuznoi knizhnoi palaty, 1960)
A. P. Doroshenko, 'Materialy izobrazitel'nogo iskusstva, khranyashchiesya v TsGAOR SSSR', *Voprosy arkivovedeniya*, 1959, no. 2, pp. 90–94
A. V. Ezhov and S. D Barer, 'Politicheskii plakat pervykh let Sovetskoi vlasti v ekspozitsiyakh i fondakh Stavropol'skogo kraevedcheskogo muzeya', in *Materialy po izucheniyu Stavropol'skogo kraya*, vyp. 14 (Stavropol' 1976)
Gosudarstvennyi muzei Tatarskoi ASSR, *Plakaty pervykh let Sovetskoi vlasti (1918–1922gg.) Katalog* (Kazan' 1959)
'Okna ROSTA' perioda grazhdanskoi voiny i interventsii v sobranii Gos.

Publichnoi Biblioteki im. Saltykova-Shchedrina. Katalog (Leningrad: GPB, 1961)

Petrogradskie 'Okna ROSTA'. Svodnyi katalog (Leningrad: GPB, 1964)

Plakaty, vypushchennye k godovshchinam Velikoi Oktyabr'skoi sotsialisticheskoi revolyutsii v Sovetskom Soyuze i za rubezhom. (Po. fondam Gos. Muzeya Revolyutsii SSSR). Katalog (Moscow: Gos. Muzei Revolyutsii, 1958)

Z. A. Pokrovskaya, sost., *Russkaya satiricheskaya periodika 1905–1907 gg.: Svodnyi katalog* (Moscow: GBL, 1980)

Putevoditel' po fondam otdela estampov (Leningrad: GPB, 1961)

Russkii sovetskii lubok v sobranii Gos. Pub. Biblioteki im. Saltykova-Shchedrina 1921–1945. Katalog (Leningrad: GPB, 1962)

Russkoe iskusstvo pervoi treti XX veka, sost. V. I. Rakitin (Yaroslavl': Muzei iskusstva, 1979)

Saratovskii oblastnoi muzei kraevedeniya. Katalog plakatov grazhdanskoi voiny (iz fondov muzeya). (Saratov 1966)

K. N. Suvorova, comp., *V. V. Makayovsky. Opisanie dokumental'nykh materialov*, vyp. 1. *'Okna' ROSTA i Glavpolitprosveta, 1919–1922* (Moscow: TsGALI, 1964)

E. M. Terer, 'Plakaty pervykh let Sovetskoi vlasti v sobranii otdela estampov GPB', in Gos. Publichnaya Biblioteka im. Saltykova-Shchedrina, *Trudy*, vol. 12 (Leningrad 1964), pp. 137–44

Tsentral'nyi muzei Tatarskoi ASSR, Kazanskii plakat (Kazan' 1929)

Tsentral'nyi muzei vooruzhennykh sil SSSR. Putevoditel' (Moscow 1969)

Books (a selective list)

Abolina, R. Ya., *Sovetskoe iskusstvo perioda grazhdanskoi voiny* (Moscow: Izd. Akademii khudozhestv SSSR, 1962)

Abramsky, I. P., *Smekh sil'nykh. O khudozhnikakh zhurnala 'Krokodil'* (Moscow: Iskusstvo, 1977)

Ades, Dawn, *The Twentieth Century Poster* (New York: Abbeville Press, 1984)

Agitatsionno-propagandistskaya rabota Glavpolitprosveta. Materialy k XII s"ezdu partii (Moscow: Glavpolitprosvet, 1923)

Alekseev, D. G., *Sovetskii politicheskii plakat – vazhnoe ideologicheskoe oruzhie Kommunisticheskoi partii v bor'be za uprochenie Sovetskoi vlasti i postroenie osnov sotsializma (1971–1927gg.)* (avtoreferat kand. diss., Moscow, 1971)

Aleshina, L. S. et al., *Russkoe iskusstvo XIX-nachala XX veka* (Moscow: Iskusstvo, 1972)

Alexander, Sidney, *Marc Chagall: a Biography* (New York: Putnam, 1978)

Alpatov, M. V., *Drevnerusskaya ikonopis'*, 2nd ed. (Moscow: Iskusstvo, 1978)

———, *Kraski drevnerusskoi ikonopisi* (Moscow: Izobrazitel'noe iskusstvo, 1974)

Aratov, B., *Iskusstvo i klassy* (Moscow: Gosizdat, 1923)

Arvidsson, Claes and Blomqvist, Lars Erik, eds., *Symbols of Power: The Esthetics of Political Legitimation in the Soviet Union and Eastern Europe* (Stockholm: Almqvist and Wiksell, 1987)

Bakhtin, V. and Moldavsky, D., *Russkii lubok XVII-XIX vv.* (Moscow-Leningrad: Gosudarstvennoe izdatel'stvo izobrazitel'nogo iskusstva, 1962)

Baldina, O., D., *Russkie narodnye kartinki* (Moscow: Molodaya gvardiya, 1972)

Barnicoat, John, *A Concise History of Posters* (London: Thames and Hudson, 1972)

Barooshian, Vahan P., *Russian Cubo-Futurism* (The Hague: Mouton, 1974)

Barron, Stephanie, and Tuchman, Maurice, eds., *The Avant-Garde in Russia, 1910–1930: New Perspectives* (Camb. Mass.: Mit Pressm 1980)

Bedny, Dem'yan, *Izbrannye proizvedeniya* (Moscow: Sovetskii pisatel', 1951)

Bird, Alan, *A History of Russian Painting* (Oxford: Phaidon, 1987)

Bogachev, A., *Plakat* (Leningrad: Blago, 1926)

Bojko, Szymon, *New Graphic Design in Revolutionary Russia* (New York: Praeger, 1972)

Bor'ba za realizm v izobrazitel'nom iskusstve 20-kh godov (materialy, dokumenty, vospominaniya) (Moscow: Sovetskii khudozhnik, 1962)

Botsianovsky, V. and Gollerbakh, E., *Russkaya satira pervoi revolyutsii 1905–1906* (Leningrad: Giz, 1925)

Bowlt, John, *The Silver Age: Russian Art in the Early Twentieth Century and the 'World of Art' Group* (Newtonville, Mass.: Oriental Research Partners, 1979)

Bowlt, John, ed., *Russian Art of the Avant-Garde: Theory and Criticism 1902–1934* (New York: Viking, 1976)

Brown, Edward J., *Mayakovsky: a Poet in the Revolution* (Princeton NJ: Princeton University Press, 1973)

Brylyakov, N. A., *Rossiiskoe telegrafnoe . . .* (Moscow: Mysl', 1976)

Chagall, Marc, *Ma vie* (Paris: Stock, 1957)

Chardzhiev, N. et al., *K istorii russkogo avangarda* (Stockholm: Hylaea Prints, 1976)

Charter, Samuel and Ann, *I Love* (London: Deutsch, 1979)

Cheremnykh, N. A., *Khochetsya, chtoby znali i drugie* (Moscow: Sovetskii kuhudozhnik, 1965)

Chistyakov, A. V., *Petrogradskie 'Okna ROSTA'* (avtoreferat kand. diss., Leningrad, 1973)

Constantine, Mildred and Fern, Alan, *Revolutionary Soviet Film Posters* (Baltimore Md.: John Hopkins University Press, 1974)

Darracott, Joseph, *The First World War in Posters* (New York: Dover, 1974)

Darracott, Joseph, and Loftus, Belinda, *First World War Posters* (London: Imperial War Museum, 1972)

Demchenko, K. P., *Politicheskaya grafika Kieva perioda revolyutsii 1905–1907gg.* (Kiev: Naukova dumks, 1976)

———, *Satiricheskaya pressa Ukrainy 1905–1907gg.* (Kiev: Naukova dumka, 1980)

Demosfenova, G., Nurok, A. and Shantyko, N., *Sovetskii politicheskii plakat* (Moscow: Iskusstvo, 1962)

Deni, V. N. *Deni. Plakaty. Karikatury*, intr. M. Savelov (Moscow: Izogiz, 1963)

———, *My, nashi druz'ya i nashi vragi v risunkakh Deni*, intr. A. V. Lunacharsky (Moscow-Leningrad: Gosizdat, 1930)

———, *Plakat na sluzhbe Oktyabrya. Deni* (Moscow: Ogiz-Izogiz, 1934)

———, *Politicheskie risunki 1922g.*, intr. A. V. Lunacharsky (Moscow-Petrograd: Giz, 1923)

Denisov, V., *Voina i lubok* (Petrograd: Izdanie Novogo zhurnala dlya vsekh, 1916)

Dinershtein, E. A. and Yavorskaya, T. P., comps., *Izdatel'skoe delo v pervye gody sovetskoi vlasti (1917–1922gg,) Sbornik dokumentov i materialov* (Moscow: Kniga, 1972)

Direktivy Glavnogo komandovaniya Krasnoi Armii (1917–1920). Sbornik dokumentov, ed. G. A. Belov et al. (Moscow: Voenizdat, 1969)

Dologrukov, N. A., *Stranitsy zhizni* (Leningrad: Khudozhnik RSFSR, 1963)

Drobashenko, S., ed., *Dziga Vertov, Stat'i, dnevniki, zamysli* (Moscow: Iskusstvo, 1966)

Dul'sky, P. M., *Grafika satiricheskikh zhurnalov 1905–1906gg.* (Kazan': Tatgosizdat, 1922)

Dunin-Borkovsky, K. I., *O gerbe i flagakh RSFSR* (Moscow: NKID, 1922)

Duvakin, V. N., *Radost', masterom kovannaya. Ocherki tvorchestva V. V. Mayakovskogo* (Moscow: Sovetskii pisatel', 1964)

———, *Rosta-Fenster. Majakowski als Dichter und bildender Künstler*, 2nd ed. (Dresden: Verlag der Kunst, 1975)

Efimov, Boris, *Karikatury*, intr. L. Trotsky (Moscow: Izvestiya, 1924)

_____, *Mne khochetsya rasskazat'* (Moscow: Sovetskii khudozhnik, 1970)

_____, *Na moi vzglyad* (Moscow: Iskusstvo, 1987)

_____, *Rasskazy starogo moskvicha* (Moscow: Moskovskii rabochii, 1981)

_____, *Sorok let. Zapiski khudozhnika-satirista* (Moscow: Sovetskii khudozhnik, 1961)

Erenburg, Il'ya, *Sobranie sochinenii v devyati tomakh*, vol. 8 (Moscow: Khudozhestvennaya literatura, 1966)

Etkind, M. L., intr., *Boris Kustodiev* (Moscow: Sovetskii khudozhnik, 1982)

Elliott, David, *New Worlds. Russian Art and Society 1900–1937* (London: Thames and Hudson, 1986)

Eventov, I., *Mayakovsky – plakatist* (Moscow-Leningrad: Iskusstvo, 1940)

Fedyukin, S. A., *Velikii Oktyabr' i intelligentsiya* (Moscow: Nauka, 1972)

Fevral'sky, A. V., *Vstrechi s Mayakovskim* (Moscow: Sovetskaya Rossiya, 1971)

Fitzpatrick, Sheila, *The Commissariat of Enlightenment* (Cambridge: Cambridge University Press, 1980)

Fülöp-Miller, René, *The Mind and Face of Bolshevism. An Examination of Cultural Life in Soviet Russia* (London and New York: Putnam, 1927)

Gallo, Max, *The Poster in History* (London: Hamlyn, 1974)

Gassner, Hubertus and Gillen, Eckhart, *Zwischen Revolutionskunst und sozialistischen Realismus. Dokumente und Kommentare Kunstdebatten in der Sowjetunion von 1917 bis 1934* (Koln: DuMont Buchverlag, 1979)

Gleason, A., et al., eds., *Bolshevik Culture* (Bloomington: University of Indiana Press, 1985)

Gollerbakh, E., *Istoriya gravyury i litografii v Rossii* (Moscow-Petrograd: Gosizdt, 1923)

_____, *Sovetskaya grafika* (Moscow: Ogiz-Izogiz, 1938)

Golynets, S. V. *Ivan Bilibin* (London: Pan, 1981)

_____, ed., *Ivan Yakovlevich Bilibin. Stat'i, pis'ma vospominaniya o khudozhnike* (Leningrad: Khudozhnik RSFSR, 1970)

Gomberg-Verzhitskaya, E. P., *Russkoe iskusstvo i revolyutsiya 1905 goda* (Leningrad: Izdatel'stvo Leningradskogo Universiteta, 1960)

Gosudarstvennoe izdatel'stvo RSFSR (Moscow-Leningrad: Giz, 1925)

Gosudarstvennoe izdatel'stvo, *Katalog izdanii 1919–1925* (Moscow-Leningrad: Giz, 1925–27)

_____, *Otchet o deyatel'nosti na 1-oe dekabrya 1920* (Moscow: Giz, 1920)

Gosudarstvennoe izdatel'stvo v 1922 godu (Moscow-Petrograd: Gosizdat, 1922, 'na pravakh rukopisi')

Grabar', I. E. et al., eds., *Istoriya russkovo iskusstva*, 13 vols. (Moscow: Izdatel'stvo Akademii nauk SSSR, 1953–69)

Graficheskoe iskusstvo v SSSR 1917–1927. Sbornik statei (Leningrad: Gosizdat, 1927)

Gramotnost' v Rossii (Moscow: TsSU, 1922)

Gray, Camilla, *The Russian Experiment in Art, 1863–1922*, rev. ed. (London: Thames and Hudson, 1986)

Gushchin, A., *Oformlenie massovykh pradnestv za 15 let diktatury proletariata* (Moscow: Ogiz-Izogiz, 1932)

Hamilton, G. H., *The Art and Architecture of Russia*, 3rd ed. (New York: Penguin, 1982)

Hardie, Martin and Sabin, Arthur K., eds., *War Posters issued by Belligerent and Neutral Nations 1914–1919* (London: Black, 1920)

Hillier, Bevis, *Posters* (London: Weidenfeld and Nicolson, 1969)

Il'ina, G. I., *Kul'turnoe stroitel'stvo v Petrograde oktyabr' 1917–1920gg.* (Leningrad: Nauka, 1982)

Ioffe, M. L., comp., *Boris Efimovich Efimov* (Moscow: Iskusstvo, 1952

_____, *Desyat' ocherkov o khudozhnikakh-satirikakh* (Moscow: Sovetskii khudoznhik, 1971)

_____, *Mikhail Mikhailovich Cheremnykh* (Moscow–Leningrad: Iskusstvo, 1949)

_____, *Mikhail Mikhailovich Cheremnykh* (Moscow-Leningrad: Sovetskii khudozhnik, 1950)

_____, *Viktor Nikolaevich Deni* (Moscow-Leningrad: Iskusstvo, 1947)

Jangfeldt, Bengt, *Mayakovsky and Futurism 1917–1921* (Stockholm: Almqvist and Wiksell, 1976)

Jangfeldt, Bengt and Nilsson, Nils Åke, eds., *Vladimir Majakovskij: memoirs and essays* (Stockholm: Almqvist and Wiksell, 1975)

Kämpfer, Frank, *'Der rote Keil'. Das politische Plakat: Theorie und Geschichte* (Berlin: Mann, 1985)

Kandinsky, Wassily, *Complete Writings on Art*, 2 vols. (London: Faber, 1982)

Karginov, German, *Rodchenko* (London: Thames and Hudson, 1979)

Karpinsky, V. A., ed., *Agitparpoedzda VTSIK. Ikh istoriya, apparat, metody i forma raboty. Sbornik statei* (Moscow: Gosizdat, 1920)

Karshan, Daniel, ed., *Malevich: The Graphic Work 1913–1930. A Print Catalogue Raisonné* (Jerusalem: Israel Museum, 1975)

Kataev, Valentin, *Sobranie sochinenii v devyatii tomakh*, vol. 8 (Moscow: Khudozhestvennaya literatura, 1971)

Katanyan, V. A., *Mayakovsky: literaturnaya khronika*, 4th ed. (Moscow: Gosudarstvennoe izdatel'stvo khudozhestvennoi literatury, 1961)

_____, comp., *Mayakovsky – khudozhnik* (Moscow: Izobrazitel'noe iskusstvo, 1963)

Katkov, N. F., *Agitatsionno-propagandistskaya rabota bol'shevikov v voiskakh i tylu belogvardeitsev v period 1918–1920gg.* (Leningrad: Izdatel'stvo Leningradskogo Universiteta, 1977)

Kauffer, E. McKnight, *The Art of the Poster. Its Origins, Evolution and Purpose* (London: Palmer, 1924)

Kaufman, R. S., *D. S. Moor* (Moscow: Izogiz, 1937)

Keirim-Markus, M. B., *Gosudarstvennoe rukovodstvo kul'turoi. Stroitel'stvo Narkomprosa (noyabr' 1917 – seredina 1918g.)* (Moscow: Nauka, 1980)

Kemenov, V. S. et al., eds., *Kukryniksy*, 4 vols. (Moscow: Izobrazitel'noe iskusstvo, 1982–)

Kenez, Peter, *The Birth of the Propaganda State. Soviet Methods of Mass Mobilization, 1917–1929* (Cambridge: Cambridge University Press, 1985)

Kerzhentsev, P. M., *Gazeta. Organizatsiya i tekhnika gazetnogo dela*, 4th ed. (Moscow-Leningrad: Gosizdat, 1925)

Khalaminsky, Yu. Ya., *D. S. Moor* (Moscow: Sovetskii khudozhnik, 1961)

Khan-Magomedov, S. O., *Rodchenko* (London: Thames and Hudson, 1986)

King, David and Porter, Cathy, *Blood and Laughter: Caricatures of the 1905 Revolution* (London: Cape, 1983)

Kolychev, V. G., *Partiino-politicheskaya rabota v Krasnoi Armii v gody grazhdanskoi voiny, 1918–1920* (Moscow: Nauka, 1979)

Kopelev, Lev, *The Education of a True Believer* (London: Wildwood House, 1981)

Koretsky, V., *Tovarishch plakat* (Moscow: Plakat, 1978)

_____, *Zametki plakatista* (Moscow: Sovetskii khudozhnik, 1958)

Kostin, V. I., comp., *Mikhail Mikhailovich Cheremnykh* (Moscow: Sovetskii khudozhnik, 1957)

Kozhin, N. A. and Abramov, I. S., *Narodnyi lubok vtoroi poloviny XIX veka i sovremennyi* (Leningrad: Obshchestvo pooshchreniya khudozhnikov, 1929)

Kozlov, A. M., comp., *Dmitri Stakhievich Moor* (Moscow-Leningrad: Sovetskii khudozhnik, 1949)

_____, *Viktor Nikolaevich Deni* (Moscow-Leningrad: Sovetskii khudozhnik, 1950)

Kratkii ocherk kul'turnoi-politicheskoi raboty v Krasnoi Armii za 1918g.

(Moscow: Litizdat, 1919)

Krupskaya, N. K., *Pedagogicheskie sochineniya v desyati tomakh*, vol. 1 (Moscow: Izdatel'stvo Akademii pedagogicheskikh nauk, 1957)

Kuchin, V. N., ed., *Iz istorii stroitel'stva sovetskoi kul'tury* (Moscow: Iskusstvo, 1964)

Kul'turnoe stroitel'stvo v RSFSR 1917–1927, vol. 1 (1917–1920), ed. L. Davydova (Moscow: Sovetskaya Rossiya, 1983)

Kupaigorodskaya, A. P., *Oruzhiem slova: listovki petrogradskikh bol'shevikov 1918–1920gg.* (Leningrad: Lenizdat, 1981)

Kuz'min, N. V., *Devno i nedavno* (Moscow: Sovetskii khudozhnik, 1982)

Lapshin, V. P., *Khudozhestvennaya zhizn' Moskvy i Petrograda v 1917 godu* (Moscow: Sovetskii khudozhnik, 1983)

Latviešu tēlotāja māksla. 1957 (Riga: Latgosizdat, 1958)

Lazarev, V. N., *Russkaya ikonopis'. Ot istokov do nachala XVI veka*, 6 parts (Moscow: Iskusstvo, 1983)

Lebedev, P. I., *Sovetskoe iskusstvo v period inostrannoi interventsii i grazhdanskoi voiny* (Moscow-Leningrad: Iskusstvo, 1949)

V. I. Lenin i izobrazitel'noe iskusstvo: dokumenty, pis'ma, vospominaniya, sost. V. V. Shleev (Moscow: Izobrazitel'noe iskusstvo, 1977)

Lissitzky-Küppers, Sophie, ed., *El Lissitsky. Maler. Architekt. Typograf. Fotograf*, 2nd ed. (Dresden: Verlag der Kunst, 1976)

Lodder, Christina, *Russian Constructivism* (New Haven and London: Yale University Press, 1983)

Lunacharsky, A. V., *Ob izobrazitel'nom iskusstve*, 2 vols. (Moscow: Sovetskii khudozhnik, 1967)

Lyakhov, V., ed., *Sovetskii reklamnyi plakat 1917–1923* (Moscow: Sovetskii khudozhnik, 1972)

Malevich, K. S., *K voprosu izobrazitel'nogo iskusstva* (Smolensk: Giz, 1921)

———, *Essays on Art 1915–1933*, ed. Troels Andersen, 4 vols. (Copenhagen: Borgens Forlag, 1971–78)

Malyutin, I. A., *Karikatury* (Moscow: Izd. Krokodila, 1964)

———, *Mastera sovetskoi karikatury: Ivan Malyutin* (Moscow: Sovetskii khudozhnik, 1978)

Marcadé, Valentine, *Le renouveau de l'art pictural russe 1864–1914* (Lausanne: L'Age de l'homme, 1971)

Marinov, A. A., *V stroyu zashchitnikov Oktyabrya. Voenno-politicheskaya kniga, 1918–1925* (Moscow: Nauka, 1982)

Markov, Vladimir, *Russian Futurism: a History* (Berkeley: University of California Press, 1968)

Massovye prazdnestva. Sbornik komiteta sotsiologicheskogo izucheniya iskusstv (Leningrad: Academia, 1926)

Matafonov, V. S., *Nikolai Mikhailovich Kochergin* (Leningrad: Khudozhnik RSFSR, 1978)

Matsa, I., ed., *Sovetskoe iskusstvo za 15 let. Materialy i dokumentatsiya* (Moscow-Leningrad: Ogiz-Izogiz, 1933)

Mayakovsky, V.V., *Groznyi smekh* (Moscow-Leningrad: Iskusstvo, 1938)

———, *Love is the Heart of Everything*, ed. Bengt Jangfeldt (Edinburgh: Polygon, 1986)

———, *Polnoe sobranie sochinenii*, 13 vols. (Moscow: Khudozhestvennaya literatura, 1955–61)

Mayakovsky: materialy i issledovaniya, ed. V. O. Pertsov and M. I. Serebryansky (Moscow: Goslitizdat, 1940)

V. Mayakovsky v vospominaniyakh rodnykh i druzei, ed. L. I. Mayakovskaya and A. I. Koloskov (Moscow: Moskovskii rabochii, 1968)

V. Mayakovsky v vospominaniyakh sovremennikov, intr, Z. S. Paperny (Moscow: Gosudarstvennoe izdatel'stvo khudozhestvennoi literatury, 1963)

Mierau, P., *Links! links! links!* (Berlin: Rütten & Loening, 1970)

Millon, Henry A. and Nochlin, Linda, eds., *Art and Architecture in the Service of Politics* (Cambridge Mass.: MIT Press, 1978)

Mitingi, sobraniya, lektsii v 1917–18gg., ed. V. V. Bush (Petrograd:

Giz, 1920)

Milner, John, *Russian Revolutionary Art* (London: Oresko, 1979)

Moor, D. S., *Azbuka krasnoarmeitsa* (Moscow: Giz, 1921)

———, *Dmitri Stakhievich Moor* (Moscow-Leningrad: Iskusstvo, 1948)

———, *Izbrannye proizvedeniya* (Moscow: Sovetskii khudozhnik, 1958)

———, *Moor. Plakat, Karikatury* (Moscow: Izogiz, 1959)

———, *Plakat na sluzhbe Oktyabrya* (Moscow: Ogiz-Izogiz, 1934)

———, *Ya – bol'shevik* (Moscow: Sovetskii khudozhnik, 1967)

Moor, D. S. et al., *Diktatory Rura i Lozanny v karikaturakh Deni, Efimova i Moora* (Moscow: Gosizdat, 1923)

Morizet, A., *Chez Lénine et Trotski* (Paris: La renaissance du livre, 1921)

Nakov, A. B., intr., *Kasimir Malevich* (London: Tate Gallery, 1976)

Naumov, E., *Mayakovsky v pervye gody sovetskoi vlasti (1917–22)* (Moscow: Sovetskii pisatel', 1950)

Nilsson, N. A., ed., *Art, Society, Revolution. Russia 1917–21* (Stockholm: Almqvist and Wiksell, 1979)

Novikov, A., *Leniniana v plakate* (Moscow: Sovetskii khudozhnik, 1970)

Ocherki po russkomu i sovetskomu iskusstvu. Sbornik statei (Moscow: Sovetskii khudozhnik, 1965)

Oginskaya, L. Yu., *Gustav Klutsis* (Moscow: Sovetskii khudozhnik, 1981)

Okhochinsky, V., *Plakat: razitie i primenenie* (Leningrad: Izdatel'stvo Akademii khudozhestv, 1926)

Otchet o deyatel'nosti literaturno-izdatel'skogo otdela PUR RVSR, s 1 iyunya 1919g. po 1 iyunya 1920g. (Moscow 1920)

Otchet o deyatel'nosti literaturno-izdatel'skogo otdela Politupravleniya Revvoensoveta Zapadnogo Fronta s oktyabrya 1919g. po aprel' 1921g. (Moscow 1921)

Otchet o deyatel'nosti Otdela voennoi literatury pri RVSR i Vysshego voennogo redaktsionnogo soveta s 1 yanvarya 1921g. po 31 dekabrya 1922g. (Moscow: VVRS, 1923)

Ovsyannikov, Yu., comp., *Lubok: russkie narodnye kartinki XVII – XVIII vv.* (Moscow: Sovetskii khudozhnik, 1968)

Partiino-politicheskaya rabota v Krasnoi Armii (aprel' 1918 – fevral' 1919). Dokumenty (Moscow: Voenizdat, 1961)

Partiino-politicheskaya rabota v Krasnoi Armii (mart 1919 – 1920gg.). Dokumenty (Moscow: Voenizdat, 1964)

Pasternak, L. O., *Zapisi raznykh let* (Moscow: Sovetskii khudozhnik 1975)

Pavlov, I. N., *Moya zhizn' i vstrechi* (Moscow: Iskusstvo, 1949)

———, *Zhizn' russkogo gravera* (Leningrad: Iskusstvo, 1940)

Pertsov, V., *Mayakovsky: zhizn' i tvorchestvo*, 3 vols. (Moscow: Nauka, 1969–72)

Pethybridge, Roger, *The Social Prelude to Stalinism* (London: Macmillan, 1974)

Petrov, V., *Vladimir Vasil'evich Lebedev 1891–1967* (Leningrad: Khudozhnik RSFSR, 1972)

Philippe, Robert, *Political Graphics: Art as a Weapon* (Oxford: Phaidon, 1982)

Plakat i reklama posle Oktyabrya (Leningrad: Izdanie vystavochnogo komiteta, 1926)

Polonsky, V. P., *Na literaturnye temy. Izbrannye stat'i* (Moscow: Sovetskii pisatel', 1968)

———, *Russkii revolyutsionnyi plakat. Khudozhestvennaya monografiya* (Moscow: Gosizdat, 1925)

Povolotskaya, E. and Ioffe, M., *Tridtsat' let sovetskogo plakata* (Moscow-Leningrad: Iskusstvo, 1948)

Punin, N. N., *Russkii plakat 1917–1922*, Vyp. 1, *V. V. Lebedev* (Petrograd: Strelets, 1922)

Radakov, A. A., *Karikatura* (Leningrad: Blago, 1926)

———, *Karikatury* (Moscow: Pravda, 1968)

Raevsky, S., *Plakat A. Strakhova* (Khar'kov: Mistetstvo, 1936)

Rickards, Maurice, *Posters of the First World War* (London: Evelyn, Adams and Mackay, 1968)

————, *Posters of Protest and Revolution* (Bath: Adams and Dart, 1970)

————, *The Rise and Fall of the Poster* (Newton Abbot: David and Charles, 1971)

Rodchenko, A. M., *Stat'i. Vospominaniya. Avtobiograficheskie zapiski. Pis'ma* (Moscow: Sovetskii khudozhnik, 1982)

Rovinsky, D. A. *Russkie narodnye kartinki*, 5 vols. (St Petersburg: Imperatorskaya Akademiya Nauk, 1881–1893)

Rudenstine, Angelica Z., ed., *The George Costakis Collection: Russian Avant-Garde Art* (London: Thames and Hudson, 1981)

Savostyuk, O. and Uspensky, B., intr., *Mikhail Mikhailovich Cheremnykh* (Moscow: Sovetskii khudozhnik, 1970)

Shcherbak, V. M., *Bol'shevistskaya agitatsiya i propaganda (oktyabr' 1917 – mart 1919gg.)* (Moscow: Vysshaya shkola, 1919)

Shklovsky, V. B., *Zhili-byli: vospominaniya, memuarnye zapiski, povesti o vremeni* (Moscow: Sovetskii pisatel', 1966)

Shleev, V. V. et al., eds., *Revolyutsiya 1905–1907 godov i izobrazitel'noe iskusstvo*, 3 parts (Moscow: Izobrazitel'noe iskusstvo, 1977–81)

Sidorov, A. A., *Russkaya grafika nachala XX veks* (Moscow: Iskusstvo, 1969)

————, *Russkaya grafika za gody revolyutsii 1917–1922* (Moscow: Dom pechati, 1923)

Sovetskie plakatisty – frontu (Moscow: Istusstvo, 1985)

Sovetskoe dekorativnoe iskusstvo. Materialy i dokumenty, 1917–1932. Farfor, fayans, steklo, ed. I. A. Pronina et al. (Moscow: Iskusstvo, 1980)

Speranskaya, E. A., ed., *Agitatsionno-massovoe iskusstvo pervykh let Oktyabrya: materialy i issledovaniya* (Moscow: Iskusstvo, 1971)

Stykalin, S. I., *Okna satiry ROSTA* (Moscow: Izdatel'stvo Moskovskogo Universiteta, 1976)

Sviridova, I. A., *Viktor Nikolaevich Deni* (Moscow: Iskusstvo, 1978)

Sytova, A., *The Lubok. Russian Folk Pictures* (Leningrad: Aurora, 1984)

Tolstoi, V. P., *Sovetskoe dekorativnoe iskusstvo 1917–1945* (Moscow: Iskusstvo, 1984)

————, *V istokov sovetskogo monumental'nogo iskusstva 1917–1923* (Moscow: Izobrazitel'noe iskusstvo, 1983)

Tolstoi, V. P., ed., *Agitatsionno-massovoe iskusstvo. Oformlenie prazdnestv*, 2 vols. (Moscow: Iskusstvo, 1984)

Trotsky, L. D., *Moya zhizn'*, 2 vols. (Berlin: Granat, 1930)

Tumarkin, Nina, *Lenin Lives! The Lenin Cult in Soviet Russia* (Cambridge Mass.: Harvard University Press, 1983)

Turkov, A. M., *Boris Mikhailovich Kustodiev* (Moscow: Iskusstvo, 1986)

Tvorchestvo Mayakovskogo, ed. L. I. Timofeev and L. M. Polyak (Moscow: Izdatel'stvo Akademii nauk SSSR, 1952)

Vaisfel'd, I. and Mikhailov, A., eds., *Plakatno-kartiinaya agitatsiya na putyakh perestroiki* (Moscow-Leningrad: Izogiz, 1932)

Veimarn, B. V. et al., eds., *Istoriya iskusstva narodov SSSR*, vols. 7 and 8 (Moscow: Iskusstvo, 1972–77)

Verzhbitsky, N. K., *Zapiski starogo zhurnalista* (Moscow: Sovetskii pisatel', 1961)

Vladich, L. V., *Ukrain'skii politichnii plakat* (Kiev: Politvidav Ukraini, 1981)

Voprosy sovetskogo izobrazitel'nogo iskusstva i arkhitektury (Moscow: Sovetskii khudozhnik, 1976)

Vos'moi s''ezd RKP(b) mart 1919 goda. Protokoly (Moscow: Gosudarstvennoe izdatel'stvo politicheskoi literatury, 1959)

Weill, Alain, *The Poster: A Worldwide Survey and History* (London: Sotheby's, 1985)

Weitzmann, Kurt, ed., *The Icon* (New York: Knopf, 1983)

Williams, Robert C., *Artists in Revolution. Portraits of the Russian Avant-Garde, 1905–1925* (London: Scolar Press, 1978)

Woroszylski, Wiktor, *The Life of Mayakovsky*, trans. Boleslaw Taborski (London: Gollancz, 1972)

Yuon, K. F. et al., eds., *Tridtsat' let sovetskogo izobrazitel'nogo iskusstva* (Moscow: Iskusstvo, 1948)

Za bol'shevistskii plakat. Zadachi izoiskusstva v svyazi s resheniem ТSК VKP(b) o plakatnoi literature. Diskussiya i vystupleniya v institute LIYa (Moscow-Leningrad: Ogiz-Izogiz, 1932)

Zemenkov, B., *Udarnoe iskusstvo Okon satiry* (Moscow: Khudozhestvennoe aktsionernoe izdatel'skoe obshchestvo AKhR, 1930)

Zhadova, Larissa A., *Malevich: Suprematism and Revolution in Russian Art, 1910–1930* (London: Thames and Hudson, 1982)

Zhitomirsky, A., *Iskusstvo politicheskogo fotomontazha* (Moscow: Plakat, 1983)

Illustration Credits

The author and publishers are grateful to the following for permission to reproduce illustrations: Imperial War Museum, London, 1.17; David King Collection, London, 1.6, 2.2; Library of Congress, Washington DC, 1.3, 2.27, 3.15, 3.20, 3.24, 5.9; Musée d'histoire contemporaine, Paris, 2.18, 3.5, 5.19; National Library of Scotland, Edinburgh, 2.16, 2.24, 4.4, 5.10, 5.15, 6.1; Radio Times Hulton Picture Library, London, 2.5, 2.6; University Library, Uppsala, 1.10, 1.13, 1.19, 2.8–10, 2.12–13, 2.17, 2.19–21, 2.23, 2.26, 3.8–9, 3.11, 3.14, 3.16, 3.19, 3.25–28, 3.32, 3.37, 4.5, 4.17–19, 5.1–7, 5.12–14, 5.16–18, 5.20–23, 5.25–32, 5.35, 5.37–51. All other illustrations are drawn from the author's own collection.

Index

Ache, Caran d', 7
Agitational barge, 23
Agitational ship, 23
Agitational trains, 22–3, 43, 61, 113–14
Allegory and myth, in Soviet posters, 32–8, 89, 92
Amfiteatrov, A., 56
Anniversaries, celebration of, 20–2, 51, 70, 88, 92, 101, 113
Antonov-Ovseenko, V. A., 41
Apsit, Alexander, 25–32
Assiette au beurre, L', 7
Athos, Mount, 26
At the Grave of the Counter-Revolution (Deni), 57, 100
At the Moment No-one is Poorer than Us (Mayakovsky), 76

Baba-Yaga, 2
Babel, Isaac, 89
Bagritsky, Edward, 89, 117
Bakst, Lev, 10, 14
Bakunin, Mikhail, 113
Barmine, Alexander, 109
Beat the Whites with the Red Wedge (El Lissitsky), 10, 88, 128
Bednota, 11, 57, 70, 108, 112
Bedny, Demyan, 3, 6, 26, 42, 57, 61, 92, 112
Before and After (Moor), 43–4
Begemot, 127
Belyaev, V. V., 14
Benois, Alexander, 10
Be on Guard (Moor), 100
Bernini, G. L., 37
Bernshtein, M. D., 85
Bezbozhnik, 7, 43
Bich, 11, 56, 57, 127
Bilibin, Ivan, 3, 8, 10, 11, 14, 15, 114
Blok, A. A., 64, 109, 112
Bloody Path of Struggle is Over, The (Moor), 104
'Bloody Sunday', 10
Bogdanov, Alexander, 36
Bolotnikov, Ivan, 29, 92
Bov, 127
Brailsford, H. N., 108–9, 126
Brik, Lili, 68, 75, 80, 117
Brik, Osip, 67
Brodaty, Lev, 81, 84, 85, 114, 127
Brodsky, Isaac, 14
Brothers-in-Arms, 32
Buchkin, P., 15
Budilnik, 7, 10, 11, 42, 43, 56, 72
Building of Socialism, The, 93
Bunin, Ivan, 8, 73
Burlyuk, David, 73

Capital (Deni), 57, 94
Capital and Co. (Kochergin), 9
Cézanne, Paul, 72
Chagall, Marc, 21, 88–9, 113
Chekhonin, Sergei, 11
Chekhov, Anton, 7
Chemodanov, M. M., 8
Cheremnykh, Mikhail M., biography of, 68–72, 80; Mayakovsky on, 72; personality of, 72; Polonsky on, 72; and Rosta Windows, 67–80, 108, 114, 124–5; other references, 11, 24–5, 57, 92, 121, 121–2, 124, 120
Chéret, Jules, 6

Chernov, Viktor, 6
Children! (Radakov), 104
Christian symbolism, in Soviet posters, 37
Christmas (Moor), 46
Chukovsky, Kornei, 8
Clemenceau, Georges, 51
Commercial posters, in Russia, 11–15
Communist International, posters on, 101
Comrade Lenin Cleans the World of Filth (Deni), 57, 70
'Comrade Muslims' (Moor), 50
Concerning the Toiler... (Cheremnykh), 24–5
Concerts, industrial, 21–2
Constitution of 1918, Soviet, 6, 18, 36
Constitutional Assembly, election posters for, 15–17, 112, 119
'Contemporary Lubok' publishing house, 3, 73
Counter-revolutionary Wrecker, The (Deni), 128
Curzon, Lord, 6
Cyril, St., 4, 21, 113

Danton, Georges, 20
Day of Soviet Propaganda, 105
Day of the Wounded Red Armyman (Apsit), 29, 93
Death to World Imperialism (Moor), 43, 64, 94, 113
Decoration, of Soviet towns, 20–2, 43, 61, 84, 112
Deineka, Alexander, 43, 128
Deni, Viktor N., career of, 55–60; personality of, 60–1; Polonsky on, 41; poster work of, 11, 17, 94–104, 114, 121, 128–9; other reference, 6
Denikin, General, 6, 26, 43, 51, 57, 67, 76, 94–6, 100, 115–16
Denikin's Band (Deni), 57, 95
Denisovsky, N., 77
Departing Gentry, The (Moor), 98–100
Devil Doll (Moor), 100
Dionysius of Moscow, 5
Dislocation and the Army of Labour (Kochergin), 61
Dmitriev-Kavkazskii, Lev, 26
Dolgorukov, Nikolai, 55, 60–1, 114
Dostoevsky, Fedor, 20
Down with Capital (Melnikov), 101
Dreiser, Theodore, 109
Druzhinin, N. M., 8
Dobrokovsky, S., 115
Dobuzhinsky, Mstislav, 8

Efimov, Boris, on cartoons, 127; on Cheremnykh, 72; on Deni, 60; diplomatic protest against, 55; on Moor, 53; and Rosta Windows, 89; other reference, 129
Ehrenburg, Ilya, 109, 112
Eighth of March, The (Strakhov), 121
Eisenstein, Sergei, 88–9
Either Death to Capital... (Deni), 94
Ekonomicheskaya gazeta, 68
Enemy is at the Gates, The (Kochergin), 61, 95–6, 124
Enemy is at the Gates, The (Moor), 44, 61, 96
Enemy wants to Capture Tula, The (Apsit), 61, 96
Enemy wants to take Moscow, The, 96
Engels, Friedrich, 20, 111, 113
Entente under the Mask of Peace, The (Deni), 17, 57, 94
Eremeev, Konstantin, 22–3, 26, 69
Esenin, Sergei, 3

Every Blow of the Hammer... (Deni), 94

Fevralsky, Alexander, 80
Fidman, Vladimir, 94, 96
First of May (Apsit), 29, 92
First of May (Kochergin), 61
1 May (Moor), 101
1st of May (Ivanov), 101
First World War, and poster art, 14–17, 23
Five Minutes to October, 11
Flagg, James Mongomery, 48
Fliegende Blätter, 7
Flit, A. M., 84
Forward, to the Defence of the Urals (Apsit), 29, 93, 95
Four Years, 104
'Freedom Loan' posters, 15, 88, 119
Fülöp-Miller, René, 113

Galchonok, 11
Garibaldi, Guiseppe, 20
George, St., 5–6, 6, 14, 89
Gilotina, 127
Give me your Hand, Deserter (Moor), 97
Glavpolitprosvet, 67, 120, 125–6
Goldschmidt, Alfons, 108, 126
Golos Moskvy, 56
Goncharova, Natalya, 3
Gorbachev, Mikhail, 6
Gorky, Maxim, 8, 15, 41, 73
Gosizdat, 39, 109, 115, 116, 120, 125, 126
Gudok, 68
Gulbransson, Olaf, 7, 43

Hammer and sickle, as symbol, 36
Hangmen torture the Ukraine (Deni), 57
Happy New Year (Kogout), 97
Happy New Year, Bourgeois!, 11
Have you Enrolled as a Volunteer? (Moor), 46–8, 97, 114, 121, 124
Heartfield, John, 121
Help! (Moor), 50, 64
Help Voluntarily! (Mayakovsky), 76
Heroes and Victims of the Revolution (Mayakovsky), 75, 84
Herzen, Alexander, 20
How have you helped the Front? (Moor), 121
How the English oppress the Peasants... (Cheremnykh), 92
How the Polish Enterprise will End (Mukharsky), 97–8
How the Tsars deceived the People (Krylov), 92
Hygiene, and Soviet Posters, 108

Icons, and Soviet posters, 3–7, 43, 44
If we don't finish off Whiteguardism... (Mayakovsky), 76
Ilf, Ilya, 89
International, The (Apsit), 32
In the Luxury Carriage (Cheremnykh), 72
In the Waves of Revolution (Deni), 56
Iskra, 7
It's Wrangel's Turn (Kochergin), 61
Ivanov, Sergei, 101, 104–5, 108
Ivanov, N. K., 67
Ivanov, Viktor, 123, 124
Izvestiya, 43, 60, 68

Judge, 7

Kalinin, Mikhail, 23
Kamenev, Lev, 112
Kandinsky, Vassily, 3, 117
Karpinsky, Vyacheslav, 22
Kasatkin, N. A., 69
Kataev, Valentin, 46, 89, 109
Kelin, Petr, 42, 73
Kerzhentsev, Platon, 65, 80, 84, 92, 111, 114, 125
Khalturin, Stepan, 112
Khvostenko, V. V., 68
Kimval, 11, 42
Kipyatok, 127
Kiselis, Petr, 97
Klutsis, Gustav, 121, 128, 129
Kniga i revolyutsiya, 115
Kochergin, Nikolai, 9, 61, 94, 100, 117, 129
Kogan, Ivan, 80
Kogout, Nikolai, 97, 100
Kolchak, Admiral, 6, 23, 57, 94–6, 100, 114, 116
Kommunar, 70
Kopelev, Lev, 6
Koretsky, Viktor, 120, 123, 129
Korovin, K. A., 69
Kozlinsky, V. I., 6, 10, 81, 84
Krasnaya niva, 60, 120, 121
Krasnoarmeets, 41, 43
Krasnyi bich, 67
Krasnyi dyavol, 84, 127
Krasnyi perets, 57, 127
Kremlin, repair of chimes of, 70–2
Krokodil, 43, 53, 55, 72, 127, 130
Krupskaya, Nadezhda, 23, 60
Krzhizhanovsky, G. M., 32
Kukryniksy, The, 43, 123
Kupka, Frantisek, 92
Kustodiev, Boris, 3, 8, 15, 34–6

Labour (Moor), 46
Labour will be Master of the World, 101
Lansere, Ye. Ye., 8, 10, 11, 14
Lapot, 127
Larionov, Mikhail, 3
Last Hour, The (Deni), 57, 70, 115
League of Nations, The (Deni), 57, 64, 94
Lebedev, Vladimir, 10, 81, 84–8, 123, 124, 128
Leete, Alfred, 48
Lenin, Vladimir, depiction of in posters, 20, 21, 25, 69, 121, 128; and monumental propaganda, 19; views on posters, 111–12; other references, 6, 15, 18, 60, 70, 109, 113, 115, 124
Lenin (Strakhov), 127
Levin, A. S., 68
Levit, T. M., 67
'Liberators' (Deni), 57, 94–5
Life, 7
Lissitsky, El, 21, 40, 88, 121, 128
Literacy, 18–19, 126; posters on, 104–8
Litizdat, 39–40, 44, 56, 60–1, 93–4, 109, 120, 126
Lloyd George, David, 6, 21, 57
Locomotive, as symbol, 36–7
Lokhov, N. N., 9
Long Live the Communist International (Ivanov), 101
Long Live the Communist International (Moor), 101
Long Live the Communist International (VKuTEMAS), 101
Long Live the Friendship of all the Peoples of the Caucasus (Kochergin), 61
Lubok, and Soviet political posters, 1–3, 44, 46
Lunacharsky, Anatoly, and Deni, 56–7, 60; other references, 6, 19, 127

Maîtres d'affiche, Les, 7
Make Proposals (Cheremnykh), 108
Makovsky, Tadeusz, 10
Maksimov, A. F., 14
Malevich, K. S., 3, 21, 75, 88–9, 128
Malone, Colonel C., 109, 126
Malyutin, Ivan, 11, 42, 67–8, 76–7, 80–1, 129

Manifesto (Deni), 57
Marches and demonstrations, 6
Marx, Karl, 20, 88, 105, 113
Master of the World is Capital, The, 92
Mayakovsky, Vladimir V., biography of, 72–6; and *lubok*, 3; Moor on, 50; and Rosta Windows, 67–81, 84–5, 108, 114, 117, 125–7; other references, 10, 92, 111, 115, 120, 127
Mayday, celebration of, 20, 29, 43, 51, 61, 101, 109, 112
Melnikov, Dmitri, 101
Menagerie of the Future, The (Cheremnykh), 70
Methodius, St., 4, 21, 113
Meyerhold, Vsevolod, 75
Mice bury the Cat, The, 2–3
Militant Pencil, 124
Millerand, Alexandre, 6
Molotov, Vyacheslav, 23
'Monumental propaganda', 19–20
Moor, Dmitri S., on Apsit, 28–9; career of, 41–3; Cheremnykh on, 43; and decline of poster, 120; and decoration, 112; on icons, 55–6, 60; and Gulbransson, 7; and icons, 6–7; on Lebedev, 85; personality of, 51–5; on Polonsky, 41; poster work of, 43–51, 93–104, 121, 128, 129–30; responses to work of, 114, 115; and Rosta Windows, 76; and satirical graphics, 10–11; other references, 3, 8, 37
Moscow School of Painting, Sculpture and Architecture, 10, 24, 69, 73
Motherland Calls, The (Toidze), 123, 130
Mukharsky, S., 97
Muromets, Ilya, 2
Mushketov, I. I., 11
Mussolini, Benito, 21

Newspaper graphics, and Soviet posters, 7–11
Nicholas II, Tsar, 11, 15, 43
Nightingale, Florence, 20
Nightmare of the Deserter, 92
Nikulin, Lev, 41
Niva, 11, 26
Noble Poland… (Deni), 97
Noulens, Joseph, 72
Novyi Satirikon, 10, 11, 73, 85
Nyurenberg, Amshei, 68, 77, 80, 81

October 1917–October 1920 (Moor), 101
Ogarev, Nikolai, 20
Old Believers, 3
Olesha, Yuri, 89
Once upon a Time the Bourgeoisie… (Cheremnykh), 25, 69–70
One hand stretches… (Malyutin), 77
Only he deserves Freedom (Malyutin), 77
Only the Red Army… (Pomansky), 95
'On poster literature' (1931), 128
On the Eve of the World Revolution, 101
Ordzhonikidze, Sergo, 55
Osmerkin, A. A., 81
Out of the Way!, 98
Owen, Robert, 20

Party Programme, of 1919, 18, 29
Pasternak, Leonid, 14–15, 23
Paul, St., 6
Pavlov, Ivan, 26–8, 43, 53–4, 72
Pavlov, S. A., 84
Pavlova, Anna, 14
Peasant! The Polish Landlord… (Deni), 57, 97
People of the Whole World…, 92–3
People's Court (Moor), 95
Pesis, B. A., 67
Pet, A., 23
Peter the Great, 2–3, 5
Petlyura, Simon, 57
Pilsudsky, Joseph, 6
Plakat, Das, 7
Platonov, Andrei, 6
Pobedonostsev, Konstantin, 8
Popular Movement in the Time of Troubles (Apsit), 29

Podvoisky, Nikolai, 61
Political posters, in the USSR: decline of, 119–30; early years of, 23–38; impact of, 108–15; origins of, 1–17; themes of, 91–108
Polonsky, Vyacheslav, on Apsit, 28; biography of, 40–1; on Deni, 60; on Lebedev, 85; other references, 11–14, 15, 17, 23, 48, 64, 96, 109, 111, 112, 113, 115, 124
Pomansky, Nikolai, 95
Poster, The, 7
Pravda, 19, 43, 57, 60, 68, 89, 110, 112, 123, 127, 128
Priests help Capital… (Moor), 51
Proletkult, 21
Publishing, military, 39, 40, 126
Publishing, in early Soviet period, 19
Pulemet, 8
Punch, 7

Radakov, Aleksei, 3, 8, 11, 84, 104, 116, 124, 129
Radishchev, Alexander, 20
Radlov, Nikolai, 10, 84
Rait, Rita, 67, 125
Rampa i zhizn, 56, 72
Rannee utro, 70
Ransome, Arthur, 112, 113
Raphael, 70
Razin, Stenka, 21
Red Army is Fighting Heroically at the Front, The, 88
Red Armyman! Attack Disorder!, 101–4
Red Armyman's Alphabet (Moor), 115
Red Army, symbols of, 36, 51
Red Moscow… (VKhUTEMAS), 101
Red Present for the White Pan (Moor), 97
Red Soldier at the Front is without Footwear and Clothing, The (Moor), 50–1, 96
Religion, posters and, 7, 11, 57, 112
Remember Red Barracks Day (Mayakovsky), 76
Remizov, Nikolai, 10, 56, 114
Repin, Ilya, 3, 8, 10, 56
Retreating before the Red Army (Apsit), 29, 94–5
Rich Man and the Paunchy Priest, The (Deni), 95
Rimsky-Korsakov, Nikolai, 3
Rire, Le, 7
Robespierre, Maximilien, 20
Rodchenko, Alexander, 116, 121
Rodina, 26
Rodzianko, M. V., 14–15
Roskin, V. O., 68
Rosta, 65–7
Rosta Windows, in Moscow, 65–89; in Odessa, 89, 109, 114, 117, 124; in Petrograd, 81–8, 114, 127; in Vitebsk, 88–9; other references, 3, 43, 91, 94, 100, 108, 109–10, 113–15, 125–6
Rovinsky, D. A., 2, 3
RSFSR: Workers of All Countries, Unite! (Kogout), 100
Rublev, Andrei, Old Testament *Trinity* of, 5, 6; other references, 3–4, 20
Russkoe slovo, 43
Russo-Polish war (1920), 51, 57, 72, 76–7, 91, 96–100, 115

St. Petersburg Academy of Arts, 10, 85, 127
Saltykov-Shchedrin, M. E., 7
Satirical journals, in Russia, 8–11
Satirikon, 7, 10, 43, 84, 85
Second World War, Soviet posters of, 121–2, 129, 130
Serov, Valentin, 8, 10, 14, 56
Serov, Vladimir, 29
Shalyapin, Fedor, 56
Shapov, A. F., 84
Shchukin, Sergei, 113
Shebuev, N. G., 56
Shevchenko, Taras, 20
Shishkin, Ivan, 26
Shklovsky, Viktor, 77, 85, 117
Sibirskaya nov, 70
Sidorov, A. A., 64, 112–13, 113
Simplicissimus, 7, 43

Skryabin, Alexander, 20
Smirnov, N. I., 80, 125
Social Pyramid, 8–9
Solntse Rossii, 56
Solovei, 11
Sosnovsky, Lev, 60, 110–11, 116, 119
Soviet Alphabet (Mayakovsky), 75–6
Soviet Russia is an Armed Camp (Moor), 51, 94
Soviet Turnip (Moor), 44–6, 97
Sow prepared in Paris (Deni), 57, 97
Spartacus, 20
Spassky, Konstantin, 94
Spassky, Vassily, 34, 94
Spider and the Flies, The (Deni), 11, 57, 94
Stalin, J. V., 128, 129, 130
Stalin's Pipe (Deni), 129
Stand up for the Defence of Petrograd (Apsit), 29, 93, 124
Stanislavsky, Konstantin, 54–5
Stenberg brothers, 121
Stepanov, N. A., 7
Story of the Bread Rings (Cheremnykh), 72
Strakhov, Adolf, 120, 121
Strekoza, 7
Stroganov Art School, 10, 61, 72
Sun, as symbol, 36
Symbolism: see Allegory
Sytin, I. D., 2

Tass Windows, 121–2, 123–4
Tatlin, Vladimir, 85
Theophanes the Greek, 4
Third International (Deni), 57–60, 128
To horse, Proletarian! (Apsit), 29
Toidze, Irakly, 123
To the Deceived Brothers (Apsit), 32, 92
To the Fallen in the Struggle, 20
'To the People of the Caucasus' (Moor), 50
To the Polish Front! (Mayakovsky), 77

To the Polish Front! (Malyutin), 77
To the Ukrainian Comrades (Kochergin), 61
Towards the Lighthouse of the Communist International (Spassky), 34
Trepov, D. S., 8
Tretyakov, S. M., 67
Trotsky, Leon, 6, 19, 29, 37, 41, 57, 70, 100, 112, 129
Trotskyist-Bukharinist Swine, The (Deni), 128–9
Tsar, Priest and Kulak, 23–4, 32, 92
Tsarist Regiments and the Red Army, The (Moor), 44
Tukhendkhold, Yakov, 72, 120, 120–1, 127

Ukrainian Torments (Kochergin), 61
Ukrainians and Russians . . . (Mayakovsky), 77
Union of Workers of the Revolutionary Poster, 128
Unshakable Fortress, The (Deni), 95
Utro Rossii, 43
Utro vechera mudrenee, 11, 42

Vandervelde, Emile, 6
Vasnetsov, Apollinary, 14
Vasnetsov, Viktor, 3, 14
Vechernye izvestiya, 70
Vengeance on the Tsars (Apsit), 32
Vereshchagin, V. V., 92
Vertov, Dziga, 114
Verzhbitsky, Nikolai, 80
Vesna, 56
Vestnik agitatsii i propagandy, 112, 115–16, 119
Village 'Virgin' (Deni), 6
Vinogradov, N. V., 70
Virgin of Vladimir icon, 4
Vladimirov, I. A., 14
Voinov, V. V., 84
Volynka, 42
Vrubel, Mikhail, 14

Vsevobuch, 61
VTsIK, publishing activities of, 23, 39, 69, 92, 109

We destroy the boundaries . . . (VKhUTEMAS), 101
Wells, H. G., 126
We shall mercilessly defeat and destroy the Enemy (Kukryniksy), 123
We will not surrender Petrograd (Moor), 44, 93
Where Wrangel sends his Bread, 100
White Guard Beast of Prey, The (Kiselis), 97
Williams, A. Rhys, 109
Wilson, President Woodrow, 25, 27
Winter Palace, 21, 23, 41
Witte, S. Yu., 42
Women, emancipation of, 108, 130
Worker and peasant, as symbol, 36
Worker kicked out the Capitalist, The (Cheremnykh), 25, 70
Workers have conquered Power in Russia, 101
Wrangel, Baron P. N., 11, 57, 76, 89, 96, 100, 115
Wrangel is Coming! (Kochergin), 61, 100
Wrangel is Still Alive! (Moor), 100

Year of the Proletarian Dictatorship (Apsit), 26, 92
Yellow Book, 7
Yudenich, Nikolai, 6, 29, 94, 95–6, 100, 124

Zelinsky, A., 17
Zemenkov, Boris, 109
Zetkin, Klara, 70
Zhdanov, Andrei, 128
Zhukovsky, S. Yu., 73
Zhupel, 8, 10
Zritel, 36
Zvorykin, Boris, 34